8/97

The Use of
Arthurian Legend in
Hollywood Film

The Use of Arthurian Legend in Hollywood Film

From Connecticut Yankees to Fisher Kings

Rebecca A. Umland
and Samuel J. Umland

Contributions to the Study of Popular Culture, Number 57

GREENWOOD PRESS
Westport, Connecticut • London

Library of Congress Cataloging-in-Publication Data

Umland, Rebecca A.
  The use of Arthurian legend in Hollywood film : from Connecticut
Yankees to fisher kings / Rebecca A. Umland and Samuel J. Umland.
    p.   cm.—(Contributions to the study of popular culture,
ISSN 0198–9871 ; no. 57)
  Filmography: p.
  Includes bibliographical references and index.
  ISBN 0–313–29798–3 (alk. paper)
  1. Arthurian romances in motion pictures.   I. Umland, Samuel J.
II. Title.   III. Series.
PN1995.9.A75U44   1996
791.43′651—dc20   96–5835

British Library Cataloguing in Publication Data is available.

Library of Congress Catalog Card Number: 96–5835
ISBN: 0–313–29798–3
ISSN: 0198–9871

First published in 1996

Greenwood Press, 88 Post Road West, Westport, CT 06881
An imprint of Greenwood Publishing Group, Inc.

Printed in the United States of America

The paper used in this book complies with the
Permanent Paper Standard issued by the National
Information Standards Organization (Z39.48–1984).

10 9 8 7 6 5 4 3 2 1

To John, Andrew, and Lauren, with love and affection

Contents

Illustrations

Preface

Hollywood's romance with Arthur now exceeds seven decades, but cogent and sensible critical studies of films that use the *Matter of Britain* are rare. Note that we say "use" and not the collocation "Arthurian films" because in this study we hope to demonstrate that the uses of the legend are not always faithful representations of it, nor do they even wish to be. Instead, we contend that most films that draw from the Arthurian legend rely on the audience's rudimentary familiarity with it; the activation of only select features of the legend serves certain purposes and achieves various ends that are often discernible by an examination of the genre in which the legend is recast.

As E. D. Hirsch points out in *Cultural Literacy*, traditional knowledge tends to be transmitted by stereotypes and clichés, so that only part of the story—its typical features—will be recalled. Hollywood, in other words, is an expert on cultural literacy in that it researches the values and lifestyles of "consumers." It employs the Arthurian legend as a vehicle for specific polemical agendas, selecting certain of its features to serve those ends. Thus, we argue, the Arthurian legend represents a heterogeneous set of materials from which filmmakers can select the portions they wish to activate and ignore the rest. Yet in his article "Mythopoeia in *Excalibur*," Norris Lacy observes that "the Arthurian myth, for better or for worse, is constantly being remade" (121). The mythopoeic nature of the legend thus extends from written representations to visual representations, and this—far from serving as a detriment to the legend's survival—guarantees its constant vitality in the general culture.

Film genre, as well as specific filmic antecedents, is the organizing principle of this study because a persistent shortcoming in discussions of "Arthurian film" is, in our view, the insistence upon assessing films by literary standards, and in so doing expecting conformity to the conventions that govern narrative. Moreover, there is a propensity to demand of filmic representations of the legend what is *not* required of their literary counterparts—namely, a strict adherence to some source perceived to be authoritative. Although there is, as we shall see, a decided tyranny of tradition, the legend's strength rests also on its adaptability to various audiences and purposes. To admire a writer for his originality but to castigate a filmmaker for his failure to produce a "faithful" representation of the Arthurian legend is surely unfair: It seems more judicious to assess films not by narrative conventions but by those that govern the visual medium chosen for expression.

Richard C. Bartone's essay "Variations on Arthurian Legend in *Lancelot du Lac* and *Excalibur*" acknowledges this myopic attitude toward film and calls for a corrective:

Unfortunately, film audiences primarily perceive narrative progression and plot elements, overlooking how other aesthetic characteristics of the medium converge with narrative to interpret myth and history. . . . Cinema's ability to thematically reveal Arthurian legend depends upon the viewer's ability to understand that the various channels of articulation converge and contribute to rigorous discourse. (144–45)

By exploring the discursive categories outlined in the table of contents— intertextual collage, melodrama, propaganda, the legend as Hollywood epic and as postmodern quest—we examine the ways in which Hollywood has activated features of the Arthurian legend employing what Hayden White has called a "performance model" of discourse analysis. As White explains in "The Question of Narrative in Contemporary Historical Theory,"

From the perspective provided by this [performance] model, a discourse is regarded as an apparatus for the production of meaning rather than as only a vehicle for the transmission of information about an extrinsic referent. Thus envisaged, the content of the discourse consists as much of its form as it does of whatever information might be extracted from a reading of it. It follows that to change the form of the discourse might not be to change the information about its explicit referent, but it would certainly change the meaning produced by it. (*The Content of the Form* 42)

We are compelled to employ a performance model because it allows us to take into account, as White puts it, "the enormous number of kinds of narratives that every culture disposes for those of its members who might wish to draw upon them for the encodation and transmission of messages" (41). For instance, although the 1949 production of *A Connecticut Yankee in King Arthur's Court* and the later *Camelot* (1967) are Hollywood musicals, we discuss them as models of intertextual collage and melodrama, respectively, because these discursive models allow us to isolate and discuss how these films have employed elements of the Arthurian legend—a discussion not available to us if we should examine how each film employs features of the Hollywood musical. Musicals, much like children's films, do make a contribution to the continued vitality of the Arthurian legend in film, but as a genre they do not afford the opportunity to explore fully exactly how Hollywood has activated various features of the *Matter of Britain*, which is the first objective of our study. Likewise, all the "Connecticut Yankee" films can be classified as science fiction films because their frame is the device of time travel, but such a category yields little insight into the various *uses* of the legend. We hope to open up new avenues of discussion about what exactly is meant—or rather, can be meant—by the ambiguous collocation "Arthurian film." Our method is not "source study," that is, we are not "template matching." In our view, much of the scholarship on "Arthurian film" has consisted heretofore of template matching, in other words, discerning the degree of one-to-one correspondence between the film and its (apparent) narrative source; determinations of the film's merit follow as a consequence. Our approach was to allow the broadest possible definition of what constitutes an "Arthurian film," including that of structural resemblance. Like Raymond H. Thompson in his study *The Return From Avalon*, we have been as inclusive as possible in our use of the word "Arthurian."

Our purpose is thus twofold. Although we focus on ways in which the Arthurian legend has been adapted to the medium of film, we also use this study to explore filmic adaptations in Hollywood, employing the example of the *Matter of Britain* as a case study or model. Because of this, the reader will notice that we have not examined a number of European films that have worked with the Arthurian legend, of which Robert Bresson's *Lancelot du Lac* (1974) and Eric Rohmer's *Perceval le Gallois* (1978) have perhaps received the most critical attention. We also wish to emphasize that our work is not intended to be an encyclopedic survey of films that use the Arthurian legend, nor is our aim to present an exhaustive discussion of every such film produced in Hollywood. Instead, we have opted to discuss in detail key films that are illustrative of the discursive models most frequently used in Hollywood productions, those that have proven to be continuously lucrative, and we trust that with this focus in mind, the reader will not find our selection of films capricious.

It is useful to begin with a brief consideration of the most influential literary antecedents of the films we plan to discuss because they necessarily precede the filmic ones. We understand "literary" to include both imaginative literature and critical/scholarly commentary on the legend and we understand both to be equally important methods of transmission. Literary antecedents help us to posit a likely or at least a logical mode of transmission to popular audiences. We must emphasize that "influence" in such a context does not necessarily or even usually mean "source." Rather we are using the term to denote ways in which the narrative tradition transmitted the legend so that it became part of our transcultural lexicon. One need not have read Sir Thomas Malory's *Le Morte d'Arthur* or Alfred, Lord Tennyson's *Idylls of the King*, for instance, to be cognizant of the legend and even the *ethos* of those works. Although the latter are extremely important, we address their influence only as they can be related to individual films and film genres. By starting with its long literary tradition, however, we can accentuate the significance of the legend's mythopoeic nature— that is, its timeless appeal coupled with its adaptability—since it is this quality that allows for its transposition to the filmic genre and helps to explain the continued fascination with the *Matter of Britain*. Our discussion of the literary antecedents is not intended to be exhaustive, lest it impinge upon and curtail our main purpose. Rather, we hope to bring to the fore the two prevalent strands of the medieval legend—one represented by Malory's "hoole booke," the other by the grail quest as recounted first by Chrétien de Troyes and then by Wolfram von Eschenbach—and its primary continuators (Alfred Lord Tennyson, Mark Twain, and T. H. White) whose influence is most apparent in Hollywood films that employ the legend.

Films that employ the quest are ultimately indebted to the medieval grail romancers listed above, but their more immediate sources are figures like composer Richard Wagner and scholar Jessie Weston, whose works popularized and/or familiarized twentieth-century audiences with this strand of the legend. These films include obvious examples such as *Indiana Jones and the Last Crusade* (1989) and *The Fisher King* (1991) but also productions that are more subtle in their use of medieval grail legends (certainly *The Natural* and arguably the *Star Wars* trilogy as well). Malory's narrative is the parent work for Mark Twain, whose *A Connecticut Yankee in King Arthur's Court* (1889) spawned an entire subgenre of Arthurian film, and also for White's *The Once and Future King*, parts of which inspired *Camelot* and *The Sword in the Stone*, and which also clearly influenced *Monty Python and the Holy Grail*. The direct result of Malory's efforts can be seen in such melodramas as *Knights of the Round Table* and in epic films like *Excalibur*, both of which also reveal a marked indebtedness to Tennyson's own revision of Malory as well.

To be sure, there are other influential writers of interest to us, such as the Pearl Poet and his relationship to portrayals of Gawain in film. But we have been constrained to discuss by way of introduction only those works that are most instrumental to our examination of the legend's use in film, and we must therefore omit a consideration of writers who have contributed greatly to the Arthurian *literary* canon but whose influence on Hollywood film has not been pronounced (e.g., William Morris). Moreover, it is imperative for us to examine the way in which the films we have selected here have been influenced by other films, many of which are not Arthurian, as the organizational categories suggest.

Having chosen to organize our discussion around generic categories, we begin each chapter by identifying the formal qualities and demands of the genre, occasionally adding historical information as well. We then examine chronologically the films we have placed in the generic category, for earlier efforts do indeed inform our understanding of later ones.

It is our hope that this book will be useful to Arthurian enthusiasts and to film scholars as well. But if we can suggest in the ensuing pages new ways to assess and even appreciate (at least upon occasion) Hollywood's use of the *Matter of Britain*, we will feel that our efforts have provided us, in the words of a one-time quasi-Arthurian, "abundant recompense."

Acknowledgments

We owe our deepest thanks to our friend Jim Fields for his tireless interest, support, and advice, and for the loan of the books from his personal film library. He was a constant source of help during the writing of this book. Our friend Valerie Lagorio, Professor Emerita at the University of Iowa, believed in this project and was an early supporter of it, and we wish to thank her for warning us about the "grail murk." We also thank Dr. Robert Luscher, Chair of the English Department at the University of Nebraska at Kearney, and Dr. Ken Nikels, Dean of the Graduate College, for their support by way of subvention for the illustrations used in this book. We owe a debt of gratitude to Dwaine Spieker who read our manuscript with great care and consideration and made several valuable suggestions—a Pict sure is worth a thousand words. Thanks to Mary Corliss, Film Stills Archivist at the Museum of Modern Art, for her assistance in choosing these illustrations. We must also mention Alan Lupack, who supplied us with a copy of David Butler's *A Connecticut Yankee*. Nina Pearlstein, our editor at Greenwood Press, gave us a lot of room and showed us great patience, and for her tolerance and aid we thank her, too, more than she imagines.

Rebecca A. Umland
Samuel J. Umland
Kearney, Nebraska
May 1996

1

The Mythopoeic Nature of the Arthurian Legend and Its Methods of Transmission

Cinema, Truffaut said, is spectacle—Méliès—and research—
Lumière. . . . I have always wanted, basically, to do research in the
form of a spectacle. The documentary side is: a man in a particular
situation. The spectacle comes when one makes this man a
gangster or a secret agent.
                              —Jean-Luc Godard (*Godard on Godard* 181)

There can be little dispute that the prevailing medieval literary antecedents for
Hollywood films are Sir Thomas Malory's *Le Morte d'Arthur*, which has been
widely consulted, adapted, and bowdlerized by writers and filmmakers alike, and
the works of two early grail romancers, Chrétien de Troyes and Wolfram von
Eschenbach. This latter strand of the legend has been used in a specialized way in
film, serving, for the most part, as a basis for those productions that focus on
the postmodern quest, the subject of our final chapter. Moreover, since each of
these contributions to the medieval legend has become familiar to modern
audiences through the efforts of postmedieval writers, we will attempt to trace
the influential contribution of Malory, Chrétien, and Wolfram through their
nineteenth- and twentieth-century popularizers. We will begin with Malory
because the effect of his *Morte* is such a pervasive one—in literature as well as
in film.

   In his groundbreaking study of the postmedieval Arthurian legend *The
Flower of Kings*, James Douglas Merriman avers that the importance of
Malory's work "would be difficult to exaggerate" because it "has been the
seminal source of nearly every worthwhile treatment of the legend in English"
(17), an assessment that can be corroborated by films that employ the legend as
well. And Eugène Vinaver claims that it is to Malory's efforts that "Arthurian
romance owes its survival in the English speaking world" (*Arthurian Literature
in the Middle Ages* 541). Before we discuss Malory's influence on later writers
who are particularly important to filmic uses of the legend (and Malory himself

bears considerable *direct* influence), it is worthwhile to explore why his version has become synonymous with the "received legend" and why the *Matter of Britain* is, in this form Malory gave it for English readers, inherently attractive to generation after generation of readers and viewers. In other words, it is useful to consider what makes the legend mythopoeic.

The most controversial issue of Malory studies (with the possible exception of his actual identity) has centered on whether his work can and should be viewed as a complete and coherent narrative. This debate was sparked by Vinaver—after William Caxton, Malory's most celebrated editor—who argued that Malory composed eight separate tales instead of a unified narrative, at least in any modern aesthetic sense. Thus, Vinaver chose as the title for his 1947 edition, based upon the Winchester manuscript discovered in 1934, *Works*.[1] The publication of the Winchester manuscript also created a debate over whether it or the Caxton manuscript, published in 1485, stands as a more faithful representation of Malory's intentions, an issue that has resurfaced in recent years.[2]

Vinaver also downplays Malory's own contribution to the legend and chooses to view him largely as a redactor. The most outspoken critics of his assertions have been R. M. Lumiansky, Charles Moorman, and John Matthews, who have taken to task both these assumptions. Vinaver's opponents argue that Malory did indeed create—out of a chaos of source materials—something that resembles a coherent narrative, and that he was often highly original in his version of the legend.[3] Arguably, there was *no* received legend until Malory created it by unifying diverse sources and by virtue of his own creativity and narrative ability, but this debate we will leave to Malorian experts and to those who specialize in editing medieval texts. What is germane to our discussion is that Malory's Arthurian version of the legend was so powerful in its effect on Arthurian revivalists from the nineteenth century to the present that it has *become* the jewel in the canonical Arthurian crown. Regardless of the considerable merits of earlier medieval Arthurian texts, Malory's was so strong as to virtually obliterate those of his precursors.

Let us first identify what we mean by the "received legend," as it is presented in Malory's version. Merriman succinctly summarizes those components that comprise what he refers to in his first chapter as "The Essential Arthurian Story" (21). These include Arthur's parentage by Uther and Igraine, his birth, his rearing by Sir Ector, the sword in the stone episode that results in his right to claim the throne and his efforts to unify Britain, followed by his fateful marriage to Guinevere and his formation of the Round Table. Also essential is the adultery between Lancelot and the queen. The grail quest is a key element, as is Gawain's vengeful feud that allows for the usurpation of the crown by Mordred. This, in turn, results ultimately in the fatal wounding of Arthur and his sailing to Avalon to be healed. Finally, the story features the death of Guinevere and then of Lancelot. According to Merriman, this adumbration represents "the essential Arthurian story or, in Platonic terms, the ideal story, as it manifests itself in Malory" (22). Merriman argues that Arthur's incestuous liaison with

Morgause, which results in the birth of Mordred, is downplayed by Malory, who understood that "the essential conflict . . . is the adulterous love of Gwenyvere and Lancelot" (23). Furthermore, he asserts, "the incest motif, clearly, remained a mere attachment to the story, never assimilated into its spirit or emotional structure" (23).

It must be noted here, that this is perhaps Merriman's most controversial view, one that has divided critics and writers alike. For instance, Tennyson— who wrote for a middle-class Victorian audience and who strived to present a "pristine" king, one who would represent "ideal manhood closed in real man" ("To the Queen" 1. 38)—omitted the incest altogether and reverted to the medieval chronicle tradition in which Mordred is merely the king's wicked nephew. For this he was criticized by his rival, Arthurian writer and critic A. C. Swinburne, who argued for the importance of this component:

It seems to me that the moral tone of the Arthurian story has been on the whole lowered and degraded by Mr. Tennyson's mode of treatment. . . . The hinge of the whole legend of the Round Table, from its first glory to its final fall, is the incestuous birth of Mordred from the connexion of Arthur with his half-sister, unknowing and unknown; as surely as the hinge of the *Oresteia* from first to last is the sacrifice at Aulis. (*Swinburne Replies*, "Under the Microscope" 57)

Swinburne referred satirically to Tennyson's *Idylls of the King* as the "Morte d'Albert" or the "Albertian Idylls" because he thought Tennyson was attempting to curry favor with Queen Victoria by using her prince consort, Albert, as a model for his depiction of Arthur.

Other writers agree with Swinburne that it is Arthur himself, and not Lancelot and Guinevere, who must shoulder the blame for his own demise. E. A. Robinson holds the king culpable, claiming in "Merlin" that he built his kingdom on "two pits of living sin" (69)—his incest and his hapless marriage. T. H. White likewise argues that because it resembles classical tragedy, the legend must show Arthur to be guilty of begetting Mordred by his incest with Morgause: "It is a tragedy, the Aristotelian and comprehensive tragedy, of sin coming home to roost. . . . He did not know he was doing so, and perhaps it may have been due to her, but it seems, in tragedy, that innocence is not enough" (*The Once and Future King* 312). It is very important to note, however, that in the films we will discuss here, the genre of melodrama demands that the focus be on the adultery of Arthur's wife and his most puissant knight, Lancelot, and the betrayal that adultery necessarily entails. Hollywood versions of the legend dwell not on the incest (with the exceptions provided by *Camelot* and *Excalibur*) but on the eternal triangle of which melodrama consists. By omitting the incest and stressing Arthur's betrayal by Lancelot and Guinevere, Hollywood renditions of the legend that use the formula of melodrama are more closely allied to Tennyson's version of the legend than to Malory's.

After identifying the elements of plot he considers central to the legend, Merriman observes that "the story of Arthur is not historical" (25). Rather, it is mythic, by which he means that "the essential Arthurian story is no arbitrary, exocogital creation of individual imagination; instead it is, in the fullest anthropological and literary sense of the word, a myth" (25). He cites, among other works, Lord Raglan's *The Hero: A Study in Tradition, Myth, and Drama* (1949), in which twenty-one heroes are considered. Twenty-two motifs or typical incidents are identified, of which Arthur's story possesses nineteen (194). Its mythic nature means that "such a legend is from the beginning relatively fixed in both form and spirit. Growing out of the unconscious but irrational mind, its configuration will reject any significanct alteration in events. And it is equally resistant to any change in spirit" (26). Moreover, this spirit is "profoundly tragic. . . . It can no more have a 'happy ending' than could the stories of Oedipus or Orestes or Hamlet. . . . The tragedy *is* the story" (26).

This is the tyranny of tradition that dictates the generic forms and conventions that must be employed to guarantee a successful Arthurian story. But our study maintains that Hollywood has rarely attempted, or even wished, to create an actual "Arthurian film," by which we mean a complete version that adheres roughly to the characterization and also presents the events in a similar chronological order with a similar cause-effect relationship as that which we find in the version that emerged in the Middle Ages. Instead, as we will show, the films that employ features of the legend are a heterogeneous collection: They have very different purposes and use the legend—or, more accurately, activate only certain features of it—to achieve their particular ends. The received legend can be seen as a repertoire of characters and potential scripts that the filmmaker chooses like pieces before the start of a game. The "fixed form" and "tragic spirit" also explains why a work that employs the legend may be an accomplished literary or filmic text (e.g., Mark Twain's *A Connecticut Yankee* or Gilliam and Jones's *Monty Python and the Holy Grail*). However, because such films violate this weight of tradition, their success as *Arthurian* texts is questionable.

The fixed core of the legend that Malory employed in his narrative is, according to Merriman, only one of two ingredients responsible for its mythopoeic nature. Like other myths, the Arthurian legend is "remarkably responsive to changes in symbolic content" (26). That is, it possesses a "flexibility" that allows for the idiosyncrasies of individual artists and for each generation to respond to it by virtue of a new idiom furnished for it. Finally, because the legend embraced and was influenced by the "secular ideal" of chivalry, it is markedly social rather than individual in its implications (26). As a result, the tragedy involves all of its constituents. When Arthur falls, so does an entire society based on a chivalric ideal, and thus there is much more at stake in the story than an individual's fate.

Perhaps this explains why the legend serves as such an apt vehicle for didactic statements about society, politics, and morality, especially for ages that perceive themselves to be suffering from continual crises. If this is so, it helps to explain why Malory—writing at the conclusion of one of England's greatest periods of social instability and political upheaval, the War of the Roses—would expend such a tremendous effort on a legend that might well have been exhausted, albeit temporarily. In addition, the apocalyptic nature of the *Matter of Britain* may have contributed to its attraction for the Victorians. We thus understand narrative in abstract terms as a figure of comprehension and follow Hayden White's statements on the unity of narrative and explanation: "Narrative might well be considered a solution to a problem of general human concern, namely, the problem of how to translate *knowing* into *telling*" ("The Value of Narrativity in the Representation of Reality" 5). Most certainly Jean-Luc Godard understands the cinema as serving a similar form of comprehension, as revealed in the quotation that serves as the epigraph to this chapter: "Research in the form of a spectacle." The employment of the various features of the Arthurian legend in Hollywood film in particular, as we note above, would seem to be associated with periods of historical catastrophe.

It was the Victorians who gave birth to a new flowering of Arthurian texts and ideas within the context of the larger Gothic revival—the inception of which may be found in the latter half of the eighteenth century—a movement worth discussing briefly before we explore those writers who, in some transmuted form, gave Malory's work new expression in modern times and who are responsible for the Malorian legacy identifiable in Hollywood film.

In recent years scholars have published excellent studies of Arthur's return from Avalon, which found full expression with the Victorians. This resurgence occurred within the context of the larger Gothic revival.[4] Before examining this renewal, though, it is important to point out that although it never died out entirely, since the publication of Malory the Arthurian legend had experienced a steady decline for over three centuries. First, there were the efforts by British monarchs to manipulate the legend for political ends by maintaining that they descended from Arthur. Monks at Glastonbury Abbey shrewdly claimed that Arthur and Guinevere were buried there. Such overtly self-serving and absurd claims defamed the legend and made it a target of ridicule. And although the political climate and aesthetic tastes of the postmedieval eras were not amenable to the legend, one might speculate that Malory, as a kind of strong Bloomian precursor, was formidable enough to intimidate later writers. Even Edmund Spenser and John Milton contemplated but discarded the idea of an Arthurian epic.

The origin of the Gothic revival, however, dates back to the latter half of the eighteenth century. An expression of interest in the Gothic may be seen in a number of ways: in an antiquarian approach to history, in architectural design, in scholarly editions of ancient texts, and in imaginative literature that bears a medieval influence. In literature and in scholarly endeavors, this antiquarian interest prompted critical inquiry into the customs, habits of mind, and historical events of the past. Moreover, ancient texts enjoyed a rejuvenation of life as they were edited and published by independent scholars and also supported by organizations such as the Early English Text Society.[5]

Insofar as this revival preferred the medieval over the classical and idealized the medieval past, it was in accord with the high romanticism of the early nineteenth century. This reaction can, in turn, be accounted for by the revulsion for the negative side effects of the Industrial Revolution, which altered English life significantly in a several ways. The most famous popularizer of the Middle Ages surely has to be Sir Walter Scott, whose interests and activities encompassed every manifestation of the medieval or Gothic revival. Scott's enthusiasm was contagious, and his influence on later generations was profound.

Mark Girourard observes in *The Return to Camelot: Chivalry and the English Gentleman*, that Scott's attitude toward the Middle Ages was ambivalent, not one of unmitigated admiration: "Emotionally he responded instinctively to the Middle Ages; intellectually he was always apologizing for them" (34). Moreover, he claimed, "one of Scott's greatest achievements was to bring chivalry up to date, and popularize a type of character which could reasonably be called chivalrous, but was acceptable as a model both by himself and his contemporaries" (34). Scott's antiquarian interests and his enthusiasm for Gothic architecture can be seen in his study of medieval customs, which appeared in the form of torturous notes to his own novels, and in his construction of Abbotsford, a castle crammed with arms. His scholarly bent is also evident in his edition of a medieval text, Thomas of Erceldoune's *Sir Tristrem* (1804), but his imaginative efforts are those that most influenced the public. Both his poems and his novels were enormous successes. It is noteworthy that one of Scott's novels set in the medieval past, *Ivanhoe* (1820), has twice been filmed by Hollywood (not including "spin-offs" such as *The Black Shield of Falworth*), in 1952 and again in 1985. Poems such as *The Lay of the Last Minstrel* (1809) and *The Lady of the Lake* (1809) made Scott a celebrity, but he always downplayed his career as a writer and preferred to be perceived as a man of leisure, a product of his love of the feudal past. When George IV made him a baron in 1820, Scott's dream of being a "laird" became viable and he set out to transform his home, Abbotsford, into a fully realized medieval estate. Because of his idealized yet vivid depictions of the medieval past, Scott's legacy was great: He instilled into later generations a wild enthusiasm for the remote past.[6]

This return to the past gained in popularity during the first quarter of the nineteenth century. For instance, Stansby's 1634 edition of Malory was the last until 1816, but between 1816 and 1817 three new editions were printed and several more soon followed. The Gothic, and particularly the Arthurian, revival reached its apex in the Victorian period, and it is Tennyson—whom David Staines has called the "father of the Arthurian renaissance in Victorian England" (*The New Arthurian Encyclopedia* 446)—who was to become the great popularizer of the legend. His influence is enormous, not only because of his effect on later writers but also because it was he who created an audience for the Arthurian legend. From the advent of his first published Arthurian efforts in his 1842 *Poems*, he set out to educate and influence a public still largely unfamiliar with the *Matter of Britain*. For this reason alone Tennyson necessarily earns a place in our discussion, but he also merits attention because as a revitalizer he introduced some extremely important changes to his primary source, Malory, that can be traced directly to Hollywood film. Most of these revisions were designed to make the medieval material more satisfying for his Victorian readers, and the fact that these innovations tended to be employed by the Hollywood melodramas of the 1950s and 1960s suggests how minimal the gap really is between Tennyson's Victorian audience and a modern one.

Early on, Tennyson was searching for the most advantageous form for his ambitious desire to recast the Arthurian material. In 1833 he composed a prose sketch he intended to use for a dramatic rendition of the legend, and his 1842 collection of poems contains short lyrics (e.g., "Sir Launcelot and Queen Guinevere" and "Sir Galahad"). More important in that collection are his "Morte Arthur" and "The Epic," the latter of which addresses objections Tennyson imagined he would incur should he attempt to publish a sustained Arthurian work. These poems may be seen as efforts to anticipate and thus neutralize resistance from his audience, but especially from hostile critics who could shape public opinion. After years of careful preparation, Tennyson published his first installment of the poems of which his Arthurian masterpiece, *Idylls of the King*, would eventually consist. As we know the work, it is an epic poem composed of twelve idylls, but it did not receive this final form until late in the poet's career, and he continued to make minor revisions almost up until his death in 1896. In its final form the *Idylls*, based on Malory but also on other sources (e.g., Geoffrey of Monmouth and the *Mabinogion*) and on Tennyson's own imagination as well, is the version that influenced so many writers and filmmakers. It is important to keep in mind, then, that Tennyson published his Arthurian epic serially, over a period exceeding four decades, and that the idylls were not initially published in the chronological order the poet supplied them in their final form.

In 1859 the four "women" idylls appeared: "Enid," "Vivien," "Elaine," and "Guinevere." These works were such an enormous success, owing in large part to their thematic appeal, that they were followed by the publication of "The Coming of Arthur," "The Holy Grail," "Pelleas and Ettarre," and "The Passing of Arthur" in his 1869 volume of poems entitled *The Holy Grail and Other Poems*. He added two new poems in 1873, "The Last Tournament" and "Gareth and Lynette," and published his "Balin and Balan" in 1885. In the work's final form, the "Enid" idyll became two poems, "The Marriage of Geraint" and "Geraint and Enid."

Tennyson used the Arthurian legend as a vehicle to reflect and explore Victorian values and concerns. In the *Idylls* he examines notions of the ideal political leader, addresses questions of religious faith, and presents various sexual and moral codes, especially on the part of his female characters. He purges the grail material of Malory's medieval Catholicism in order to suit his middle-class, largely Protestant audience, and he emphasizes the subjective nature of religious faith in order to satisfy the growing number of skeptics among his readers, surely a result of the increased scientific inquiry that threatened traditional spiritual ideals (e.g., Darwin). Throughout his Arthurian work, he presents those qualities possessed by an ideal ruler as they are manifested by Arthur, using the Carlylean principle of the divinely inspired, visionary leader who commands obedience from his subordinates. This concern reflects the Victorian compulsion for order and inspired leadership. The most pervasive issue in this epic poem, however, is the degree to which the domestic realm influences Arthur's kingdom. Women in the *Idylls* are micro-managers—either for or against Arthur's principles—and the king's success or failure to rule depends upon the moral fabric created by the women who dwell in this decidedly Victorian Camelot.

Tennyson's major departure from Malory is his depiction of Arthur as the "blameless king" whose ideals are undermined almost exclusively by the adultery of Lancelot and Guinevere. The poet excises any unsavory elements relating to Arthur's character: He removes the illegitimacy of his conception and birth and omits the king's incestuous liaison with Morgause: As in Geoffrey of Monmouth's account, Mordred is only Arthur's treacherous nephew. Arthur's other minor sexual infractions found in Malory also vanish. The king reminds his tainted queen, "I was ever virgin save for thee" ("Guinevere" 1.554). It is the betrayal of Arthur by his adulterous queen and his "chief of knights," as well as the sexual license of other characters, that corrupts Arthur's realm from within and leads to its downfall. Equally counterproductive, though not *morally* reprehensible, are characters who insist upon celibacy instead of fruitful marriage and healthy offspring (e.g., Elaine and Perceval).

An emphasis upon the love triangle at the expense of other major elements of plot is Tennyson's main legacy to filmic versions of the legend, even those that claim to be "based on Sir Thomas Malory" such as *Knights of the Round Table* and *Excalibur*. Does the indirect and convoluted manner of transmission of these films, which owe much to Tennyson, unwittingly circumvent him in their credits? Or is it the pejorative connotation associated with "Victorian" that creates the omission—the assumption that a writer who comes from an age perceived as priggish and repressed, especially in matters of sex—wouldn't "sell" movies that emphasize the sexual torpor and torment of its Arthurian characters? Finally, is it possible that Malory cast a shadow so great as to obscure not only his precursors but also his epigones? Perhaps it is merely a legal issue, a question of copyright. This is, of course, difficult to answer, and it may not be possible to do so, but the influence of Tennyson is so pronounced—in the two films above, but also in others we will discuss—that it invites such speculation.

Another enormously influential nineteenth-century writer is Mark Twain, whose satirical novel *A Connecticut Yankee in King Arthur's Court* (1889) has served as the basis for many Hollywood productions. Like that of his contemporary, Tennyson, Twain's main source was putatively understood to be Malory.[7] His target has been a matter of considerable debate, however. In his "Notebook" Twain records a dream in which he was "a knight errant in armor in the Middle Ages." He contemplates the disadvantages of wearing such attire, and then written in ink five years later across this note is an account of the inception of his now famous "Arthurian" novel:

Fall of '84—while Cable and I were giving readings, Cable got a *Morte d'Arthur* and gave it to me to read. I began to make notes in my head, for a book. Nov. 11, 1886, I read the first chapter (all that was then written) . . . and closed the reading with an outline of probable contents of the future book. Wrote a book "The Yankee at Arthur's Court" in '87 and '88, and published it in December 1889 (shall, anyway). (171)

Apparently, in 1880, four years before Cable exposed him to Malory's *Morte*, Twain had read Sidney Lanier's *The Boy's King Arthur* (*Arthurian Encyclopedia* 478), one of many bowdlerized versions available for consumption by young readers. Whatever Twain might have thought of Malory's politics (his disdain for monarchs is notorious), the book must have fired his imagination; further, his relationship with the chivalric past is not as uncomplicated as has been supposed by many scholars, who have averred that *A Connecticut Yankee in King Arthur's Court* is merely an attack on the Middle Ages in general and the Arthurian legend in particular. Commentaries that argue that the novel applauds or even believes in an idea of "progress" and likewise see Hank Morgan as an unambiguous hero result in a reductive understanding of a complex work. As Donald L. Hoffman argues so persuasively in his essay, "Mark's Merlin: Magic vs. Technology in *A Connecticut Yankee in King Arthur's Court*":

Such readings of the novel fail to comprehend its irony, for as the novel progresses its dark undercurrent becomes apparent by Hank's inability to transcend the shortcomings of the age he is so quick to criticize: "Choosing to become *The Boss*, he seeks to acquire the authority of function freed from the fallibly human. In his desire to attain the divine objectivity he associates with the machine, Hank ignores the limits of his own subjectivity. In striving to transcend the human, Hank merely succeeds in becoming inhuman. (*Popular Arthurian Traditions* 54)

To illustrate Hank's lack of progress, Hoffman points to Hank's admiration—and partial emulation—of Morgan le Fay's cruelty and to the fact that he is seduced by power, evinced, for example, when he violates the rules of the joust and shoots Sir Sagramoure with a pistol or when he employs his technological know-how to electrocute his unsuspecting enemies. Regardless of Twain's aversion to monarchs, feudal systems, and religious patriarchs, he was not foolish enough to assume that humankind was marching toward some grandiose perfection that would, by comparison, shame our medieval ancestors. Hank may be able to expose the cruelty and superstition of a past age, but he cannot escape entirely many of the same impulses that drove medieval knights to acts of carnage and barbarity. Progress, in other words, is an illusion, and Twain knew it.

Twain's main influence on Hollywood film was to reveal the comic possibilities that could arise by using the device of transporting a modern man back into the past, albeit a past that never really existed. It was an ingenious ploy because it allowed for virtually endless opportunities to expose modern folly while ostensibly debunking the ancient past. Twain's story was thus tailor-made for Hollywood, since the device of placing a modern in medieval times is a variation of what in Hollywood lingo is a "fish out of water" story, one that dramatizes the clash of values that allows for social commentary. Examples of such popular Hollywood films are *Coogan's Bluff* (1968), in which Clint Eastwood, as a sheriff from the West, comes to New York City (adapted with modifications in 1986 as *Crocodile Dundee*); and *Beverly Hills Cop* (1984), in which Eddie Murphy, playing a cop from Detroit, goes to Beverly Hills.[8] Hollywood thus acknowledges the didactic possibilities inherent in such a method, though it has used it more frequently for comic purposes. Twain's contribution to the popularity of the legend was to show the potential in exploiting its idealized view of the past for comic ends.

Although this created a work of some hilarity, Twain violates the "tragic spirit" of the legend, which means that its success cannot be attributed to its use of Arthur at all but to Twain's superior talent as a satirist. *A Connecticut Yankee in King Arthur's Court* is a great and influential literary work, but it is not a great Arthurian work. Perhaps it is for this very reason that the novel has had such an enormous effect on Hollywood productions that use the Arthurian legend. As we shall see in the next chapter, Twain's was a work with great liberating capacity, even though it never attempted to be viewed as an Arthurian work. Its main contribution belongs to the category we identify as intertextual collage, a category that has proven to be an enormous success for Hollywood filmmakers.

If Twain's work is forceful enough to have spawned an entire subgenre of Hollywood films, T. H. White's Arthurian efforts have been no less influential. White first published what is now known as *The Once and Future King* (1958) in separate parts: *The Sword in the Stone* (1938); *The Witch in the Wood* (1939), later titled *The Queen of Air and Darkness*; *The Ill-Made Knight* (1940); and *The Candle in the Wind* which completed the work as it was printed in its final form. Published posthumously was *The Book of Merlin* (1977). Just as Tennyson might be considered the greatest revitalizer of the nineteenth century, White is surely in the vanguard of twentieth-century popularizers, and his contribution to the *Matter of Britain* is profound, even though he once told his friend, David Garnett, that he "never pretended to be more than a footnote to Malory" and that his Arthurian fiction would serve as "a kind of literary criticism of him" (*The White-Garnett Letters* 91). White was an avid and astute reader, and his novel does provide some of the finest Malory criticism to date, yet *The Once and Future King* is also a work of great originality.

White's major contribution to the legend includes his detailed portrayal of Arthur's childhood, as well as of the early years of both the Orkney clan and of Lancelot, and his depiction of Merlin as Arthur's endearing and wise but comically forgetful mentor, a wizard who lives backwards in time. This depiction of Merlin has since been exploited widely in literature and in film. He emphasized the families and role models (or lack of them) as formative influences on the children, relying heavily on Freudian psychology to elucidate character. And though he was not the first writer to feature anachronisms for comic ends (Twain had earlier exploited the juxtaposition of historical periods), White certainly did employ the device freely and perhaps with even greater liberty than Twain. For instance, one adventure the young Arthur (nicknamed "Wart") experiences involves "Robin Wood" and the "Maid Marian"—the latter a separate legend and one not traditionally associated with Arthur and his *entourage*. This grafting on of the Robin Hood legend appears in such films as *Siege of the Saxons*. *Monty Python and the Holy Grail* and *Knightriders* also do this: The former includes a character named Sir Robin, while the latter uses Friar Tuck.

Another significant feature of *The Sword and the Stone* is its forceful anti-war theme. Certainly White is not the only writer to exploit and emphasize the devastation of a country divided against itself—this is, after all, what causes Arthur's kingdom to self-destruct—but his work, along with that of other twentieth-century Arthurians like E. A. Robinson's, for instance, does employ the legend as a vehicle for forceful pacifist statements. In fact, it was the rise of fascism in Europe that in 1936 prompted White to set to work in earnest on his Arthurian novel, although his interest had begun much earlier, at the age of eight when he read Malory, and he had written his thesis on the subject when he was at Cambridge in the 1920s (Nathan Comfort Starr, *King Arthur Today* 115).

More obvious, however, is White's role as a popularizer in films that credit his Arthurian work as their ostensible source, though only as a marginal source. These include the Disney children's film *The Sword in the Stone* (1963) and the musical melodrama *Camelot* (1967), itself based on the earlier Broadway musical production (1960). Because of the success of these filmic efforts, it is reasonable to assume that White often serves, albeit indirectly, as a first exposure to the legend. In her 1996 feature article on the legend published in *Smithsonian*, for instance, Caroline Alexander recalls: "I have spent years more or less in thrall to the Camelot story. Walt Disney's film *The Sword in the Stone* set me on the path, imparting beyond the comedy and magic a sense of something grave and wondrously tragic. Based on T. H. White's *The Once and Future King*, it opened up Arthur's life and world" ("Waiting for Arthur: A Winter Vigil at Camelot" 34). It is also noteworthy that through the Disney film and then White's novel, Alexander became interested in Malory and Tennyson, whom she read as an adult.

Each of the writers who ultimately owe their inspiration to Malory—Tennyson, Twain, and White—have also contributed significantly to our collective Arthurian heritage and therefore to filmic adaptations of the legend, as we shall see in the ensuing chapters. The extent of their influence varies greatly, depending on a number of factors: genre, targeted audience, and time of release. Moreover, films that employ the Arthurian legend, however much they may rely upon a specific narrative version, nonetheless tend to owe much more to filmic antecedents that are not necessarily, or even often, themselves Arthurian. It is important to keep in mind that most of the films that employ the legend activate only certain portions of it, and what is repressed is often as revealing in purpose as what is used. It is a striking fact that in recent years the aspect of the medieval legend that has emerged frequently in film is the grail quest, a trend that deserves special attention. The history and growth of the grail material is too complex (and too muddled) to trace in detail here, nor is it possible, for the most part, to cite specific "sources" for particular films, as the transmission of this strand of the Arthurian legend is convoluted indeed: The holy grail, it would seem, has assumed a life of its own, often functioning autonomously (and subtly) in Hollywood productions. Despite this, one can identify certain models that have been presented in the literature of the Middle Ages and, curiously enough, one model prevails in filmic adaptations.

A late twelfth-century French writer, Chrétien de Troyes, would certainly be both astonished and pleased at the influence his last romance, *Perceval*, or *Le Conte del Graal*, has exercised on imaginations up through the late twentieth century, especially considering that although his work exceeds 9,000 lines, Chrétien himself did not finish it. His own death may have prevented its completion and it remained for other "continuators" to add to the text and/or to attempt a conclusion.[9] Versions of Chrétien's grail romance appear in a number of Hollywood films, though not without significant alteration. Richard LaGravenese, who composed the screenplay for *The Fisher King*, states that he became interested in the subject when he read a popular psychology book, *He: Understanding Masculine Psychology*, by Robert A. Johnson, ostensibly a Jungian reading of Chrétien's romance, but one that takes great license with the latter and borrows freely from a number of tales. For instance, Johnson begins with the Irish story of the Salmon of Wisdom, which is not a part of grail lore proper.

The other primary grail romancer to emerge from the Middle Ages was Chrétien's immediate successor, the German writer Wolfram von Eschenbach, who acknowledges Chrétien's work, even though he boasts that his precursor's version is inferior to his own. He also claims that he employed what is now known to be a fictitious source, a Provencal poet named "Kyot," who purportedly furnished most of the material for Wolfram's "superior" grail story, *Parzival*, a staggering 25,000 lines in length. Wolfram's expansion and completion of the legend is important, but it is primarily through composer Richard Wagner's transformation of it, and his identifying it as part of what he calls the "German mythos," that Wolfram's influence appears in Hollywood film.

Other popularizers include Jessie Weston, who published what is now a sort of museum piece but was initially an influential study of the grail's origins, *From Ritual to Romance* (1920), that inspired T. S. Eliot's monumental poem "The Wasteland" (1922). The grail's journey from twelfth-century France to twentieth-century Hollywood is difficult to trace, but an adumbration of the manner in which it evolved is useful in understanding its lasting appeal, one that can be explained in part by the innovations of a few writers.

It is to Chrétien de Troyes that we will turn first for the story of a grail quester. Perceval is a beautiful but extremely naïve youth raised in seclusion in the forest by a doting mother. She suffers from anxiety because she fears she will lose her "darling son" to the wanderlust that robbed her of her husband and two other sons. In spite of her protective efforts, Perceval sets out to become a knight, an act that results in his mother's death. He understands little of the moral code that governs knighthood but is fascinated instead with the outer trappings of chivalry. During his travels, Perceval arrives at the grail castle and witnesses the grail procession in the company of the wounded king, the "Fisher King," but because he has been told that it is unmannerly to talk too much, Perceval fails to ask the question that would have cured the Fisher King and rejuvenated his land. Once he is castigated for this failure, Perceval becomes embittered with God. However, he later meets a hermit who instructs him of his error and explains the significance of the grail castle.

It is important to note that whereas the grail is a marvelous dish or platter that possesses mysterious powers, it is not yet, in Chrétien's romance, associated with the chalice of the Last Supper and the cup with which Joseph of Arimathea collected the drops of blood from the side of the crucified Christ. It is possible that Chrétien was influenced by stories of nourishing vessels of Celtic origin (e.g., cornucopias and horns of plenty), but he is the first to connect it to an elaborate ritual (the grail procession) with spiritual overtones (the grail king is served a single mass wafer, which sustains his life indefinitely). It is also Chrétien who connects Perceval with Arthur's court, for that is where Perceval goes to become a knight when he departs from his mother.

Perceval's story allows for great humor because it provides the "fish out of water" situation alluded to earlier. Perceval is, surely, the pure fool who insists upon taking advice literally, which creates many comic but also serious consequences. Those writers who immediately succeeded Chrétien attempted either to complete what he had begun, by charting Perceval's journey from ignorance to knowledge and portraying him as the next keeper of the grail, or to add to the rich tradition of the grail's history, as is the case with Robert de Boron, who made the grail the cup from which Christ drank at the Last Supper, a cup that also held Christ's blood collected by Joseph of Arimathea.

In Wolfram's *Parzival*, the grail is no longer a vessel but a stone that produces savory food, possesses healing powers (any one who beholds it cannot die for a week after), and by virtue of its ability to create inscriptions upon itself governs world affairs by appointing leaders and also by naming those who are destined to guard it in the grail castle. The knights who do guard it are referred to as templars, and Wolfram expands upon the history of the grail family, naming the current king Anfortas. Anfortas suffers from a wound in the testicles because the grail demands celibacy while it is being guarded, and his *cupiditas* causes his disobedience. Moreover, Wolfram intensifies family relationships, and Parzival learns eventually that Anfortas, whom he cures, is his uncle; Parzival himself then becomes the grail king.

Wolfram begins with a long narrative of the adventures of Parzival's father, Gahmuret, who travels widely in the Middle East, serves an infidel, and rescues an African queen, whom he marries and with whom he has a pagan son, Feirefiz (curiously, because of his interracial parentage, Feirefiz is speckled black and white). It is Wolfram who introduces the exotic and oriental components as well as the templar knights into the grail legend. Moreover, along with the Third Continuator of Chrétien's unfinished romance, known as Manessier, Wolfram provides a conclusion to Perceval's adventures: The wounded king is healed miraculously, after which Perceval himself assumes the role of grail keeper.

In the works of Chrétien and Wolfram, Perceval is a compelling figure, one who through his naïveté and his imperfect human nature errs, but one who nonetheless eventually finds the path of redemption. In both works he must ask a critical question that will heal an ailing king, and the audience wants Perceval to succeed—for his own sake and for that of the suffering grail guardian. Perceval's success, however, depends upon his own spiritual growth, so that his quest becomes one for self-enlightenment.

For this reason, as we shall see in our final chapter, films that feature the postmodern quest tend to rely upon these early medieval versions of the quest for the holy grail and bypass the later versions (best known perhaps by Malory's *Queste del Sanc Graal*) in which Galahad, a product of the imagination of Cistercian monks, largely usurps Perceval's role as the grail knight *par excellence*. Galahad's purity and his perfection render him a less sympathetic character than his precursor, Perceval. Unlike Perceval, who fails before he accomplishes this task, Galahad succeeds the first time. Engendered by a liaison between Elaine (the grail king's daughter) and Lancelot, who is tricked into believing she is Guinevere, Galahad, a bastard, is raised by nuns with the sole purpose of achieving the quest: He heals the wounded king and is translated to heaven, *à la* Enoch and Elijah, with the holy grail itself in tow. When Galahad appears in Hollywood productions, he is most often presented satirically and only in passing (e.g., in the 1949 version of *A Connecticut Yankee in King Arthur's Court* he is a minor character who is vain and humorless, and in *Monty Python and the Holy Grail* he is a fop and a dandy). This is because his perfection, as presented in the later medieval versions like Malory's, renders him an uninteresting character, and his healing of the wounded king is underemphasized. The story of the king is likewise lost in a confusing and convoluted history of the grail. It is little wonder that the preferred models for Hollywood films that activate the Arthurian grail quest are the earlier works, not the later ones.

If Tennyson was the father of the Arthurian revival in England, it was surely the composer Wagner who brought the grail legend to the fore in the nineteenth century, not only for his German audience but for the world. In fact, Tennyson was reluctant to compose a poem on the holy grail at all, and it was only through the persistent prompting of prestigious readers, such as Prince Edward's wife, that he wrote "The Holy Grail." The quest is not central to Tennyson's scheme in his *Idylls*, and although he radically alters his "source," it is still recognizably Malorian. But Wagner returned to the earlier quest model, his nationalist sentiments leading him to seek inspiration in the work of the great German medieval romances, in this case Wolfram's *Parzival*.

Wagner's famous opera *Parsifal* (1882) reduces the story to its ritualistic essentials and focuses on its Christian spirituality.[10] There are far fewer characters than those found in his source, and he eliminates long sections that in the romances of both Chrétien and Wolfram are devoted to Gawain and thus digress from the main story. In this way Wagner can present more fully developed characters and can bring out the dramatic potential in this story of sin and redemption. Notable also is that the grail king, Amfortas (Anfortas in Wolfram's work), while suffering from an affliction that will not heal, is wounded not in the testicles but in the side and, in order to augment his guilt by comparison, with the same spear that putatively pierced the side of Jesus. Another key substantive change is in Wagner's insistence that complete sexual abstinence is required of the keeper of the grail. (In Wolfram's work, only obedience to the grail's commands about whom the king can marry and chastity within this designated marriage are required.) Trevor Ravenscroft's 1973 work, *The Spear of Destiny*, examines the occult beliefs in the spear as used by artists from Wolfram to Wagner and by the Nazis as well. Ravenscroft's book was apparently an influence on *Indiana Jones and the Last Crusade* (1989) and is discussed in our final chapter.

Wagner's genius thus helped to resurrect the earlier grail model in the public imagination, one that has prevailed well into our own century. In "Whom Does the Grail Serve? Wagner, Spielberg, and the Issue of Jewish Appropriation," Martin B. Shichtman suggests the vast importance of Wagner by asserting that "the twentieth century is haunted by Wagner's intentionally unmediated vision of the Grail" (288), and remarks that Wagner was a grail "popularizer" (295). Although some may take issue with this assessment as hyperbolic, Wagner's significance to the renewed interest in grail studies cannot be denied. It is also important to note that he worked in a dramatic rather than a narrative medium: His opera may be viewed as a precursor of filmic transpositions of the grail legend.[11]

Jessie Weston's publications on medieval romance and her enthusiasm for grail studies exceeded thirty years. *From Ritual to Romance*, published in 1920, was awarded the Crawshay Prize for that year, and more germane to our purposes, it prompted T. S. Eliot's poem "The Wasteland" (1922). But other evidence of Weston's dispersal of the grail legend—whether directly or through Eliot's use of it—may seen in the work of Eliot's contemporaries and in that of later writers. For example, in F. Scott Fitzgerald's pristine novel, *The Great Gatsby* (1925), the narrator, Nick Carraway, observes that Gatsby "had committed himself to the following of a grail" (149).[12]

Weston's insistence that the grail's origins may be traced to pre-Christian vegetation and nature cults, especially those of Attis, Mithra, and Adonis, initiated vast scholarly debate, but it is her focus on the motif of the wasteland as it emerges in medieval romance, that exercised perhaps the greatest influence on modern grail studies. Weston points out that as the grail romances evolved, the wasteland motif—the infertility of the land connected with the afflicted grail king in the earlier romances—became associated more with the failure of the hero in later medieval works. She posits that the ritual that has become identified with the grail procession existed historically and became incorporated into the medieval romances, sometimes without the writer's awareness that the work he composed served as testimony to the survival of ancient cults. Weston cites, not surprisingly, Sir J. G. Frazer's *The Golden Bough* as influential on her thinking (vii). (Both Weston's and Frazer's texts are shown together in a scene in Francis Ford Coppola's 1979 Vietnam war epic *Apocalypse Now*.)

What Weston suggests about the survival of ancient pagan customs is in imaginative literature anticipated by Tennyson's portrayal of Vivien as a Druidic worshipper who is hostile to Christianity. This is especially apparent in her song in the idyll that introduces her, "Balin and Balan," after which she turns to her squire and remarks: "This fire of heaven,/This old sun-worship, boy, will rise again,/And beat the Cross to earth, and break the King/And all his table" (ll. 467–70). Even earlier, it can be seen in the figure of Duessa in Spenser's *The Faerie Queene*. Imaginative writers who have recast the Arthurian legend more recently, such as Marion Zimmer Bradley, have also been indebted to Weston's grail study. Bradley's emphasis upon the antagonism between the new Christian faith and an older matriarchal quasi-Druidic cult in her novel *The Mists of Avalon* (1982) arguably owes a debt to Weston, who theorized that maidens of a sacred pagan ritual may have been violated sexually, an act which drove their religion underground, although secretly it may have survived (*From Ritual to Romance* 172). One might also argue that in Boorman's film, *Excalibur*, Morgana's rancor for Arthur and his entourage (even her animosity toward her fellow pagan Merlin, who is the king's adviser) is prompted, in part, by this conflict between religious beliefs. And in an earlier film, *Siege of the Saxons* (1963), we witness the hatred of the Druids against the Christian usurpers of the land: They burn a church and execute the priests, then attempt to sacrifice Arthur's daughter, Katherine, at Stonehenge. Surely Weston's theory must be credited or blamed for the existence of this clash as portrayed in Hollywood film.

Moreover, in his book *He: Understanding Masculine Psychology*, Robert Johnson contrives a story in which "the Fisher King is wounded" when, as an adolescent, he came upon a salmon roasting on a spit and, hungry, he was burned when he took a piece to eat. Yet this morsel filled him with a gnosis. Johnson identifies this as "the myth" (2), which he credits to Chrétien and Wolfram, but this component of the story cannot be found in either of those grail works. This leaves two options for explaining how Johnson came by this story: Either he read of it in Weston (*Ritual* 130), who identifies and discusses it—only to rule it out as a source for the grail story—or somewhere he came across the Irish story of the Salmon of Wisdom involving Finn Mac Cumhail and Finn Eger, but refused to identify it as such, instead deliberately wedding it to the grail romances without acknowledging that he has done so. This is an important detail because Johnson is the source of inspiration that Richard LaGravenese cites for his *Fisher King* script. It is doubtful that Johnson knows the Irish story, or why would he not identify it as such? Unless, of course, he perused Weston's book and used its still fascinating—though sometimes confusing—discussion of the grail. We add here that another famous Celtic scholar, Roger Sherman Loomis, can also be understood as a popularizer of the legend. Loomis and his followers believed that their efforts acted as a corrective to Weston's scholarship, arguing that they themselves had identified the more plausible Celtic sources for Arthurian romances.[13] We suspect that in the general culture issues about the nature and identity of the grail are far from settled, even if, in the halls of academe, Jessie Weston's book is seen as no more than a curiosity or museum piece.

Certainly there are other figures who have, arguably, contributed to the popularity of the grail legend and whose work one can see, albeit indirectly, in films that employ the grail legend—or rather, some variant of it. Among them, one should count Carl Jung himself, not only because Johnson uses his method in *He* but because of Jung's interest in esoteric and occult religions, his interest in archetypes, and his personal identification with Merlin.[14] Even more indebted to Jung is John Boorman's *Excalibur*, the script to which Boorman repeatedly said, in interviews, was heavily influenced by Jung's thought (chapter 5 contains our discussion of Jung's influence on the film).

We cannot claim to be all-inclusive in our study of the literary antecedents that have influenced Hollywood film; we have tried only to sketch a logical route of transmission. The reader, it is hoped, can fill in any minor lacunae, as we have strived to identify major popularizers who have influenced filmic versions. As we shall see in our final chapter, the grail has been featured most prominently in Arthurian films. Since 1981, Jessie Weston's words have proven prophetic, at least in Hollywood:

The Grail is a living force, it will never die; it may indeed sink out of sight, and, for centuries even, disappear from the field of literature, but it will rise to the surface again, and become once more a theme of vital inspiration even as, after slumbering from the days of Malory, it woke to new life in the nineteenth century, making its fresh appeal through the genius of Tennyson and Wagner. (188)

Were she alive today, might Weston not include the George Lucas-Steven Spielberg and Richard LaGravenese-Terry Gilliam efforts as well?

NOTES

1. James Douglas Merriman and others have pointed out that there may be a connection between Vinaver's decision to give the manuscript what he calls "the

appearance of a modern novel" by employing paragraphs and the reader's impulse to approach the work with modern expectations (188).

2. For a discussion of the publication history of Malory's book, see the special issue of *Arthuriana* 5:2 (Summer 1995), which is devoted to the subject.

3. This is explored comprehensively by several scholars in *Malory's Originality: A Critical Study of Le Morte Darthur*. R. M. Lumiansky (Baltimore: Johns Hopkins University Press, 1964). Although it is true that one cannot expect modern conventions of the novel to apply to Malory's work, Malory himself did refer to it as a "hoole booke," and an astute reader will find ample connections among these tales or books. There are some inconsistencies, to be sure, but they are far outweighed by the remarkable degree to which foreshadowings and prophecies are fulfilled. Moreover, one can frequently explain "slips" by the confusing and often contradictory sources with which Malory had to contend.

4. See, for instance, Kenneth Clark, *The Gothic Revival: An Essay in the History of Taste* (New York: Scribner's, 1929); Alice Chandler, *A Dream of Order: The Medieval Ideal in Nineteenth-Century English Literature* (Lincoln: University of Nebraska Press, 1978); and Debra Mancoff, *The Arthurian Revival in Victorian Art* (New York: Garland, 1990).

5. Examples of these efforts are Richard Hurd's *Letters on Chivalry and Romance* (1762) and Bishop Percy's *Reliques of Ancient English Poetry* (1765). Creative imitations of medieval texts were enormous successes, witnessed by Horace Walpole's *The Castle of Otranto* (1765); Walpole also exemplified the renewed interest in Gothic architecture with the construction of his castle, Strawberry Hill (1748–1777).

6. See Mark Girouard, *The Return to Camelot: Chivalry and the English Gentleman*, especially Chapter 5, "The Broad Stone of Honour," in which he discusses in detail the influence of Kenhelm Digby's book on Morris, Burne-Jones, and the formation of the Boy Scouts.

7. Recent research by critics indicates that Twain borrowed heavily—the term "plagiarized" has been been invoked—from the work of one of his contemporaries, the minor humorist Max Adeler (*nom de plume* of Charles Heber Clark) and his story "Professor Baffin's Adventures" (1881), a story that predates Twain's 1884 notebook entry regarding the proposed novel by three years. See David Ketterer, "'Professor Baffin's Adventures' by Max Adeler: The Inspiration for *A Connecticut Yankee in King Arthur's Court*?," *Mark Twain Journal* 24:1 (Spring 1986): 24–34.

8. Examples of Hollywood films that use this device could be multiplied, but the device has also been used to drive the plots of many banal television series as well: *Gilligan's Island*, *Green Acres* (and its inverse, *The Beverly Hillbillies*), *McCloud* (which took the *Coogan's Bluff* formula and reconfigured it as a television series), and so on.

9. Scholars recognize five continuators of Chrétien's Grail romance. For a useful summary of the continuators and their contributions, see Norris Lacy, ed., *The New Arthurian Encyclopedia*, and the entry titled "Continuations of Chrétien de Troyes's *Perceval*."

10. See Edward R. Haymes, "From Romance to Ritual: Wolfram, Arthur, and Wagner's *Parsifal*," in *The Arthurian Revival: Essays on Form, Tradition, and Transformation*, ed. Debra N. Mancoff (New York: Garland, 1992): 174–204.

11. It is also important to note that music has been a medium through which the legend has gained popular appeal. Although Wagner's opera may belong to the realm of "high culture," popular music has played an equally significant role in the transmission of the Arthurian legend. See, for instance, Michael P. Rewa, "The Matter of Britain in English and American Popular Music (1966–1990)," in *Popular Arthurian Traditions*, ed. Sally K. Slocum (Bowling Green, OH: Bowling Green State

University Popular Press, 1992) 104–110; and also see Rebecca Cochran and Sam Umland,"Rick Wakeman: *The Myths and Legends of King Arthur and the Knights of the Round Table*," in *Quondam et Futurus: A Journal of Arthurian Interpretations*, 1:2 (summer 1991): 88–92.

12. See Letha Audhuy, "*The Waste Land*: Myth and Symbols in *The Great Gatsby*," in *Etudes Anglaises* 33 (1980): 41–54; John W. Bicknell, "The Waste Land of F. Scott Fitzgerald," in *Virginia Quarterly Review* 30 (Autumn 1954): 556–72, rpt. in *F. Scott Fitzgerald: A Collection of Criticism*, ed. Kenneth E. Eble (New York: McGraw-Hill, 1973), 67–80; Barbara Tepa Lupack, "F. Scott Fitzgerald's 'Following of a Grail,' " in *Arthuriana* 4:4 (Winter 1994): 324–347; and also Kim Moreland, "Courtly Love in America: Ernest Hemingway and F. Scott Fitzgerald Present the Lady and the Vamp," in *Selected Papers on Medievalism*, eds. Janet E. Goebel and Rebecca Cochran (Indiana, PA: Indiana University of Pennsylvania Press, 1988), 19–32.

13. Loomis was an enormously influential scholar, and one might observe that his view of the origins of Arthurian materials stands in opposition to Weston's. Clearly the Loomis school has prevailed in scholarly circles—although Weston's ideas have been widely disseminated through imaginative and popular media. Loomis's most famous contribution is, perhaps, *Arthurian Literature in the Middle Ages: A Collaborative History* (London: Oxford University Press, 1959).

14. See Gerhard Wehr's *Jung: A Biography*, trans. David M. Weeks (Boston: Shambala, 1988), and his discussion of Jung's interest in the figure of Merlin and in the grail as a symbol of healing (378–79). Emma Jung, together with Marie-Louise von Franz, Jung's student, co-authored *The Grail Legend*, which was published in translation by Andrea Dykes in 1971 (London: Hodder & Stoughton), although the impact of this particular text on the popular imagination is uncertain. Certainly Jung's commentaries on oriental esoteric religious texts (such as *The Tibetan Book of the Dead*) was one of the reasons for rise in the popular interest in oriental philosophy in the 1950s and 1960s; whether his interest in aspects of the Arthurian legend caused a similar resurgence is more difficult to ascertain. His influence on the secularization of the grail is certainly immense.

2

The Arthurian Legend
as Intertextual Collage

Now what a radical reversal of things this was; what a jumbling together of extravagant incongruities; what a fantastic conjunction
of opposites and irreconcileables—the home of the bogus miracle
become the home of a real one, the den of a medieval hermit turned
into a telephone office!
> —*A Connecticut Yankee in King Arthur's Court*,
> Chapter 24, "A Rival Magician"

Every narrative discourse consists, not of one single code
monolithically utilized, but of a complex set of codes the
interweaving of which by the author . . . attests to his talents as an
artist, as master rather than servant of the codes available for his
use. Whence the "density" of such relatively informal discourses
as those of literature and poetry as against those of science. . . . At
the same time . . . the artistic text . . . directs attention as much to
the virtuosity involved in its production as to the "information"
conveyed in the various codes employed in its composition.
> —Hayden White, "The Question of Narrative in
> Contemporary Historical Theory"

Films that use elements of the Arthurian legend arguably trace their roots back
to French film pioneer Georges Méliès (1861–1938), a magician who was also
an early artist working in film. Méliès was among the first to exploit the film
medium's potential for the fantastic, as opposed to the Lumière brothers' interest
in the documentary recording of everyday life. Méliès's first films date from
1897, and he was the first to translate into cinematic representations certain
noted works in science fiction, such as fellow Frenchman Jules Verne's 1865
novel *De la terre à la lune* (filmed as *Voyage dans la Lune*). His is an important
contribution to the history of science fiction in that he was translating the genre

from its origins in narrative literature into the language of the cinema. His early short films were whimsical inventions, a magician playing with light, but this, too, affected films that would use the Arthurian legend.[1] Thus, we argue that films which use the Arthurian legend are largely fantasies of the Mélièsian sort.

Méliès did not film Twain's *A Connecticut Yankee in King Arthur's Court* (1889), although it is a work of science fiction; however, when Twain's novel was filmed, it became a part of the Mélièsian tradition in the cinema.[2] As such, Twain's novel has *indirectly* influenced every film employing the Arthurian legend since. Several of the directors whose films we discuss in this book— David Butler, Nathan Hertz Juran, John Boorman, Steven Spielberg and Terry Gilliam—have worked exclusively within the Mélièsian tradition. John Boorman has said that all his films have used the Arthurian legend as a "template," and Terry Gilliam twice has filmed quests for the grail, *Monty Python and the Holy Grail* (1975) and *The Fisher King* (1991).[3]

We believe that Mélièsian whimsicalness in part affected the earliest attempts to translate Twain's novel to the screen, first as a Fox silent released in 1921, *A Connecticut Yankee at King Arthur's Court* (see illustration 1), and its sound remake (by Fox) in 1931 starring Will Rogers, *A Connecticut Yankee*. We say "in part" affected the filmatizations because no doubt part of the whimsy of these films is a result of Twain's popular reputation as one of America's greatest humorists, so the pessimistic, apocalyptic views of technology in Twain's novel have been removed and the films have instead exploited the "fish out of water" aspects of the story, as mentioned in chapter 1. Thus, while Twain's *A Connecticut Yankee in King Arthur's Court* has been remade as a film almost as many times as Shakespeare's *Hamlet*—which, incidentally, was first filmed by Georges Méliès—it has always been translated to film in a highly compromised, bowdlerized fashion.[4]

The first attempt to film Twain's novel was a silent version released by Fox in 1921 and directed by Emmett J. Flynn. It starred Harry Myers (perhaps most famous as the drunken millionaire who befriends, only to later reject, Charlie Chaplin in the 1931 *City Lights*), Pauline Starke, and Rosemary Theby (a Fox regular), and it is probably lost. However, the reviewer for the *New York Times* who addressed the Will Rogers version in 1931 observed, "As might be expected there are some sequences that are anticipated by those who saw the silent film, in which Harry Myers figured as Sir Boss, but these stretches are invariably put forth in a different fashion" (*The New York Times Directory of Film* 39). Luckily, this reviewer provides us a hint as to what the "different fashion" is: "Ten years ago and more the silent version of this same fantasy was brought up to the times, but here it has been still further modernized with helicopters, radios, fliverettes and other recent inventions" (*New York Times Directory* 39). Fortunately, the *Times* reviewer had double vision, able to remember the silent version as a palimpsest over which he could juxtapose the sound remake.

Herein we can see the paradigm for all future remakes of the film, a repeated attempt to "modernize" the story by references to contemporary events, tech-

1. Harry Myers (Hank) and Rosemary Theby (Morgan le Fay) in the 1921 Fox silent, *A Connecticut Yankee at King Arthur's Court*. The film is most likely lost, but served as the basis for Fox's 1931 sound remake. Photo courtesy of The Museum of Modern Art/Film Stills Archive.

nologies, and fads and fashions, with the effect that the film becomes a cipher through which to read the cultural preoccupations of the age in which it has been remade. Of course, even the first translation of the novel to film, in 1921, as the *New York Times* reviewer so astutely noted, "was brought up to the times." We turn to Gregory L. Ulmer for help in understanding the remake, which he indicates, in *Heuretics*, is a "specifically American practice" (86). One is tempted to view the practice of the remake as an illustration of Hollywood's voracious hunger for profits, but Ulmer argues that "the motive for a remake goes beyond the market system to the dynamics of collective memory, having to do with the way a story ages, becomes dated, or is revived, depending on the mentality of a society at a given historical situation" (86). Indebted to Derrida's thought on the related concepts of *chora* and *Geschlecht*, Ulmer uses the remake to illustrate the individual's creative drive in a dynamic tension with the spirit of the age.[5] The remake is an American practice because it reveals the continual "evolution of [American] national identity" (91). Thus, we view the "Connecticut Yankee" films as being very much alive in the cultural consciousness; they are still shown, they are still watched and, as our own act of criticism reveals, they are still discussed. They are not "dead" cultural artifacts on display like a corpse but fantasies, vehicles through which a culture interrogates itself, or reveals itself thinking about things that matter to it.

Remarkably, a version of the "Connecticut Yankee" story has been (re)made as a feature film five times in the seven decades since the 1921 silent: in 1931, in 1949, 1979, 1989, and 1995.[6] All use a contemporaneous setting with the exception of the 1949 remake, in which the frame story is, interestingly, set in 1912. In this version, Hank is presented as a belated blacksmith who is practicing as a (rather inept) automobile mechanic. Yet this setting, harkening back to an earlier time, before the world wars, is highly suggestive of what is arguably the film's subtext: A highly idealized form of romance and courtship, which is also suggested by its being cast in the form of the Hollywood musical.

The title of this chapter contains a deliberate allusion to Umberto Eco's "*Casablanca*: Cult Movies and Intertextual Collage."[7] It thus suggests the method of our discussion of the films which have putatively used Twain's novel as a source text. From Eco's essay we have extracted the following features as those essential to the making of a cult film. These four do not represent a magic number; other critics may find more, perhaps fewer, and a particular film need not display all of these features to qualify as a "cult movie." We found the following to be the most important features of the principle of intertextual collage. For purposes of exposition we present them here in a highly truncated fashion.

Eco avers that such films: 1) must have "a completely furnished world," so that its fans "can quote characters and beliefs as if they were part of the beliefs of a sect; 2) must demonstrate "some organic imperfections"; in other words, it must have disjunctions, dehiscence, a dislocatable "series of images"; 3) must not partake of "a central idea but many," resulting in part from an incoherent, ambiguous, or plural authorship, and "live on in and because of its glorious incoherence"; and 4) must have memorable moments that can be enjoyed in and of themselves even after they are removed from the original text, which can be taken apart or dismembered. These are the features that we will use most frequently in our discussion.

Remarkably, much of what Eco argues here is independently validated by a practicing and highly successful screenwriter, William Goldman, in a book about the practice of screenwriting, *Adventures in the Screen Trade* (1983).[8] Screenwriter of such films as *Butch Cassidy and the Sundance Kid* (1969) and *All the President's Men* (1976), Goldman writes in the section titled "Moments": "I believe it was the late Rosalind Russell who gave this wisdom to a young actor: 'Do you know what makes a movie work? Moments. Give the audience half a dozen moments they can remember, and they'll leave the theatre happy.' I think she was right" (*Adventures* 134). To Russell's anecdote, Goldman adds the wry comment, "And if you're lucky enough to write a movie with a half a dozen moments, make damn sure they belong to the star" (134).

In what can only be understood as a matter of convergence of thought rather than intersubjective (mimetic) influence, Eco and Goldman supply us with an illustration of the concept of the moment by referring to the scene in Steven Spielberg's *Raiders of the Lost Ark* (1981) when Indiana Jones (Harrison Ford), confronted by a scimitar-wielding Arab giant and seemingly trapped, nonchalantly draws his pistol and shoots him down. This moment, which can be dislocated from the film and cited by its fans, is memorable precisely because of its singularity and its unexpectedness.

Note that we are not suggesting that the "Connecticut Yankee" films we discuss in this chapter are cult films, nor are we interested in this study with cult films at all. Rather, we are using the "Connecticut Yankee" films as illustrations of the principle of intertextual collage. The performance model we shall employ is analogous to the collage model advocated by W.J.T. Mitchell, who urges that we think of pictorial representation "not as a homogeneous field or grid of relationships governed by a single principle, but as a multidimensional and heterogeneous terrain, a collage or patchwork quilt assembled over time out of fragments" (*Picture Theory* 419). In the words of Mark Twain, who was an early practitioner of the technique of collage, we shall think of the films as "a jumbling together of extravagant incongruities . . . a fantastic conjunction of opposites and irreconcileables."

THE "CONNECTICUT YANKEE" FILMS

The "Connecticut Yankee" films—those films which have reinterpreted Mark Twain's 1889 novel over the past century—represent a subgenre of film and hence constitute an intertextual intercinematic network. As Eco observes, "Cinema also comes from cinema" ("Cult Films" 4), and this is a particularly apt way to express the relationships that exist among the "Connecticut Yankee" films discussed in this chapter. The films have established their own tradition without much regard to their great literary antecedent, and an exploration of this subgenre of Hollywood films reveals the influence of a powerful film legacy.

The crucial underpinning that links the films is the narrative device of the timeslip, a device that was Twain's invention. At the time he composed *Connecticut Yankee*, Twain was among the first nineteenth-century authors to employ the narrative device of time travel.[9] H. G. Wells, of course, was to invent the gadget of the time machine a few short years after the publication of Twain's novel, in *The Time Machine* (1895). Most importantly, Twain's particular use of the timeslip was to exert a powerful influence on American literature and film ever after. We agree with David Ketterer when he states that *Connecticut Yankee* is Twain's "best and most influential work" of science fiction, saying that the novel may be "the first *genuine* time-travel story (the destructive ending takes care of the anachronism issue) and certainly established the pattern for that kind of sf [science fiction] . . . in which the hero, more or less single-handedly, affects the destiny of an entire world or Universe" (*Encyclopedia of Science Fiction* 1247). Given Twain's apparent conviction that time travel can occur instantaneously, Ketterer argues that "it seems logical that some loss of faith in the physicality of existence might occur, augmenting . . . [Twain's] notion that reality is insubstantial . . . a dream." Ketterer then acknowledges—and rightly so—that Twain's movement toward the derealization of the physical world lead to Twain's exploration in the paranormal and in other psychic possibilities, "including the whirligig of schizophrenia" (*Encyclopedia* 1248).

As we stated above, Twain's notion of the timeslip has exerted a profound influence on American literature and film, and in so doing contributed to the way American culture has imagined its relationship to the cosmos. Philip Klass was among the first critics to realize the vast importance of Twain's literary innovation, and he did in so in a way that anticipated literary theoretical trends in the last quarter of this century, among them what is now known as cultural studies.[10] In his article, "An Innocent in Time: Mark Twain in King Arthur's Court," Klass follows Jorge Luis Borges's suggestion that the work of certain writers modifies our reading of the past as much as it contributes to the future, and then provocatively suggests the way Twain's cultural influence was accomplished. Klass asks:

Suppose we consider science fiction in this light—modifying our conception of the past, and most particularly of one of its own ancestors, the *Connecticut Yankee*? What do we learn about the real problems Twain faced in the writing of *Connecticut Yankee*, problems which neither he nor any of his contemporaries could have suspected; what do we learn about the real nature of the book as seen through the lens of the science fiction which derives from it; and, most important, what do we learn about the real nature of science fiction itself, especially science fiction as it is developing today? Our reading of *Connecticut Yankee* must be both sharpened and deflected by our knowledge of today's science fiction. (24)

Twain's *Connecticut Yankee* most certainly contributed to the formation of a genre now called science fiction; in turn, science fiction has become one of the primary vehicles American culture uses to depict its relationship with the rest of the world and to imagine its own collective future.

We are exploring the influence of Twain's thought and work largely through what might be called an etymological excavation. Yet we can take a clue from a rather unlikely and for some perhaps even an outrageous source—Jacques Vallee's *Dimensions: A Casebook of Alien Contact* (1989). Vallee, a computer scientist who has written several books on the UFO (unidentified flying object) phenomenon, was the model for the character Claude Lacombe, played by Francois Truffaut, in Steven Spielberg's *Close Encounters of the Third Kind* (1977). A UFOlogist and author of several books on the subject, Vallee examines the phenomenon of alien contact through a comparative study of world religions and mythologies. Vallee writes:

It would be nice to hold on to the common belief that the UFOs are craft from a superior space civilization, because this is a hypothesis science fiction has made widely acceptable. . . . Unfortunately, however, the theory that flying saucers are material objects from outer space manned by a race originating on some other planet is not a good answer. However strong the current belief in UFOs from space, it cannot be stronger than the Celtic faith in the elves and the fairies, or the medieval belief in *lutins*, or the fear throughout the Christian lands, in the first centuries of our era, of demons and satyrs and fauns. Certainly, it cannot be stronger than the faith that inspired the early contributors to the Bible—a faith that seems rooted in personal experiences regarded as angelic visitations. Those who assume that modern UFO sightings must be the result of alien experiments—of a "scientific" or even "superscientific" nature—conducted by a race of space travelers may be the victims of their ignorance of the old folklore. (70)

Vallee makes several important cultural observations here, namely to identify the widespread cultural myth that UFOs are alien spacecraft from an enlightened and hence superior civilization. Note that we are not saying that the belief is widely accepted among the members of the population; rather, we are saying that the claim about the identity of UFOs is widely dispersed. This does not mean, however, that it is widely believed. As an assertion, the claim that UFOs are avatars of an enlightened and superior civilization can be understood as a manifestation of the doubled consciousness characteristic of paranoia. C. G. Jung posited the notion of doubling (without using the term) forty years ago in his study *Flying Saucers* (1958), using the term "projection." Jung states that projection is a "drastic" measure used by the unconscious "to make its contents perceived." Projection is accomplished when the unconscious extrapolates

its contents into an object, which then mirrors what had previously lain hidden in the unconscious. Projection can be observed at work everywhere, in mental illnesses, ideas of persecution and hallucinations, in so-called normal people who see the mote in their brother's eye without seeing the beam in their own, and finally, in extreme form, in political propaganda. Projections have what we might call different ranges, according to whether they stem from merely personal conditions or from deeper collective ones. . . . Collective contents, such as religions, philosophical, political and social conflicts, select projection-carriers of a corresponding kind—Freemasons, Jesuits, Jews, Capitalists, Bolsheviks, Imperialists, etc. (24–25)

To the above list, we might add the alien *doppelgänger*. Following Jung's lead, we can understand the (outer space) alien double as the collective projection of what we might call the Imperial myth, that is, that the more technologically advanced civilization discovers the less advanced first. As a result, the more technologically advanced civilization sees itself as morally superior, and often uses this view as a justification for its cultural and missionary zeal, inflicting its own ideologies and values on the vanquished. H. G. Wells dramatized this myth in an ironic fashion in several of his early works of science fiction, especially in *The War of the Worlds* (1898). Years later, the myth animated several early "saucer craze" films made in Hollywood, among them perhaps the best example being *The Day the Earth Stood Still* (1951). Even later films, such as Stanley Kubrick's Fortean film *2001: A Space Odyssey* (1968), employed the myth. Kubrick's film is hailed by many critics as one of the greatest films of all time.[11] Yet behind all these forms of cultural expression is Twain's trope of ironic reinscription, the timeslip.[12]

To be sure, Twain's *Connecticut Yankee* is an anti-romantic work that is largely an attack on the highly idealized Middle Ages of the Pre-Raphaelites and the chivalric ideal promoted by authors such as Alfred, Lord Tennyson. Yet Twain's relationship with the Gothic revival—and also with Tennyson—is not that banal and certainly not that simple, particularly when we see in Tennyson's conception of the Arthurian legend certain dissociated moments that must have appealed or perhaps contributed to Twain's own tendency to derealize the physical world. For example, in "The Coming of Arthur" (1869), the first poem of *Idylls of the King*, note the imagery Tennyson uses in the depiction of Arthur's birth:

Then from the castle gateway by the chasm
Descending thro' the dismal night–a night
In which the bounds of heaven and earth were lost–
Beheld, so high upon the dreary deeps
It seem'd in heaven, a ship, the shape thereof
A dragon wing'd, and all from stem to stern
Bright with a shining people on the decks,
And gone as soon as seen. And then the two
Dropt to the cove, and watch'd the great sea fall,
Wave after wave, each mightier than the last,
Till last, a ninth one, gathering half the deep
And full of voices, slowly rose and plunged
Roaring, and all the wave was in a flame;
And down the wave and in the flame was borne
A naked babe, and rode to Merlin's feet,
Who stoopt and caught the babe, and cried, 'The King!
Here is an heir for Uther!' And the fringe
Of that great breaker, sweeping up the strand,

Lash'd at the wizard as he spake the word,
And all at once all round him rose in fire,
So that the child and he were clothed in fire,
And presently thereafter follow'd calm,
Free sky and stars. (ll. 369–391)

Despite the Christian iconography of heavenly accompaniment, this passage, containing such imagery as the "dragon-wing'd" heavenly ship bright with "shining people" can only be an uncanny experience for twentieth-century readers well-used to the imagery of science fiction films and reenactments of alleged contacts with alien visitors. Even Tennyson's "The Passing of Arthur" can be read in a similar fashion.

Thereat once more he [Sir Bedivere] moved about, and clomb
Even to the highest he could climb, and saw,
Straining his eyes beneath an arch of hand,
Or thought he saw, the speck that bare the King,
Down that long water opening on the deep
Somewhere far off, pass on and on, and go
From less to less and vanish into light. (ll. 462–468)

We also remind the reader that in his famous poem "Locksley Hall" (1842), Tennyson envisioned commercial and military air transport (ll. 119–128).

Again we take a cue from Vallee's work. In the midst of a discussion of world myths that illustrate the paradox of the relativistic time traveler, Vallee invokes the pattern of the story of Ossian, or Oisin. In the story, Oisin awakens from his sleep to find himself inhabiting two worlds that possess asynchronous time tracks: On the one hand, he exists in the exotic land of Tir na n'Og, and yet he can simultaneously see his own land that is suffering from violence and oppression. Oisin learns that in terms of his own, subjective time, he's been in Tir na n'Og for "thrice seven days," but in terms of his own land's (asynchronous) time, it has been "thrice seven years." Forgetting the warning not to alight from his horse when he returns to his own land, Oisin dismounts "and at once . . . became a feeble, blind, and helpless old man" (119).

Remarkably, Vallee then pauses to observe: "It is not necessary to spend time here, to dwell in detail, on the tales of the island of Avalon, Morgan the Fay, the legend of Ogier the Dane, and the magical travels of King Arthur. All these traditions insist on the peculiar nature of time in the 'other world' " (119).[13] The point is that Vallee invokes the Arthurian legend in the context of a discussion of parallel but asynchronous time tracks, implying that Avalon, the place where Arthur is taken to be healed, is analogous to the land of Tir na n'Og. Once in Avalon, Arthur exists in asynchronous, but evidently parallel, time track, but it is also a fluid time, for he can be both "the once" and "the future" king simultaneously. The timeslip Hank Morgan experiences is subjective in that many years elapse in Camelot, but when he awakens it is scarcely a few moments in "real" or "objective" time in Connecticut. The trope of parallelism that leads to the violation of normal experience is a common one in science fiction literature and hardly needs to be stated. More importantly, behind the possibility of asynchronous but parallel worlds is the idea of plural worlds.[14]

What is clearly *not* part of Twain's novel but rather has become an intertextual frame made possible by filmic history alone is the bowdlerizing done to the protagonist's character. As we discussed in chapter 1, Twain's protagonist is named Hank Morgan, and critics have noticed that this is a deliberate surname, intended to show that in many ways and despite his claim to be enlightened, Hank is a double of the seductive but evil Morgan le Fay.[15]

David Ketterer argues, in *New Worlds for Old*, that an important dimension of Twain's novel is its preoccupation with what he calls "apocalyptic revelation":

There are two disconnected worlds or realms of experience in sixth-century England, since the romantic experience of Arthur, his knights, and the aristocracy is quite distinct from the actual living conditions of the majority of the population. The nineteenth-century experience is similarly dual: there is the technological utopia in which Hank believes, his own form of romanticism, and the dehumanized Armageddon that is much closer to a possible future reality. There are, then, essentially four worlds in *A Connecticut Yankee*: two negative visions—of the sixth century and of the nineteenth century—and two corresponding positive visions. Twain's purpose is to have Arthur undergo an apocalypse of mind in recognizing the negative reality of his time, and subsequently to have Hank experience a similar apocalyptic revelation concerning the negative reality of his epoch. (219)

The "Connecticut Yankee" film tradition suppresses the darker aspects of Hank Morgan's (or his analogue's) character altogether, substituting Twain's rather unsettling depictions of an American inventor for a more romantic view. The films opt to portray the character as a person of simple virtue, often chaste, straightforward, and therefore possessing an ultimately superior character. Hank Morgan's impressive powers of guile and his ability to dissemble, as well as the qualities he shares with the flim-flam man are downplayed if not utterly avoided. In all the films, Hank's (or his analogue's) goal is merely to induce Arthur's "apocalypse of mind," to use Ketterer's phrase; the protagonist undergoes no similar *dianoia*. This dimension removed, the films generally end up merely pitting Enlightened Yankee guile against an alien culture of rampant ignorance and superstition (a double of the protagonist's own culture), generally substituting the erotic satisfaction of the protagonist for any sort of cultural critique. In *Casablanca* (1943), Rick Blaine (Humphrey Bogart) is finally forced to admit to Ilsa Lund (Ingrid Bergman): "It doesn't take much to see that the problems of three little people don't amount to a hill of beans in this crazy world." Yet the "Connecticut Yankee" films force the opposite conclusion— especially in the 1949 remake, which can be seen as a response to the earlier war time film.

Hank Morgan is renamed Hank Martin in the Will Rogers version apparently to remove all taint of his double Morgan le Fay, and this alteration

2. Will Rogers as Hank Martin and Myrna Loy as Morgan le Fay in Fox's 1931 sound remake of its earlier *A Connecticut Yankee at King Arthur's Court*, retitled simply *A Connecticut Yankee*. Rogers was acting in silent films at the time of Fox's first filmed version. Photo courtesy of The Museum of Modern Art/Film Stills Archive.

3. Myrna Loy as Morgan le Fay and Will Rogers as Hank Martin in David Butler's *A Connecticut Yankee* (1931). Photo courtesy of The Museum of Modern Art/Film Stills Archive.

has remained consistent in the films we examine, although the remakes after 1949 freely reinvent the protagonist's name, age, and gender as well. (With the sole exception of the 1995 remake, Merlin remains Hank's rival, that is, his mimetic double.) In spite of the antiquated charm of the era into which the protagonist timeslips, the hero or heroine of the "Connecticut Yankee" films is always presented as superior by virtue of the pieces of technology he or she happens to have carried along—the technology thus functions as a metonymy of an enlightened age, the darker aspects of the future age having been repressed. For instance, in the 1949 *A Connecticut Yankee*, Hank Morgan happens to have on him some stick matches that he uses to amaze the crowd and intimidate Merlin. Calvin Fuller, the youthful Hank Morgan/Martin analogue in *A Kid in King Arthur's Court* (1995), is transported along with a portable compact disc player and a disc of heavy metal music that he ingeniously uses to terrify Arthur's court—here figured as an older generation that can't comprehend the subtleties and nuances of the music of Calvin and his generation.

A Connecticut Yankee (1931)

> Willy: Sure. Certain men just don't get started till later in life. Like Thomas Edison, I think. Or B. F. Goodrich. One of them was deaf. *He starts for the bedroom doorway.* I'll put my money on Biff.
> —Willy Loman, *Death of a Salesman*, Act I (1949)

As stated earlier, a silent version of *A Connecticut Yankee at King Arthur's Court* was released by Fox Film Corporation in 1921. Following the advent of sound motion pictures, it was only logical for William Fox decided to remake one of his own films using the new technology. Will Rogers, a popular star who had acted—and would act—in other Fox films, starred with Myrna Loy (Morgan le Fay), who would achieve her greatest success beginning with *The Thin Man* series that debuted in 1934. We suspect that the 1931 remake cast Will Rogers as Hank Martin because at the time he was seen as the great purveyor of homespun American wisdom and common sense, and what is more, a worthy heir to the title of vernacular humorist that had earlier been enjoyed by Twain himself. (See illustrations 2 and 3.) No doubt Rogers was cast in the part for this reason, which also betrays the film's primary purpose, namely, not only to provide humor and to bolster patriotism but to celebrate the virtue of the American common man. In any case, the remake was named one of the "Ten Best" films of 1931 by the *New York Times*.

The film was directed by the prolific David Butler (1894–1979), a late Victorian whose birth virtually coincided with the invention of the motion picture. He worked as a child actor and later appeared in a few silent films for D. W. Griffith and John Ford. His long tenure at Fox Studios (1927–1938) occurred when John Ford, Raoul Walsh, and Frank Borzage were also directors there. He was probably on the Fox lot during F. W. Murnau's stay, from August 1926 to March 1927, the period during which Murnau filmed his famed *Sunrise* (1927). Butler starred in Frank Borzage's Academy Award-winning *Seventh Heaven*, released in May 1927, with Janet Gaynor (of *Sunrise* fame), a film directly influenced by Murnau's style. Butler also had a featured role in John Ford's *Salute*, a film that Tag Gallagher indicates was Fox's top-grossing film of 1929 (*The Films of John Ford* 68).

Butler directed several silent features for Fox, all light comedies, beginning with *High School Hero* in 1927. He also directed the backstage musical *Fox Movietone Follies* (1929), one of Hollywood's earliest musicals. He wrote and directed the Cinderella romance *Sunny Side Up*, released early in 1930, the first of three popular musicals starring Janet Gaynor and Charles Farrell. Butler's *Delicious* (1931), the third Gaynor-Farrell musical, featured George Gershwin's first score written for the screen. Perhaps his most interesting contribution to the Mélièsian cinema is *Just Imagine*, a science fiction musical he wrote and directed, which was released late in 1930, the film he finished before beginning *A Connecticut Yankee*. Most of Butler's career, however, was spent directing musicals, in addition to directing some of the Shirley Temple comedies of the 1930s: *Bright Eyes* (1934), *The Little Colonel* and *The Littlest Rebel* (both 1935), and *Captain January* (1936). He also directed Robert Taylor in his first major film role in *Handy Andy* (1934) when Taylor was a mere twenty-two years old. Butler's long career in the cinema ended in 1967, with the making his final film, *C'mon, Let's Live a Little*.

It is appropriate that the singular *Just Imagine*, a science fiction musical, was the film Butler directed before *A Connecticut Yankee*, for it reveals that he was interested in inventing hybrid genres, or intertextual collages. Butler no doubt was drawn to the story because of its science fictional elements, and perhaps found that he could yoke these elements with the plot formula that John Clute calls an "edisonade." The edisonade, Clute argues, "can be understood to describe any story which features a young US male inventor hero who uses his ingenuity to extricate himself from tight spots and who, by so doing, saves himself from defeat and corruption and his friends and nation from foreign oppressors" (*Encyclopedia of Science Fiction* 368). Clute goes on to observe that the pattern of the edisonade can be found in Twain's *Connecticut Yankee*, asserting that Twain's depiction of Hank Morgan, or Sir Boss,

and the self-image of Edison expressed in his writings is most striking. In his later years Edison was, in short, something of a fraud; he may have served as a model when L. Frank Baum was creating the Wizard of Oz. . . . Like Edison himself, the hero of the edisonade is at some level, conscious or unconscious, an impostor or confidence-man. (369)

Was the film made as a tribute to the American hero-inventor Thomas Alva Edison, who died on October 18, 1931 at the age of eighty-four—six months after the its release? The speculation is not outside the realm of possibility. It is a well-known fact that it was Edison (1847–1931) and his associate W.K.L. Dickson (1860–1935) who played an essential role in the technological development of the American cinema. Indeed, the laboratory experiments that lead to the invention of the Kinetophonograph, or Kinetophone, occurred in October, 1889—two months before the publication of *Connecticut Yankee*—although Edison did not apply for patents on the Kinetoscope until April 1891. As a viewing apparatus, the Kinetoscope was a peepshow "in which fifty-foot loops of film could be seen by individual viewers" (C. W. Ceram, *Archaeology of the Cinema* 179). Edison and Dickson built the world's first film studio, nicknamed by their co-workers "Black Maria" because of its resemblance to a police van, near Edison's West Orange, New Jersey laboratories, in 1893. The first Kinetoscope parlor opened in New York City in 1894 (*Archaeology* 183), the year of David Butler's birth. It was not until 1906, however, that Edison invented the "cameraphone," a gadget that synchronized a phonograph and a projector and made sound motion pictures possible. (Note that all these events occurred in Twain's lifetime; Twain was Edison's senior by twelve years, though he died over twenty years before Edison.) Thus it is a rather remarkable serendipity that the first *sound* version of *Connecticut Yankee* virtually coincides with Edison's death. It is important to note that

it is one of the curiosities of technology that Edison, when he requested 'film', was not working on cinematography at all; he was merely thinking of an improvement to his phonograph (which he later renamed 'gramophone'). He had already learned how to preserve sounds and language, and he now wanted to supplement them by pictures. (*Archaeology* 83)

Ephraim Katz says that the Frenchman W.K.L. Dickson—who was assigned by Edison to develop a motion picture apparatus—was employed first in New York City's Edison Electric Works after his arrival, in 1879, in the United States. (Edison had founded The Edison Electric Light Company in 1878, and shortly after, in 1882, developed the world's first central electric light-power station.) In 1885 Dickson "was transferred to Edison's private research laboratory in Menlo Park, New Jersey" (*Film Encyclopedia* 338) By 1885, of course, Edison himself had already been nicknamed "The Wizard of Menlo Park" and it is worth keeping in mind that the "wizard" Merlin in Twain's novel is in many respects Hank's double—"a rival magician." Six years before the publication of *Connecticut Yankee*, in 1883, Edison made the discovery that is the basis of modern electronics: Named the "Edison effect," he had discovered that an electric current could flow from a heated filament across a vacuum to a metal wire. Given that the apocalypse in *Connecticut Yankee* is accomplished through the mass electrocution of armored knights, the Hank Morgan character in Twain's novel can be considered something of a composite of both Dickson and Edison.[16]

   The film versions of the novel, however, are another matter. A thirty-year period separates the publication of the novel and the (first) silent version released in 1921; moreover, the Hollywood of the 1930s in which the remake was made is not that of the 1920s. Roger Dooley notes that one of the features of 1930s films was a "Nostalgia for the Prewar Era." He says that "the gentler, more pastoral side of the prewar years" resulted in an "idealized semirural America," and it was Will Rogers who became a "perfect . . . symbol of the small-town virtues of prewar America" (*From Scarface to Scarlett: American Films in the 1930s* 116, 117) Dooley cites such films as *David Harum* (1934), *Judge Priest* (1934), *The Country Chairman* (1935), *Steamboat Round the Bend* (1935), and Rogers's last film, *In Old Kentucky* (1935) as illustrating Rogers's screen persona: "Rogers' sly country-codger maneuvers in uniting the juvenile and the ingenue were considerably enhanced by the homespun period atmosphere of various regions of the country" (*Scarface to Scarlett* 117). To this list we must also add *A Connecticut Yankee* because Rogers brings about the uniting of the juvenile and the ingenue in this film as well—a plot device in turn borrowed from musicals and what Roger Dooley calls the "college caper," both of which David Butler had previously directed. There was a successful Rodgers and Hart Broadway musical based on Twain's novel that debuted in November 1927 (and was revitalized in 1943), but Dooley avers that there is no apparent influence of the 1927 musical on the 1931 remake. However, we must note the use of the aforementioned convention from the Hollywood musical in the film.

In the frame story, on a stormy night Hank Martin (Will Rogers) is asked to deliver a radio battery to a rather eccentric fellow who lives in a Gothic style mansion outside of town. While there, Hank is struck on the head and knocked unconscious by a suit of armor when the wind blows open some French doors, thus providing the means by which the timeslip occurs. The wealthy eccentric who lives in this mansion suffers from the peculiar delusion that "every sound that has ever been uttered is still vibrating somewhere in the air." He believes that if he can build a radio set "sensitive enough" he can "tune back into the past" and recover actual speeches and sounds from earlier eras. This wealthy lord of the manor (William Farnum) also plays the part of Arthur in Hank's time travel experience in Camelot. In the frame story he might be described as a character who has read too many Walter Scott novels (he is obsessed with an idealized past and dwells in a Gothic mansion crammed with armor and other memorabilia from the chivalric past) fused with a mad scientist figure such as Victor Frankenstein. (The film adaptation of *Frankenstein*, starring Boris Karloff, was released a few months after *A Connecticut Yankee*, though Bela Lugosi's *Dracula* had been released two months earlier.)

We suggest that the lord of the manor can be seen as the first of the series of American crackpot inventors consistently invoked, and perhaps even originating with, this subgenre of Hollywood film. His theory that the radio is a means to "tune back" and recover a past that still floats around as vibrating sounds is an attempt to rationalize mysticism into science—an idea that is expressed in a highly compressed form in labeling Thomas A. Edison, for instance, "The Wizard of Menlo Park." His delusional belief may also be an indirect means of addressing the chicanery of the spiritualist craze of the twenties. We must note, however, that radio broadcasting was certainly not a new invention in 1931. One of the first national radio broadcasts occurred in the United States occurred in 1921—the year the silent version of *Connecticut Yankee* was released. This broadcast, on July 2, 1921, consisted of the ringside commentary of boxer Jack Dempsey's heavyweight title as he defended against Georges Carpentier. Remarkably, radio and in turn television broadcasting links all of the films of this subgenre: Beginning with the first national radio broadcast in 1921, radio appears as an important topical allusion in the 1931 remake; television broadcasting—which united the radio with visual information—was just beginning in the late 1940s, and the star of the 1949 remake, Bing Crosby, one of the most successful singers of this century was (like Will Rogers), immensely popular as a result of the radio. The 1989 remake, made specifically for television, finishes the sequence that began in 1921. All the films of this subgenre will link together in interesting and rather unexpected ways, as we shall see.

Despite its topical references and its obvious efforts to feature Will Rogers's special genius, this 1931 "Connecticut Yankee" initiated several enduring patterns that can be seen in later remakes, thus contributing significantly to what has emerged as an entire film subgenre, one that is in many ways independent of its literary source, Twain. We will remark on a few of the features that seem to have influenced later efforts, but we would first like to provide a few examples of ways in which this 1931 version brings the material "up to the times."

When he arrives in Camelot Hank finds himself in a hostile, even deadly environment, and he must use his Yankee wits and ingenuity to keep himself from being burned at the stake. He does so by relying upon his knowledge of the eclipse that is going to occur (has occurred) on the day in which his execution is slated. This follows Twain's novel, as does the portrayal of Merlin (Mitchell Harris) as his rival and as Arthur's would-be nemesis who is working with Morgan le Fay (Arthur's sister) and the evil knight Sagramoure (Brandon Hurst), to grab the king's power. Once he becomes famous and secures a position at court, Hank becomes a medieval analogue of Henry Ford: He introduces a factory that produces bathtubs as Model-Ts. Through the devices of the assembly line and automobiles Hank becomes linked to a long line of American inventors. He also introduces telephones, chewing gum, hot-dogs (via vendors in the stands at jousting tournaments)—and methods of advertising. Although advertising is satirized in Twain's novel, it is here designed to feature Will Rogers's peculiar brand of humor: He defines advertising to a baffled King Arthur as what "makes you spend money you don't have for things you don't want." Later the film features as part of the rescue effort to save Hank, Arthur, and his daughter Alisande (Maureen O'Sullivan) helicopters, cars, bombs, and knights brandishing Tommy guns, revealing the influence of gangster films (*Little Caesar* was released in 1930, *The Public Enemy* in 1931). Its use of an aircraft to drop bombs on Camelot provides an uncanny allusion to the realities of modern (i.e.,

World War I) warfare. This impression is augmented when Hank, liberated by the "heavy artillery" of the "allied troops," takes the time to free those "POWs" who have been held captive in Morgan's prison.

The plot in the Camelot adventure focuses on the forbidden love between Arthur's daughter Alisande and a page named Clarence. Because Clarence is considered inferior by birth, the couple are not permitted to wed ("My crime is that I'm not of noble birth"). Hank persuades Arthur to dub Clarence a knight and, when he is given the title "Sir Rogers de Claremore," Hank recognizes that Clarence is the ancestor he's been searching for, Claremore being the name not of Hank's but of Will Rogers's birthplace in Oklahoma. Once he discovers that his own (future) existence depends upon the survival and the marital union of Alisande and Clarence, Hank takes a decided interest in protecting them and agrees to rescue Alisande from the treacherous Morgan le Fay. (Since Alisande is Arthur's daughter Hank can claim to be a direct descendent of Arthur as well.) Although this relation to Clarence and Alisande supplies a comic twist to the plot, their love provides a serious indictment of the rules that govern courtship and marriage in a decadent aristocratic world. Yankee ingenuity (American democracy) provides the solution when Clarence, using the means Hank has taught him, saves Arthur, Hank, and his beloved Alisande from the gallows. In its criticism of the European class system, the film remains true to the spirit of Twain's novel, but it also reflects American patriotism and pride after World War I, the need for which might have been prompted by the low morale brought on by the advent of the Great Depression after the stock market crash in 1929.

There are several references to history and politics, as one might expect in a film that stars Will Rogers. Soon after he arrives in Camelot and displays his "know-how," Arthur asks Hank if he is a magician, to which Hank replies, "I'm just a democrat." (Rogers was instrumental in helping Franklin D. Roosevelt get elected to the presidency.) Later the film features a newspaper printed by Hank that refers to a "Dark Horse" political victory. Earlier, when Hank first meets the character whom he dubs Clarence he learns that his name is "Aimee," and upon hearing his name avers that "one Aimee is enough." Hank's response is a topical allusion to the famous religious flim-flam artist, Aimee Semple McPherson (1890–1944). She was Canadian born but arrived in Los Angeles in 1918 (with her mother as her business manager) and was soon known as "the Barnum of religion" for her flamboyant preaching and "miracle" faith healing. McPherson began with nothing, but by 1923 she attracted crowds as large as 5,000 people who came to hear her preach at her multi-million dollar Angelus Temple, the headquarters of the International Church of the Foursquare Gospel. Married three times, she became notorious for her trysts, and skimmed funds from the collection plate. Nonetheless, McPherson founded some 400 churches and even established a radio station, a fact that connects her nicely with the frame and star of the 1931 version. She also serves as an archetype of the religious figure as con-artist, a subtext of Twain's novel (in the form of Merlin) and carried over into this film. Later in the 1930s the archetype (re)emerges as the title character of *The Wizard of Oz* (1939).

In addition to the moments cited above that were tailored to Rogers's public *persona*, the film compliments the *persona* he had established prior to 1931 in another significant way, and becomes part of the filmic tradition. Although Morgan le Fay is strongly attracted to Hank and tries to seduce him, he remains chaste; his role instead is to unite the true lovers, Clarence and Alisande, who have encountered a social barrier. It is true that Hank takes an active interest in them for the pragmatic reason that his own future existence depends upon their marital union, but his role as matchmaker is also carried over into the frame story. Once returned to his own time Hank makes a hasty departure from the Gothic mansion, only to discover that two lovers (one of which is the eccentric's daughter) have hidden in his truck with the intent to elope. When they explain to Hank that they have not been permitted to marry, Hank loans them his truck and points them towards a justice of the peace. As we stated earlier, his role as matchmaker is a reprisal of Rogers's character in most of his 1930s films. Moreover, a variation of his role occurs, for instance, in the 1995 remake when Calvin (the Hank analogue) is instrumental in finding a solution to the class barrier that prevents the marriage of Arthur's daughter Sarah and Master Kane (the latter is of the court but not of noble birth). We note in passing that Twain was fascinated with the idea of love that was impeded by social constraints evinced, for instance, by the Hatfield-McCoy feud in *The Adventures of Huckleberry Finn* (Huck helps the lovers elope), itself modeled on the Romeo-Juliet story—in turn modeled on the Tristram and Iseult myth.

A Connecticut Yankee in King Arthur's Court (1949)

> There was nothing to look at from under the trees except Gatsby's enormous house. . . . A brewer had built it early in the "period" craze, a decade before, and there was a story that he'd agreed to pay five years' taxes on all the neighboring cottages if the owners would have their roofs thatched with straw. Perhaps their refusal took the heart out of his plan to Found a Family—he went into an immediate decline. His children sold his house with the black wreath still on the door. Americans, while occasionally willing to be serfs, have always been obstinate about being peasantry.
> —Nick Carraway, *The Great Gatsby* (1925), Chapter V

Bing Crosby, the star of the 1949 Paramount remake, *A Connecticut Yankee in King Arthur's Court*, was born in 1903, the same year as the first great white jazz musician, Bix Beiderbecke. Crosby had joined the Paul Whiteman orchestra in 1926 as one of The Rhythm Boys. Beiderbecke was to join the Paul Whiteman orchestra sometime in 1927 and remain for a couple of years. Hence, he and Crosby were with the orchestra at the same time.

Beiderbecke died in 1931 at the age of twenty-eight, approximately the year Crosby began his solo singing career as a "crooner" and commenced his ascent as one of the most economically successful entertainers of the twentieth century. James Lincoln Collier, in his biography of Louis Armstrong, posits that Crosby had met Louis Armstrong by 1929 and that "certainly they were aware of each other as musicians." He states that "Crosby unquestionably took much from Armstrong," but that Armstrong in turn may have taken much from Crosby, who was "an obvious model for any young singer—in the end he created a whole school of 'crooners,' who eddied in his wake." He asserts that Armstrong was unquestionably influenced by Bing Crosby's "smooth casual style, which a later generation would have termed 'laid back.'" (*Louis Armstrong* 239; see also 240). The point is that while he was a pop "crooner" rather than a jazz singer, Crosby's early career was associated with jazz music and jazz musicians (besides Beiderbecke, Jimmy and Tommy Dorsey). We have already noted how the film industry drew heavily from popular talents in competing media; both Will Rogers's and Bing Crosby's immense popularity was a result of the radio, but in the case of Crosby, his singing style (as well as jazz singing in general) was to reconfigure popular music. It is worth noting that his early popularity was a result of his singing ability, not his acting ability.

Bing Crosby had first appeared in a Hollywood film in Universal's extravaganza *The King of Jazz* in 1930, a film that featured the Paul Whiteman orchestra. Crosby left the orchestra that year for Los Angeles, where he worked with Gus Arnheim at the Coconut Grove. He appeared in several short comedies directed by Mack Sennett while simultaneously beginning a more popular singing career on the radio. In 1935 he began to host NBC's popular variety show, *The Kraft Music Hall*, and was to stay with Kraft for the next ten years. John Dunning reports that during Crosby's period of hosting the Music Hall, many of the great names of jazz appeared: Duke Ellington, Artie Shaw, the Dorsey Brothers, Jack Teagarden, and Joe Venuti (*Tune in Yesterday* 73). Crosby appeared with Louis Armstrong in the comedy *Pennies From Heaven* (1936), a film in which Crosby was beginning to work on his troubadour image.

Through the 1930s until 1945 Crosby was considered a radio star more than a film actor; however, the series of "Road" movies he made with Bob Hope and Dorothy Lamour, the first of which, *The Road to Singapore*, appeared in 1940, reinvented him as a Hollywood star. Remarkably, the "Road" series continued until 1962, the last one being *The Road to Hong Kong*. David Butler directed *The Road to Morocco* (1942) featuring the music of Jimmy Van Heusen and Johnny Burke ("Moonlight Becomes You"); the two went on to write the music and lyrics for many other "Road" movies as well. More importantly, they also wrote the music for *Going My Way* (1944), the film for which Crosby won an Academy Award as Best Actor. This film also won Academy Awards for Best Picture, Best Supporting Actor, and Best Song—for Van Heusen-Burke's "Swinging on a Star." The Van Heusen-Burke team was to write the music for the 1949 "Connecticut Yankee" remake, which included "If You Stub Your Toe on the Moon," "Once And For Always," and "Busy Doing Nothing."

The 1949 remake was produced in the years following America's victory in World War II, and thus can be seen as a celebration of Yankee ingenuity coming to the aid of a decadent and effete British aristocracy. The American is suave and competent in world affairs in the tradition of Twain, and not a gullible, naive upstart who is taken in by Europeans as in a Jamesian novel. Yet we believe that the remake is also, and more interestingly, a celebration of post–World War II American culture, the culture of "cool." The Will Rogers version sought, as we observed earlier, to express an American language that, as Raymond Chandler once observed, was "alive to clichés." In a sense, American language is also the subject of the 1949 version, but in an entirely different way, because in the 1949 film the language expresses an entire world view, one that is wisecracking, emotionally distant, unruffled, and ultimately more sophisticated than prewar America. The 1949 "Connecticut Yankee" replaces Rogers's flat, toneless, deadpan, colloquial, and homespun wisdom with Crosby's cool detachment.

One noteworthy feature about this version is that it is the only "Connecticut Yankee" film discussed which does not use a time frame contemporaneous with its own debut. The frame with which the film opens is 1912, not 1949, and the events Hank recounts in the flashback (including the bump on the head that sent him back to Camelot) must have occurred some years prior to 1912, during which he visits Pendragon Castle, relates his adventure to the current Lord Pendragon (Cedric Hardwicke, who also plays Arthur), and is finally reunited with Sandy who is, in modern times, Lord Pendragon's niece. All of the other films provide a frame that is easily identifiable with its own temporal point of entry. What makes this discrepancy in time even more noticeable in the 1949 remake is that although it is set some thirty-seven years prior to its release date, the language used in the film is very current, recognizably "1940s," as we will discuss in detail. Perhaps in this way the 1949 "Connecticut Yankee" displays a nostalgia for a *recent* prewar past, one that stands in contrast to the superstitious and barbaric medieval past of Camelot but also to the horrors introduced by technology and two world wars that directly preceded the film. In its idealization of an Edwardian past, this work may be likened to 1930s films, which frequently contained the same nostalgia.

The word "cool" emerged from 1940s American jazz culture known as "bebop," a form of jazz which jazz historians claim developed in the 1940s. Bob Yurochko observes:

Another phenomenon that rose from bebop [of the 1940s] was a new language or slang used by musicians called "bop talk." Musicians communicated with each other with words like "hip," "cool," "man," "cat," or "dig" to form their own lexicon, which became part of the jazz musician's heritage. Boppers became so aloof that many of their social and musical antics were largely exaggerated, finding much disfavor elsewhere in musical circles. (*A Short History of Jazz* 103)

To be fair, many of the these words were probably invented or perhaps popularized by Louis Armstrong (as Gary Giddens observes in his book *Satchmo*) but that isn't really our point. "Cool" became in turn a word to describe an entire way of behaving and managing the self, in short, a style. Robert S. Gold calls the word the "most protean of jazz slang terms" and meant, among other things, "convenient . . . off dope . . . on dope, comfortable, respectable, perceptive shrewd—virtually anything favorably regarded by the speaker." The word is the "linguistic parallel of the new post–World War II musical temper" that was "more relaxed, cerebral, sophisticated" (*A Jazz Lexicon* 65). The now historic recording sessions lead by Miles Davis in January and April of 1949, and concluded in 1950, were gathered under the album title *Birth of the Cool*, the term here referring to "cool jazz." In fact, one of the songs recorded during these now famous and historic sessions was "Darn That Dream," written by Jimmy Van Heusen and Eddie DeLange, a song taken from Van Heusen and DeLange's flop 1939 Broadway musical *Swingin' the Dream*, a jazz treatment of Shakespeare's *A Midsummer Night's Dream*.[17]

Lewis Porter, Michael Ullman, and Edward Hazell have argued that for a number of factors, many of which were precipitated by World War II, the jazz and swing audience began "splintering," and that after the war there were "factions in the jazz world" (*Jazz* 186). They write:

By the end of the thirties, the music was ready for a revolution, and for a counterrevolution: For the new music, which was called first rebop and then bebop, and for the New Orleans or Dixieland revival. (Black musicians, who tended to be less sentimental about the old South and more sensitive about the implications of "Dixieland," with its reference to the old Mason-Dixon line . . . preferred to call it "New Orleans" music.) Perhaps tired of the formulas and clichés of the lesser big bands, some jazz fans took a fond look backwards. Perhaps the cataclysm of the war fed a desire for an older, simpler music, made in a stable, relaxed community. (186)

This observation is corroborated by James Lincoln Collier, who in his biography of Louis Armstrong writes:

By 1946 jazz, both bebop and the revived New Orleans style in the Dixieland variant were getting a good deal of media attention. A vague comprehension of jazz as part of the American heritage was beginning to seep into the public mind. The legends of Storyville, of the riverboats, of the blues played for whores in smoky dance halls, of funeral hymns jazzed on the way home from the graveyard were becoming part of the American mythology. . . . It was romantic stuff, and inevitably Hollywood decided to capitalize on it. In 1946 producer Jules Levy announced he would produce a full-dress jazz movie, to be called *New Orleans*. (305-06)

While the film was unquestionably responsible for the resurgence of popular interest in Louis Armstrong after the war, Collier indicates that *New Orleans*—released in June 1947—"turned out to be precisely as bad as the most supicious [sic] fans had expected . . . Billie Holiday played a maid, a role understood to be suitable for blacks" (308). A novel loosely based on the life of Bix Beiderbecke, *Young Man With A Horn*, was published in 1938 and reissued as a Penguin paperback in 1945. It was then adapted as a film starring Kirk Douglas that was released early in 1950. The point is not to show that Hollywood had begun to capitalize on the cultural interest in jazz, which has been observed before us in any case; more importantly, jazz culture was contributing to the reinvention of American cultural identity after the war.

Again we emphasize that we are not trying to argue for Bing Crosby's stature as a jazz singer (which he was not), nor are we claiming that Crosby was the epitome of cool in post-World War II America; in fact, from a contemporary perspective, he might seem decidedly *uncool* as an icon of American culture—and certainly not cool like James Dean was cool, for instance. While Crosby and Dean share the quality of reserve and a certain "grace under pressure" (to use Hemingway's expression), as part of their screen *personae*, Crosby's is mature, sophisticated and conservative, in contrast with James Dean's juvenile, naïve, and rebellious posture. In fact in 1945, four years before the release of *Connecticut Yankee*, Crosby had won an Academy Award for his role as a Catholic priest in a sentimental melodrama, *Going My Way*. And later that year, he starred in its sequel, *The Bells of St. Mary's*.

Simultaneously, however, Crosby was starring in the smart-ass, wise-cracking, and largely self-reflexive "Road" movies with Hope and Lamour. Indeed, these movies had become virtually an institution in the mid-1940s, so that even while Crosby accepted the Academy Award for Best Actor, Hope

sneaked out on stage and began making faces behind Crosby's back. Crosby didn't know why the audience was laughing, but he started chuckling himself and, pipe in hand, continued, "This is a real land of opportunity when [director] Leo [McCarey] can take a broken-down old crooner and make an Academy Award winner out of him." After Crosby and [Gary] Cooper exited, Hope cracked that Crosby's winning an Oscar was like hearing that Sam Goldwyn was lecturing at Oxford. (Mason Wiley and Damien Bona, *Inside Oscar* 147)

The scene recounted in this quotation reveals several dimensions of American cool: A refusal to sentimentalize, self-deprecation and self-effacement, wisecracks, emotional distance and restraint, and self-reflexivity (the Sam Goldwyn allusion and the "broken-down old crooner" allusion). Thus, Crosby himself does not have to embody or epitomize cool or even be associated with cool (though in Crosby's case this latter point is debatable) to *act* cool in *Connecticut Yankee*. Bing Crosby's Hank Martin is, and is not, Will Rogers's Hank Martin. Their language is American English: It is alive to clichés, of occasional slang, and to some degree both characters are self-deprecating and self-effacing. Yet aside from flourishes, significant comparisons end there.

To be sure, one reason for the lasting popularity of the 1949 "Connecticut Yankee" remake is its talented cast of characters: Besides Crosby as Hank Martin (or Sir Boss), Rhonda Fleming starred as his beloved Lady Alisande (Sandy), Sir

Cedric Hardwicke as King Arthur, and William Bendix as Sir Sagramoure, dubbed Clarence by Sir Boss. The role of the "heavy" was supplied by Sir Lancelot, played by Henry Wilcoxon. Wilcoxon had for years played heavies in Cecil B. DeMille films and was also one of DeMille's close friends. His Sir Lancelot is in part a playful spoof of the *persona* he had cultivated for years in previous films. Also lampooned is the figure of Galahad (Richard Webb), here a smug but humorless bore; eventually this caricature culminated in the hilarious portrayal of Galahad as a repressed prig in *Monty Python and the Holy Grail*, discussed later in this chapter.

At a very general level of approximation the 1949 remake follows the plot formula of the edisonade, discussed earlier, but its more interesting formal innovation was to tie Twain's time travel device to the Pythagorean principle of transmigration, or migration of the soul, employed by Edgar Allen Poe in his story "Ligeia." This frame device was used again in Disney Pictures' 1995 remake, and both remakes depend upon the sentimental tradition of "love at first sight." In the 1949 version the "love at first sight" is established through a series of longing gazes exchanged between Hank and the Lady Alisande when they first lay eyes on each other, a series of actions closed off by Hank winking. Moments later, Hank explains to Alisande ("Sandy") what a wink signifies ("a token of affection"), which Sandy herself uses at a critical moment in order to reveal her true feelings for Hank. Of course, their love remains unconsummated because a bludgeon over the head sends Hank back to his own time. At the conclusion of the film, however, through a contrived event orchestrated by Lord Pendragon Hank meets Pendragon's niece—who looks exactly like Sandy. In fact, the niece *is* Sandy, as we discover when she winks at Hank. Sandy's soul has thus both traveled in time and also transmigrated, thus bringing about a comic ending consisting of libidinal satisfaction. The metonymy of the wink connects the frame device used in the film to Poe's story, for the obsessed narrator of Poe's "Ligeia" realizes that his lost love has returned only because he recognizes her haunting eyes in the body of another—the eyes being the very sense which makes "love at first sight" possible.

Crosby's Hank Martin ridicules British manners and formality through his perversions of British (or "King's") English. For instance, like his forerunner in the 1931 version, who refers to King Arthur as "Artie," here Hank uses terms of familiarity and endearment instead of a formal mode of address: Sir Sagramoure is called "Saggy" or "Clarence," the Lady Alisande is called "Sandy," and almost immediately "honey," and Sir Lancelot is "Lance," and at one point "big fella." He inflects "dost" and "dust," employs "hight" and "zounds," and peppers his speech with "thees" and "thous." When a contrite Sir Sagramoure visits Hank in prison just before the latter is slated to be burned, he confesses that he wishes there were "aught" he could do to help Hank, to which the latter replies, "Well ain't there aught?" thus juxtaposing the substandard "ain't" with the antiquated "aught." He refers to Merlin (Murvyn Vye) as "Bub" and Sir Galahad (Richard Webb) as "Buster," and when he is told that Sir Lancelot, Sandy's betrothed, is absent from Camelot on a quest, he quips, "Oh, a travelin' man." He refers to the ball at Camelot as a "clam bake" and later tells Arthur that Sir Logris and his henchmen are "gunnin' for" him.

The film also uses to humorous effect moments of self-reflexivity and deliberately jumbles together a highly stylized English with colloquialisms and slang: At the "clam bake," Sir Boss asks Clarence to introduce him to "the cast of characters," an obvious allusion to the movies. And when Clarence tells Sir Boss about Merlin's treachery, he responds knowingly, "Oh, the villain." In another scene he refers to the "musical comedy personalities that hang around the castle." Later, when he is about to be beheaded, the executioner advises him, "Die humbly, my son," to which Hank replies coolly, "That's the old routine." He is able to speak confidently at such a moment because only seconds before, when he discovered in his almanac that an eclipse was about to take place, he had gleefully informed Arthur that he was about to make a "comeback," a self-reflexive remark about the vicissitudes of the entertainment business. Just before he begins a joust with Lancelot, he asks Arthur whether he must do his "scrufflin' in all that scrap-iron."

What also makes this version memorable are those "moments" Eco and Goldman identify, those scenes that are self-contained and can be enjoyed in their own right, dislocated from the rest of the film. There are at least a half-dozen such moments in this version, one of which surely occurs at the ball or "clam bake" when Sir Boss, bored by the music provided, takes it upon himself to "straighten these fellas out." He approaches the band, comprised entirely of medieval instruments, and instructs each musician. He whistles to the flautist, hums to the violinist and, disappointed with the results of his efforts to reform the piccolo player, Sir Boss pockets the instrument and quips, "Have to file this away until 1776, I guess." He then turns to the "rhythm section," and teaches them to switch from three beats (the waltz) to four. Finally, he summons the herald and adds the horn to complete the big band sound, averring that there is nothing like brass to get the lead out. Satisfied with his directorial efforts, Sir Boss tells Sandy, "Tomorrow I might even teach them the turkey trot," still another of the modern allusions with which the film is riddled. He and Sandy dance cheek to cheek and, when Arthur follows suit, it sets a new trend in Camelot. It is a testimony to the success of this "moment" that this element becomes incorporated into the film tradition. Music is used in later versions for similar humorous effects, though never with any results that can match Bing Crosby's timing.

Another unforgettable (and self-reflexive) scene occurs when Hank is challenged to a joust by Lancelot, Sandy's betrothed. Hank witnesses another joust as he prepares for his own. He hears a crash and as a litter with a groaning victim who has a truncheon in his chest passes by his tent Hank mutters, "Tough luck, old boy." "But sire, this man is the winner," exclaims Clarence, after which the loser, who is dead, is carried by. Shaken by this and by his inability to be hoisted by rope onto his war steed (himself dressed in armor),

Hank suddenly sees the spotted pony Tex who has also been miraculously transported to Camelot. Tex's presence gives Hank his great idea and he appears for his joust with only Tex and a lasso, no "scrap-iron." "What kind of lunacy is this?" asks Lancelot, but Hank's only response, again calculated to show his cool reserve and his belief in his own resourcefulness, is "Let's get started." What follows is one of the funniest scenes in any of the "Connecticut Yankee" versions, depending for its humor on the discrepancy between a highly codified yet cumbersome method of settling disputes and the more pragmatic method employed by Sir Boss, who only wants to keep his head. As Lancelot (ironically a thug in this film) takes swipes at him with his sword and Sir Boss dodges him, the latter taunts the knight with the remark, "*I* was there. Where were *you*?" He lassos his opponent's lance, circles him, slaps Lancelot's horse on the rear and, through these antics, has the court in stitches. When Sir Boss and Tex take a tumble as they attempt to turn too sharply Lancelot, the heavy, mutters to his horse, "C'mon boy, let's trample him," a remark worthy of any villain found in a Saturday morning shoot-out film. At last Sir Boss lassos Lancelot, pulls him to the ground, and hog-ties him as Tex (a true cow-puncher's pony) backs up to tighten the rope. The entire court is by now in hysterics and when Arthur pronounces the winner he says, "A neat trick Sir Boss." Sir Boss then swaggers up to Sandy expecting to collect the reward for his victory in the form of her approval and confidently inquires, "Proud, honey?" But Sandy is scandalized and embarrassed by his "unchivalric" manner.

A similar scene had occurred in the 1931 "Connecticut Yankee," in which Will Rogers, dressed in full cowboy regalia, roped and dragged his opponent, Sir Sagramoure (depicted as a villain and not, as in the 1949 version, as Sir Boss's sidekick). Certainly there is humor in the 1931 episode, but it lacks the comic gags and sophistication Bing Crosby brings to the joust–lasso scene in the 1949 remake. Moreover, in the earlier version Hank Martin (Will Rogers) is not engaged in the joust because of a love rivalry, so there is no counterpart to Sandy, whom Sir Boss tries so hard to impress in the 1949 remake.

These are some of the enduring moments of the film. Though the screenplay is credited to Edmund Beloin, we suspect that many of its gags were contributed by the film's director, Tay Garnett (1894–1977). Like David Butler's, Garnett's birth virtually coincided with the invention of the American cinema. Unlike Butler, however, Garnett did not enter the cinema until 1920, when he began his career as a screenwriter. Ephraim Katz reports that Garnett wrote "numerous screenplays and gag material for [slapstick directors] Mack Sennett and Hal Roach" and that as a director "even his less accomplished productions were often noted for their flowing narrative and effective integration of background and plot (*Film Encyclopedia* 469). A scene in Sir Boss's blacksmith shop, for instance, is a brilliant comic sketch that would have worked in the days of silent film, and is illustrative of the sort of contribution to the film that we suspect Garnett made. The scene begins when Sir Boss is called away, leaving Sir Sagramoure (Clarence) in charge of the blacksmith shop. Sir Boss had been busy crafting and test firing a pistol, an unfamiliar object to Clarence, who loads it, spins the chamber, cocks it—and then fails to figure out how to fire it. He points the pistol right between his eyes, then tries to dislodge the hammer by prying the hammer back as he holds the gun against his chest. Finally, frustrated, he throws it down in disgust only to have it discharge and leave a hole in a helmet that happened to be in the bullet's path. Realizing his close call, he faints.

In scene that links the film to *The Wizard of Oz* (1939), Arthur, Clarence, and Sir Boss, disguised as peasants, set off on a "yellow brick road" singing "Busy Doing Nothing" and skipping along as Arthur goes to survey the true condition of his country, although at this point the film has begun to take on a decidedly pessimistic tone, one that provides some affinity between it and Twain's novel. In other words, while the 1949 version is a musical comedy and does qualify as an intertextual collage, unlike later film versions its bowdlerization of Twain is not quite complete.

While it opts for the comedy of the "Connecticut Yankee" tradition this film—the last before the material was reappropriated for young audiences—in its final twenty minutes or so it does take a sobering turn towards social criticism similar to that found in Twain's novel. This begins when a young peasant girl implores Sir Boss, whose reputation as a magician has outstripped Merlin's, to make a house-call on her plague-ridden family. Touched and overwhelmed by compassion, the cynical facade of the jocular Sir Boss vanishes and he enters the cottage where the girl's father has just died of the pestilence. Sir Boss says he will try not to wake the victim, to which the wife responds, "That you'll not. He's dead." This scene contains no comic relief for its stark presentation of the fear and cruelty the plague must have carried with it: The family has been abandoned by neighbors and left to die. Moreover, the hapless widow tells him the story of her two sons, falsely accused of a crime and left to rot in Arthur's dungeon. This would seem to leave only death by plague or starvation for the peasant woman and her daughter.

Stirred by this tale of injustice and calamity, Sir Boss returns to Camelot and storms into Arthur's private chamber to inform the king of the corruption in his realm. Arthur is past his prime, suffers from a chronic cold, and is hyper-sensitive to noise (a trait this Arthur shares with Roderick Usher). He has allowed his kingdom to be ruled *de facto* by Morgan, Merlin, and Logris and is thus ignorant of the abuse visited upon his subjects. Sir Boss persuades him to venture out *incognito* so that he may learn the truth—that his subjects loathe him because they believe him to be responsible for their misery—and redress the wrongs Camelot has suffered. Sir Boss, Clarence, and Arthur, disguised as peasants, depart. The impetus for this moment of truth is dark indeed, and carries with it lessons about the individual's responsibility to help others in need and about the evils that can befall a country when its leadership is weak and ineffective (all related thematically to a post–World War II sensibility).

Two more sobering episodes occur before the film returns to the light-hearted comedy that marked its beginning. On the way to London, the travelers are assaulted by a noble who is offended because the three "peasants" showed a lack of respect by refusing to bow low enough as he passed by. Arthur recognizes the noble as Bedivere and at first assumes he is taking his wife on a shopping trip to London, but he then discovers that the lady who is being escorted in the litter is not Bedivere's wife. He chuckles at this apparent infidelity, but is soon enraged when Bedivere whips Clarence in the latter's attempt to protect Arthur from a blow prompted by the fact that Arthur's bow was not obsequious enough.

The situation gets worse when the corrupt noble Sir Logris (Joseph Vitale), conspiring with Merlin and Morgan le Fay, abducts and imprisons the three. Next day, he places them on the auction block where they are sold as a package for the humiliating amount of ten pounds. This slave trafficking scene is another of those that contains social commentary, all of which are concentrated towards the end of the film. Although this "Connecticut Yankee" film ends happily these three incidents—at the plague-ridden cottage, on the road to London, and on the auction block—all serve to give the film didactic "teeth" and thus to emulate something of the spirit of Twain's work, one aimed at a mature and not a juvenile audience. Twain teaches with humor, as does Chaucer, though the nineteenth-century novel is decidedly darker in its outlook on human nature.

It is significant that while the 1949 film does recover the comic spirit that it displays at the outset, implying that the villains are vanquished and the kingdom set to rights, and ends with the reunion of Hank and Sandy, it does nonetheless digress in order to send a didactic message to its audience. The remakes of 1979, 1989, and 1995 suppress this element, as we shall see, largely because of the radical shift in the targeted audience that occurred after 1949.

Unidentified Flying Oddball (1979)

Unidentified Flying Oddball was released by Disney Studios during what is commonly identified as the "After Walt" period, putatively understood as an eighteen year period of artistic decline and stagnation following Walt Disney's death in December 1966 that was not reversed until Michael Eisner became chief executive officer of the company in September 1984. Because of its immeasurable power as a cultural force and its vast wealth as a media giant, the Disney organization has received much scrutiny both by the economic world and by film and cultural critics. For both sets of critics, the period before Walt Disney's death is likened to the mythical Golden Age, rich in critical ore. The "After Walt" period is, conversely, viewed as chaotic, uninspired, and banal.

Following Walt Disney's death on December 15, 1966, the company was managed by his brother and business partner, Roy Disney, until the latter's death in December, 1971. After 1971, the company was managed largely by Donn B.

Tatum and E. Cardon (Card) Walker, until Ron Miller, Walt Disney's son-in-law, was named chief executive officer in 1982.[18]

Ron Miller (1933–   ), the producer of *Unidentified Flying Oddball*, was a football star at the University of Southern California in the early 1950s who played for a short time for the Los Angeles Rams. He married Walt Disney's daughter, Diane, in 1954 and become a second assistant director in 1957. He produced or co-produced many of Disney Studios' live action features in the 1960s and 70s. Miller was named by Card Walker as president and chief executive officer of the Disney organization in 1982. He is evidently responsible for having initiated and developed a number of costly film projects, such as the computer animated *Tron* (1982), that did poorly at the box office. Asked to resign his position in August 1984, he was subsequently replaced by former Paramount executive Michael Eisner. Shortly after resigning, Miller quit the film business altogether. Under Miller's leadership, however, a number of important events occurred from a financial point of view: In 1983 he formed the Disney subsidiary, Touchstone Pictures, and also instituted that same year the pay-cable Disney Channel.[19]

Kathy Merlock Jackson, in *Walt Disney: A Bio-Bibliography*, provides a complete listing of the "After Walt" feature film production up to 1992 (286–290). For purposes of contextualizing the period when *Unidentified Flying Oddball* emerged, we abstract the following twelve films released in roughly a three year period (not complete for the years 1978 or 1981):

The Cat From Outer Space (1978)
Hot Lead and Cold Feet (1978)
The North Avenue Irregulars (1979)
The Apple Dumpling Gang Rides Again (1979)
Unidentified Flying Oddball (1979)
The Black Hole (1979)
Midnight Madness (1980)
The Last Flight of Noah's Ark (1980)
Herbie Goes Bananas (1980)
The Devil and Max Devlin (1981)
Amy (1981)
The Fox and the Hound (1981)

Ron Miller produced, co-produced, or saw to the development of virtually all of these films. To us this list reveals something very important about the potential Miller saw in *Unidentified Flying Oddball* as a "Connecticut Yankee" remake. Evidently, he surmised that Twain's source novel had been reinvented by American culture between 1950 and 1979 as children's entertainment.[20] Indeed, the two times it has been remade after, in 1989 and then again by Disney Pictures in 1995, it has been specifically designed for young audiences.

We are not trying to employ a tautology, namely to say that the 1979 remake became a children's entertainment because it was remade as a Disney Studios' picture. Rather, we are saying that in the roughly thirty years between the 1949 musical and 1979 remake, the cultural memory had rethought Twain's source novel, and as a result it became possible for the novel to be remade as a children's picture. In 1949, shortly after the end of World War II, the Arthurian legend was used to invoke a nostalgic, turn-of-the-century America that was an uncomplicated world of courtship and romance. (The same revision of America, incidentally, that inspired the "Main Street" of Disneyland.)[21]

The 1979 remake draws together a number of American cultural preoccupations in the intervening years between the two films. The American title alludes deliberately to an "unidentified flying object" (UFO), exploiting the culture's fascination with the subject. In contrast, the British title was *The Spaceman in King Arthur's Court*, perhaps titled as such to attract a British audience by alluding to one of its national heroes. In the immediate context of the late 1970s, the immense success of *Star Wars* (1977) had renewed Hollywood's interest in producing science fiction films, but the film that drew extensively on UFO mythology was Steven Spielberg's *Close Encounters of the Third Kind* (1977). It may be that *Oddball* was devised to capitalize on the success not only of *Monty Python and the Holy Grail* (1975) but also on Terry Gilliam's next project that used a "medieval" setting, *Jabberwocky* (1977). Note, however, that the cultural fascination with "flying saucers" or UFOs predates even the 1949 *Connecticut Yankee*. While mysterious flying objects in the sky were not a sudden invention in 1947—indeed, Twain himself had an intense interest in the phenomenon—the first noted UFO citing of the "modern era" occurred on June 24, 1947 when a pilot named Kenneth Arnold sighted a group of flying objects—that were later dubbed "flying saucers" by an anonymous journalist—near Mount Rainier in Washington State.

According to Pierre Lagrange, in his article "It Seems Impossible, But There It Is," after Arnold's reported sighting had made national headlines, reports of UFOs "proliferated" (*Phenomenon: Forty Years of Flying Saucers* 30). Lagrange details the national media attention given to the question of the existence of flying saucers and states that by August 19, 1947, "a Gallup Poll . . . revealed that though only one out of two Americans had heard of the Marshall Plan, nine out of ten had heard about the saucers" (35). Writing in July, 1955, Edward J. Ruppelt—who from early in 1951 until September 1953 was Chief of the United States Air Force's Project Blue Book—claims that by early 1949 there was such popular confusion and suspicion about the government's role in the UFO phenomenon that the Air Tactical Intelligence Center (ATIC) commissioned author Sidney Shallet to write an article on "the UFO story" for *The Saturday Evening Post* (*The Report on Unidentified Flying Objects* 85). Ruppelt reports that Shallet's article, which largely debunked the phenomenon, appeared in two parts in the April 30, and May 7, 1949 issues of the *Post*—three and four weeks, respectively, after the release of the 1949 *Connecticut Yankee*. Ruppelt reports that the public reaction to Shallet's article wasn't what the Air Force and ATIC expected. They had thought that the pubic would read the article and toss it, and all thoughts of UFO's, into the trash can. But they didn't. Within a few days the frequency of UFO reports hit an all-time high. People, both military and civilian, evidently didn't much care what Generals Vandenberg, Norstad, LeMay, or Colonel McCoy thought; they didn't believe what they were seeing were hallucinations, reflections, or balloons. What they were seeing were UFO's, whatever UFO's might be. . . . A few days after the last installment of the *Post* article the Air Force gave out a long and detailed press release completely debunking UFO's, but this had no effect. It only seemed to add to the confusion. (87)

The vast number of publications on the subject of UFOs indicates the extent of public interest and fascination with the subject and the extent to which writing books on the subject was a cottage industry. Donald E. Keyhoe published three books on UFOs in the five year period 1950–1955: *The Flying Saucers Are Real* (1950); *Flying Saucers From Outer Space* (1953); and *The Flying Saucer Conspiracy* (1955). Aimé Michel published *The Truth About Flying Saucers* in 1956 as well. And Kenneth Arnold, the man whose report of seeing flying objects started the saucer craze, published *The Coming of the Saucers* (1952). Even C. G. Jung found the subject compelling, and showed an active interest in UFOs from 1954 when he published an article on the phenomenon. He eventually published *Ein Moderner Mythus von Dingen, die am Himmel gesehen werden* in 1958, one of his last writings, published as *Flying Saucers: A Modern Myth of Things Seen in the Sky* in translation in 1959. (We suspect that the title head *Flying Saucers* was added to appeal to American audiences.) Jung was trying to work the UFO problem from the discipline of psychology. He indicates that he had read all of the aforementioned books on the subject—Ruppelt's, Keyhoe's, and Michel's—as well as media reports. Earlier, in 1953, Harvard University Press had published D. H. Menzel's *Flying Saucers*, a book whose function was analogous to Shallet's 1949 articles: To debunk the phenomenon. And as we noted earlier in this chapter, Hollywood exploited the cultural fascination with the subject almost immediately. *The Thing* and *The Day the Earth Stood Still* (both 1951) were among the first Hollywood films to configure an alien spaceship as a flying saucer.

Like certain 1950s saucer craze films that have now achieved cult status—*Earth vs. the Flying Saucers* (1956), *20 Million Miles to Earth* (1957), *Plan 9 From Outer Space* (1958)—*Unidentified Flying Oddball* was released during the month of July. Edward J. Ruppelt reports data regarding UFO sightings from the years 1947–1955 that indicate July was the peak month for UFO sightings (*Report* 315). As an institution of cultural literacy, the Disney organization was probably aware of these statistics. The release of *Unidentified Flying Oddball* after thirty years of cultural fascination with UFOs reveals how it partakes in a cultural ritual.

It is a film that consists of many heterogeneous features. It contains elements of the screwball or slapstick comedy (as alluded to in its title), features of science fiction films that employ the devices of space travel and time travel, and a handful of characters drawn from Twain's novel. The film uses the device of a spaceship that can travel at the speed of light—which, as expressed in the popular version of Einstein's theory of relativity—can possibly lead to a "time warp." This is precisely what happens: Tom Trimble (Dennis Dugan, playing the Hank Martin analogue) is accidentally transported via "time warp" into the mythical past. Moreover, it features a simulacrum of Tom Trimble, named Hermes. Through a series of rather contrived accidents, Trimble ends up on board the spaceship—named Stardust—along with the Hermes simulacrum. (Naming the spaceship the Stardust links the film to the jazz era and one of its hits, Hoagy Carmichael's "Stardust.") The function of Hermes can only be understood by examining the particular features of the Disney science fiction film.

We turn for help in understanding the special nature of Disney science fiction to Brian Attebury's article, "Beyond Captain Nemo: Disney's Science Fiction," in which Attebury identifies two broad plot formulae used in Disney science fiction films. He calls one "the Exploding Gadget" formula and the other the "Stranded Extraterrestrial" formula (151).[22] For purposes of exposition, we quote two passages from Attebury's article. In films using the Exploding Gadget formula

the gadget does not literally explode; rather it sends out emotional and social shock waves until the hero can disarm it at the end. The hero is a boyish inventor . . . who creates or acquires the Gadget, which flies, reads minds, transforms things, or causes people to behave in inappropriate ways. When the Gadget is made public, it leads to the temporary estrangement of the hero's girlfriend or wife and subjects him to pursuit by various agents of the government, the military, or the business world. In the end, the Gadget's powers are tamed, the roused military-industrial establishment is appeased or evaded, and the hero's personal life settles down. . . . As is common in Hollywood plots, a romantic resolution substitutes for the social change that the initial situation seemed to demand. (151–52)

In contrast, the Stranded Extraterrestrial formula (which we shall refer to as the Stranded ET formula) "leads to a more unsettling depiction of American middle-class life." In this plot formula

the same boyish inventor . . . in the Gadget formula is brought face-to-face with the alien Other, whom he must assist in repairing a space ship or finding a way home. The execution of the plot closely resembles that of the Gadget plot. . . . But because the disruptive agent is an individual rather than a mere gadget, the hero's social and psychological tensions can be acknowledged by being displaced onto the Extraterrestrial, rather than being buried in a comic resolution. In addition, the most significant interaction within the plot is between the hero and alien, so it is not so easy for erotic satisfaction to substitute for social change. (152)

Attebury discusses three films that he argues are paradigmatic of the Stranded ET formula: *Moon Pilot* (1962), *The Cat From Outer Space* (1978), and *Flight of the Navigator* (1986). He concludes that these films "are virtually the same movie three times over" (153). *Unidentified Flying Oddball* occurs between *The*

Cat From Outer Space and *Flight of the Navigator* in the above sequence, but contains many features of *Moon Pilot*. We know that Ron Miller, producer of *Oddball*, was involved in the making of the first two; his participation in the development of the latter is uncertain, but it is clear in any case that some of the creative projects such as *Flight of the Navigator*, released during the Eisner period (1984 and after), still adhered to plot formulae that Disney films had used two decades earlier.

As stated above, *Unidentified Flying Oddball* contains many features of *Moon Pilot*, most importantly the reluctant astronaut/boyish inventor figure. This character was Richmond Talbot in *Moon Pilot*, played by the late Tom Tryon. It is Tom Trimble in the latter: Note the wordplay between Tom Tryon and Tom Trimble, revealing another way the films are linked. Other similarities include a corporate or military hierarchy (NASA in both films), the alien woman (Lyrae in the earlier film, Alisande in the latter). In *Oddball*, the master criminal character functions are performed by Sir Mordred (Jim Dale) and Merlin (Ron Moody).[23] The atypical character in *Oddball* is Hermes, Tom Trimble's simulacrum, yet the function of Hermes can be explained by understanding how Disney science fiction films resolve the psycho-sexual tensions in the male protagonist. In this sense, *Unidentified Flying Oddball* represents an interesting variant on the Stranded ET formula.[24]

As Attebury observes, the male protagonist of the Stranded ET plot confronts the alien Other, usually figured as a female presence. In *Moon Pilot*, the alien Other is an alien Woman, Lyrae, sexually aggressive and hence intimidating to the male protagonist. The analogue to Lyrae in *Oddball* is Alisande, but in contrast to Lyrae, she is portrayed as a virginal maiden who is attracted not to Tom Trimble but to Hermes, Trimble's unemotional and asexual simulacrum. Hermes thus represents Trimble's own displaced sexuality, and it is only after Alisande shows erotic interest in Hermes that Trimble begins to approach her in an overtly sexual way. For much of the early action in the film, Trimble remains in his prophylactic-like space suit—indeed, he emerges from the Stardust dressed in the space suit at the moment that coincides with the appearance of Alisande—and only later does he pass on the suit to Hermes. When he appears for the first time without the space suit, he is dressed, anachronistically—anachronisms being one of the characteristic features of all the "Connecticut Yankee" films—in a pair of trousers, a plaid jacket, and huge bow tie. Attebury notes that the Richmond Talbot character of *Moon Pilot* dresses in a gray suit and red bow tie only after visiting his mother, who chastens him and effectively reduces him to about age twelve. He interprets the change in dress as having a symbolic significance that later inspired Paul Rubens to create "the perpetually pre-pubescent Pee-Wee Herman" character (154). We believe that Trimble's change of costume has a similar symbolic significance.

That Hermes is Trimble's own displaced sexual self is illustrated in several moments in the film. Early in the film, after Trimble (the boy-genius) invents and builds the simulacrum Hermes, he is "educating" Hermes by showing him a series of slide projections that consist of pictures of various objects of cultural significance: An automobile, a passenger jet, and a young blonde girl in a rather revealing bikini. Hermes' immature reaction—coded as sexual by a series of short electronic bleeps and whistles—causes Trimble to gloss the picture in the most perfunctory fashion, saying "This is a woman. I am a man. That is a woman. You are modeled after me. She is the opposite sex," at which point he moves on to the next slide. Later in the action, after Sir Mordred has challenged Trimble to a joust, Trimble substitutes Hermes for himself while he scours Camelot for evidence of Mordred's treachery. Before the joust begins, Alisande approaches Hermes—whom she mistakenly believes is Trimble because Hermes is now wearing the space suit–and confesses to him her romantic interest. Hermes' reaction is to lift her off her feet and attempt to kiss her, although the kiss is necessarily chaste because their lips are separated by the thin prophylactic shield on the space suit's helmet. Trimble, spying on the two from the castle, becomes irritated and gives orders via his communicator for Hermes to cease the kiss and get on with the joust.

Incidentally, the action of the joust seems to be borrowed from the Black Knight sequence of *Monty Python and the Holy Grail*. On each pass, Mordred's lance manages to knock off a piece of Hermes' body: First his arm, then his head, and finally, in the *coup de grace*, the lance punctures Hermes' chest and shorts out his circuits. Later, after Trimble repairs the resilient Hermes (like the resilient "droids" of the earlier *Star Wars*, Hermes is dis-membered and then re-membered), Alisande approaches the simulacrum and says, "You are so brave, Hermes." Hermes sighs; Trimble's gaze betrays his jealousy of their obvious mutual attraction. He immediately switches off Hermes. Thus, Hermes serves to prompt Tom's own passion for Alisande.

Shortly after, Trimble approaches Alisande and awkwardly expresses his interest in her, saying he's just an "average American boy." Alisande, however, evinces little interest. However, by the film's conclusion, Alisande realizes that it is Trimble she wants, not the asexual Hermes. Before Trimble takes off in his spaceship, she orders a note be given to Hermes, which reads, "I think you are sweet and I will always remember you fondly. But there can never be anything serious between us. I have given the matter a lot of thought and I like Tom best. But it was not an easy decision."[25] The note is not without an important symbolic significance, for in effect Alisande is saying that she is in love with a Tom Trimble who has integrated his sexual self with the self that is an "average American boy." Realizing that Alisande can travel through the "time warp" without aging—as we shall see—and hence return with him to his own time, Trimble turns the spaceship around in order to retrieve her. The film ends as a romantic comedy.

That *Oddball* concludes this way is not without significance. Just as the Richmond Talbot character of *Moon Pilot* can reenter his own time—that is, the masculine world—"no longer in a subservient and juvenilized position," so too can Tom Trimble. The integrated Tom Trimble, like Richmond Talbot of *Moon*

Pilot, "has been inducted . . . into adult sexuality, autonomy, and even paternity" (Attebury 155). The latter event is presented figuratively, as the "gander" that Alisande had carried around during much of the film turns out to be a "goose" which, as a "stowaway" onboard the Stardust, lays an egg. Realizing that the goose has passed through the time warp without aging, Trimble reverses the ship's course in order to get Alisande and bring her back to the future. The symbolic import of the egg as an emblem of paternity can hardly be missed. We can only conclude that the Arthurian material is no more than the epiphenomena of a more fundamental *rite de passage* that is centuries old.

A Connecticut Yankee in King Arthur's Court (1989)

This made-for-television remake was adapted by Paul Zindel, the Pulitzer-prize winning playwright (*The Effect of Gamma Rays on Man-in-the-Moon Marigolds*) and novelist known for his books for young adults. It appeared on television in December 1989, apparently to coincide with the centennial celebration of the publication of Twain's novel. This film breaks with some of the traditions in the productions discussed heretofore, doing so to capitalize on the popular interest in the film's now female protagonist, Karen Jones (Keshia Knight Pulliam of the then popular *Cosby Show*) and to cash in on the liberal stance it takes on issues of gender and race equality. Karen Jones is a young (twelve year old) black female. Thus we have a change in gender, ethnicity, and also the timely theme of the single-parent home.

This "Connecticut Yankee" film contains a number of features characteristic of Zindel's fiction (as opposed to Twain's) as outlined by Jack Jacob Forman in his study, *Presenting Paul Zindel*. First, the stories are often related in part to school environments. This film opens in Karen's science class, where she is studying eclipses. Later, when she employs her knowledge to save herself from the execution Morgana (Jean Marsh) has planned for her, Karen laments the fact that she "didn't pay more attention," because she cannot be certain whether the eclipse will occur on June twenty-first or June twenty-second. In Zindel's works, Forman observes, parents tend to be in the background. Here, we have the single-parent family and the theme of the broken home: Karen's mother is a realtor, and her father is absent. Moreover, in Camelot Karen (known there as Sir Boss) is treated by friend and foe alike as an adult, not a child. Believed to be a sorceress, she acts as karate and aerobics instructor and reforms the court's views on ecology and politics. Her enemies plot to behead her and later to burn her at the stake.

Forman also notes that Zindel's stories are told from the viewpoint of the teenage protagonist: In the film, Sir Boss's point of view prevails. Zindel's fiction employs language and dialogue that is "contemporary" but not "trendy." Again, the film complies with this tendency. Even the Camelot characters use little "antiquated" language but speak like contemporary characters, in contrast to the 1949 version. And while there are timely allusions to "cop shows" and "gismos," such language is not specific to a particular decade, nor is it inappropriate for Sir Boss's age. Forman argues that romance and the characters' awkward attempts at it are present in Zindel's stories. Sir Boss's alliance with the young boy Clarence (Bryce Hamnet) has romantic undertones, at least, and he sails away with her in the balloon at the end of her adventure in Camelot. Mischief and rebellion are present in Zindel's fiction, as they are here. In this version, Karen Jones incurs a bump on the head after being thrown from a horse she has been forbidden to ride because she lacks the requisite skill to do so; ignoring this, her ensuing mishap causes the timeslip that transports her to Camelot. When she regains consciousness, Karen seems to have matured from her experience in Camelot and is prepared to take responsibility for her mishap, much to her older sister's dismay. Finally, Forman asserts that Zindel's fiction features fast-paced action, suspense, and is also short, all qualities that can be said of the film as well.

As we shall see, the changes introduced in this 1989 remake serve as examples of the way in which the "Connecticut Yankee" films are continually being brought up to date to speak to a new generation of viewers, but they also suggest the degree to which the story was reinvented for a young audience.

Karen Jones is still a pre-adolescent: She enjoys her "boom box" and her bicycle, a far cry indeed from an adult male who invents guns and repairs automobiles. Moreover, in the 1931 version, Will Rogers introduced roller skates and model-Ts to Camelot; in the 1949 version, Bing Crosby introduced safety pins and the big band sound; here, Sir Boss introduces disco, aerobics, and karate—all of which she teaches to the court ladies—as well as a facile feminism. The disco music she introduces to Camelot updates the big band music of the 1949 version; as we shall see, in the 1995 remake the rock music becomes heavy metal. These intertextual references illustrate our point that films come from other films as much as they derive from literary sources.

Moreover, we see political correctness in that Sir Boss, who admonishes the queen for carving ivory and calling elephants "ghastly," teaches Guinevere (Emma Samms) to needlepoint in order to participate in a campaign to "Save the elephants." She instructs the queen in karate, a skill that saves Guinevere's life when Morgana, late in the film, assaults her with a knife. There is at least one black knight in Camelot, and a black female peasant whom Arthur (Michael Gross) interviews in a tavern. Finally, Sir Boss invents a bicycle as a rescue vehicle, an answer to the jeeps and model-Ts in the 1931 version. Other devices that "bring the film up to the times," include a Polaroid camera (that she calls a "lightning box") Sir Boss uses upon her arrival (replacing the matches in earlier versions) to convince the court of her occult powers, and a tape recorder, both of which she brought to Camelot with her in her backpack.

The villains in this film are Arthur's step-sister Morgana and her son Mordred (Hugo E. Blick), both of whom are resentful of Arthur's position. Also working with them is Merlin (René Auberjonois), who completes the anti-

Arthur trinity. In all the films, the reigning monarch, Arthur, is supposed to come to his senses about the deplorable corruption of his nobles. Although he himself is not evil, his trusting nature makes him an easy target for the heavies. When he discovers the way in which Mordred has abused the peasants, Arthur is converted to a "democratic" way of thinking. As in earlier versions (and in the 1995 remake), Arthur believes himself to be beloved of his subjects, but his image has been undermined by those who rule *de facto* with harshness and heavy taxes. Thus, Sir Boss convinces him to disguise himself as a peasant and learn first-hand of this corruption. As in the 1949 version, Arthur encounters a cruel noble who is intent upon punishing him because he refuses to humble himself. Sir Boss vanquishes the nobleman with her tape recorder, and Arthur finally arrives at the truth when he sits with some of his subjects in a tavern.

In this film, the king creates a "democratic" Round Table while he is imprisoned a second time by Morgana and Mordred, who have engineered an insurrection. When the characters escape, the villains are defeated, and Karen and Clarence evade Merlin by escaping in a hot air balloon. At the end, Karen wakes from her concussion, but before she does so she sees Guinevere look meaningfully at Lancelot (Whip Hubley) and, knowing the story of their ill–fated love, she mutters, "Uh, oh, guess you can't argue with destiny," which reveals that she knows that Lancelot and Guinevere, innocent throughout her adventure, will begin their adultery and create discord in the kingdom. It is noteworthy that this is the only "Connecticut Yankee" film to allude to the illicit love. It is possible that the producers of the film assume its viewers will be familiar enough with the love triangle component of the legend that it must be somehow included. Here it is treated lightly, but nonetheless an allusion to the ill-fated love is made. That the love triangle is downplayed, though, suggests that this version intends to court a juvenile and not an adult audience. Although technology often assists Sir Boss, in this film it is but the antiquated device of a homing pigeon introduced by Clarence (and not a modern communication system) that helps alert the court that the wicked Morgan has imprisoned Sir Boss, King Arthur, and his *entourage*. This is fitting, however, considering that this "Connecticut Yankee" film insists upon the policy of sound ecological practices and also on humane treatment of animals, timely concerns designed to speak to a young viewer of 1989.

A Kid in King Arthur's Court (1995)

> "See!" he cried triumphantly. "It's a bona fide piece of printed matter. It fooled me. This fella's a regular Belasco. It's a triumph. What thoroughness! What realism! Knew when to stop, too–didn't cut the pages. But what do you want? What do you expect?"
> –Owl Eyes, *The Great Gatsby* (1925), Chapter III

When F. Scott Fitzgerald made his first trip to Hollywood in 1927, he was asked by producer John Considine to write a "flapper" comedy for actress Constance Talmadge (1900–1973). Unfortunately, the silent era was at the beginning of its end, and Constance Talmadge never made a single "talkie." Of course, the forty-four page script that Fitzgerald produced, titled *Lipstick: A College Comedy*, was by all accounts a weak and hence forgettable effort that was rejected. The script's subtitle indicates that it was a college caper, a form of comedy at which David Butler had some success. John Considine was later to produce the two Thomas A. Edison biographies released by M-G-M, *Young Tom Edison* and its sequel *Edison the Man*. Both films were released in 1940, the last year of Fitzgerald's life.

Fitzgerald's third stint as a writer in Hollywood commenced in July, 1937, working for M-G-M. His first task was a rewrite of a screenplay originally penned by Frank Wead titled *A Yank at Oxford* (1938), a college caper set overseas, starring Robert Taylor. Taylor had become a Hollywood star two years earlier as a result of his appearance in the highly successful sentimental melodrama *Magnificent Obsession* (1935), later remade in 1954 and starring Rock Hudson and Jane Wyman. (In 1954 Taylor starred in *Knights of the Round Table*, discussed in chapter 3). We assume that *A Yank at Oxford* is a film that employs the popular formula that began with Will Rogers and, in turn, Mark Twain. Roger Dooley writes:

Several Rogers vehicles dealt with American-European cultural contrasts, not in the Jamesian sense, but very much in the tradition of Twain, as the not-so-innocent abroad exposes the phony nobleman and wins the respect of the real one. It would be pointless to discuss all his films [of the 1929–1932 period], since most were cut from much the same pattern, tailored expertly to his nationally familiar personality and allowing him every opportunity to ad-lib timely witticisms, as he did in his widely syndicated column. (*Scarface to Scarlett* 525)

After Will Rogers's accidental death on August 15, 1935, it was Robert Taylor (among others) who carried on the Rogers tradition—certainly not as the homespun humorist but most certainly as the American abroad. Robert Taylor's first film, *Handy Andy*, released in August 1934—Taylor was a mere twenty-two years old—was directed by the ubiquitous David Butler and starred Will Rogers. In May 1936 Twentieth Century-Fox rereleased Rogers's 1931 *A Connecticut Yankee*, and in 1937 Robert Taylor appeared in *Lest We Forget*, a short feature tribute to Will Rogers. *A Yank at Oxford* contains virtually every feature characteristic of Rogers's 1929–1932 output as delineated above (minus the ad-libbed witticisms) but it is set on a college campus.

The extent of F. Scott Fitzgerald's work on *A Yank at Oxford* is unclear; seven writers received a writing credit on the film, although Fitzgerald was not one of them. However, the fact that he was asked to do a rewrite on the film is not entirely a result of coincidence. Sheila Graham, a Hollywood columnist with whom Fitzgerald was romantically involved during his last years, writes:

Eddie [Mayer] told me later that Scott [Fitzgerald] had . . . come west on a six-month contract to write the screen play for *A Yank at Oxford*. Eddie smiled a little sadly as he told me this. They had hired Scott Fitzgerald, he went on, because Scott's first novel, *This Side of Paradise* [1920], a remarkable first novel which made him famous as a young man just out of Princeton, dealt with college youth. But from *This Side of Paradise* to *A Yank at Oxford*—Eddie shook his head. It was obvious that he thought it a great waste of this man's time to write for pictures. (*Beloved Infidel* 135)

Despite Eddie Mayer's misgivings about Fitzgerald's involvement, the film was a popular prewar success. (It was remade in 1984 as *Oxford Blues*.) Roger Dooley indicates that during the years 1921–1930, seventy films were released with subjects having to do with college: During that decade, this works out to an average of seven films a year had college as a subject, meaning that such a film was released approximately every seven weeks for ten years. Dooley writes:

The basis of all this fascination with college was the convergence of two national passions: for youth and for sports, never more frenzied that in the '20s. College football as played by the Ivy League was followed by millions of fans every Saturday on radio, then a few days later watched in newsreels. Thanks to the jazz orchestras of the day (many of which looked and sounded collegiate), like Rudy Vallee and his Connecticut Yankees and Fred Waring and his Pennsylvanians, as well as theater organ recitals, vaudeville, band concerts and radio programs, college medleys, especially during the football season, were almost as popular as those from the Gay '90s. (*From Scarface to Scarlett* 432)

This brief background places Disney Pictures' *A Kid in King Arthur's Court* (1995) in the context of a number of decades-old cultural preoccupations, in particular with youth and sports. Thomas Ian Nicholas, who plays Calvin Fuller (the youthful Hank Martin analogue) in the film, had met with previous success in *Rookie of the Year*, a box-office hit in 1993. Will Rogers was fifty-one years old at the time *A Connecticut Yankee* was released; Thomas Ian Nicholas was only a teenager in 1995. However, the more significant intertext for the film is *The Natural* (1984), given that Calvin's baseball team, like Roy Hobbs's team in the earlier film, is named the Knights. We discuss *The Natural* in chapter 6 as an example of the postmodern quest, but as we shall see, the film also shows a marked indebtedness to traditions established by its forerunners of the same or similar titles, and to *The Black Knight* and *Siege of the Saxons*, two films we examine in chapter 4 as examples of forms of agitational propaganda.

In this remake the protagonist is accidentally transported across time by an inept Merlin (Ron Moody) who, fooled by the "Knight" logo on Calvin's uniform, mistakenly believes he has summoned a puissant knight from the future, not a kid who has just struck out in a baseball game. Thus, the motif of the reluctant hero and the accidental nature of his time travel adventure is preserved in this film. The function of the master criminal of the Stranded ET plot is fulfilled by the evil Lord Belasco (Art Malik), a noble who has won Arthur's confidence and is the *de facto* ruler of the kingdom as a result of the king's incessant mourning over his deceased wife. Belasco wants to marry Arthur's older daughter, Princess Sarah (Kate Winslet) and also to be named the king's successor, and he will stop at nothing to achieve his goal. Since Merlin is benevolent, and is presumably rendered virtually powerless by his entrapment in the cult "Well of Destiny," Belasco is the character who sees Calvin—the interloper—as his rival and vows to kill him. In this way the film departs from earlier versions, and from Twain's novel, in which Merlin and Hank (or his counterpart) compete for court favor and fame.

A melancholy and uxorious King Arthur (Joss Ackland) has lost his desire to live after the death of Guinevere. As one of the peasants says early in the film, "the king is no longer a man of the people." This situation, in which an impostor manipulates the king at the expense of his subjects, occurs in several filmic versions. As we have seen, one challenge for each "Connecticut Yankee" film is how to deal with the love triangle. In the 1949 remake, for instance, it is suppressed, or rather displaced onto the rivalry between Lancelot and Sir Boss for Sandy's love. The 1989 remake portrays a "good" Guinevere but hints at the impending disaster, as we discussed earlier. *A Kid in King Arthur's Court* apparently modifies the 1931 version, in which Guinevere is Arthur's deceased wife. She is not alluded to in the Will Rogers version, but Arthur does have a daughter, so one can assume there was at one time a queen Guinevere. That Arthur has two daughters in the 1995 remake is one way that it hearkens back to the 1931 version. Here, the king loved his queen and there is no intimation that she was unfaithful to him but she is, at least indirectly, the reason the kingdom is neglected. Of course the shift to younger viewers is in part responsible for the omission of adultery, but the 1949 version, aimed at an adult audience, also ignored this feature of the legend by having Guinevere conveniently absent.

The "heavy" or villain of the film, Lord Belasco, is not a figure drawn from the Arthurian legend, nor does he have a precedent in the filmic tradition. Instead, the name is drawn from the cultural memory, invoking the famous theater director, playwright, and set designer, David Belasco (1853–1931). Belasco's autobiography, *The Theatre Through Its Stage Door*, was published in 1919, preceding Fitzgerald's *Gatsby* by about six years. Thus Belasco was so well known in Fitzgerald's time, one might well assume, that Fitzgerald could invoke Belasco's name in order to suggest something about his titular protagonist, Jay Gatsby. Gatsby's mansion is his own self-designed set, the set of a movie in which he also plans to star. Like David Belasco the set designer, Gatsby has attended to every detail in order to impress upon his guests that he is the genuine item, a man of culture and taste, and not a racketeer. When Owl-Eyes, then, refers to Gatsby as a "regular Belasco," he is saying that Gatsby is a master illusionist, a confidence man, not unlike the Wizard of Oz—a flim-flam artist. Likewise, the name is surely no accident in *A Kid in King Arthur's Court*: Lord Belasco subsumes the role of Merlin in earlier films and in the tradition begun by the novel, as he is both the villain and rival magician to the Yankee interloper, in this case Calvin Fuller. The name Belasco also comments on his deceptive nature, in that he pretends to be Arthur's closest, most trustworthy council, but in fact is the king's enemy.

As we have seen, each remake of the "Connecticut Yankee" material attempts to work the angle of modern technology as it is introduced to the world of King Arthur, one of the ways that this material is constantly being "brought up to the times." The gadgets, or inventions, also reflect the age of the targeted audience for each film.

In addition to the aforementioned rock music, *A Kid in King Arthur's Court* shares with its 1989 forerunner the practice of karate that is, interestingly, introduced to female members of the court. In the 1989 version, Sir Boss teaches karate to Guinevere and her ladies in waiting, while in the 1995 remake Princess Katey (Paloma Baeza) sees Calvin as he hones his skill and thinks he is dancing. In the 1995 version, roller blades replace roller skates, and bicycles also make an appearance, though in the updated form of the mountain bike. The three innovations this film introduces are Calvin's use of the Swiss Army knife to escape prison (replacing, for instance, the magnet used by Bing Crosby's character in the 1949 remake), chewing gum (though Will Rogers chew gum in the 1931 version), and hamburgers. Calvin introduces the pleasure of "Mad Dog Bubble Gum" to the king himself who, like a child, at first tries to swallow it. In his scene Arthur is perplexed to learn that the gum is not a food to be swallowed and asks, "What is its purpose?" Calvin, at first daunted by the question, replies, "There *is* no purpose." The young hero also prepares "a double cheeseburger with lettuce and tomato on a whole wheat bun," in order to impress Katey, who finds it delicious. When she asks what it is, Calvin says a "Big Mac," an innovation directed at a young and contemporary audience. Such innovations serve as cultural registers, and it is not surprising that the sandwich metonymically associated with the "Golden Arch" appears in this film.

Each of the innovations helps to create those "moments" that will communicate with and establish a loyal audience, while the use of modern devices and the motif of the genius inventor is one feature present in all of the "Connecticut Yankee" films, so that some measure of continuity may be seen in all of these versions, despite the varied approaches to the material.

Other features this film shares with its forerunners is its propensity to allude to other films and its use of colloquialisms for humorous ends. For instance, when Katey leads Calvin through a passageway in order to show him the "Well of Destiny" where Merlin appears, Calvin refers to the room as the "temple of doom," a reference to the "Indiana Jones" film. While in the room, Calvin recognizes Excalibur, much to Katey's dismay, but he tells her by way of explanation," I watch a lot of CNN." He mistakes the "Well of Destiny" for a hot tub and later, when he and Arthur engage in a scuffle in their attempt to rescue Katey—who has been abducted by Belasco—Calvin fruitlessly tries to cut a chandelier so that it will crush their adversaries, and he utters "Gee, this always works in the movies." Finally, at the tournament designed to decide who will marry Sarah, Arthur mutters to himself, "Kick his butt," as his (and Sarah's) choice, the commoner Master Kane (Daniel Craig) prepares to battle Bealsco, the other finalist. It is interesting to note that the ongoing intercinematic network continues in this scene. Here, Master Kane is defeated by Belasco only becasue the latter cheats. He wears a jewel in his helmet that reflects the sun; this spooks Master Kane's horse and causes him to lose the joust. Earlier, in the 1989 version, Sir Boss assists Lancelot in his joust with Mordred by polishing his armor; this blinds Mordred and his horse, so that he loses. In this version the device serves the cause of good, but the trick is carried over to serve evil in the 1995 remake.

As we mentioned, the frame of this film—with its baseball game and its team called the Knights—is indebted to *The Natural* and, of course, we have seen how it also continues and adapts other features found in previous "Connecticut Yankee" films. However, *A Kid in King Arthur's Court* also seems to have borrowed for a few of its plot innovations and details from two 1950s films that we discuss in detail in chapter 4: *The Black Knight* (1954) and *Siege of the Saxons* (1963). From the latter comes, we suppose, the name of Arthur's younger daughter Katey (Katherine). *Siege of the Saxons* revolves around a would-be usurper who abducts Arthur's daughter and heir-apparent, Katherine (or Kate). The villain attempts to force Katherine into marriage and, when she refuses, plans to undermine her. Here, too, the villain Belasco kidnaps Katey in an effort to force her older sister Sarah to marry him. Since there is no tradition for these names or for this forced marriage plot that stems from Twain's novel or from previous "Connecticut Yankee" productions, we assume that *Siege of the Saxons* may well have suggested it.

The Black Knight focuses on a blacksmith named John (Alan Ladd) who falls in love with Lady Linnet, daughter of the knight under whom he serves. Moreover, Camelot is threatened by infiltrators who plan to make it vulnerable to invaders, and John is recruited by one of Arthur's faithful knights to work undercover as the Black Knight so that he may expose the threat. By doing so, he earns his knighthood and wins Linnet as well. In *A Kid in King Arthur's Court*, there is a Black Knight—also incognito and also a good force—who turns out to be none other than Arthur's daughter Sarah. Thus, the gender issue is raised to show that this is a politically correct Camelot, one in which women can excel at the traditionally masculine role of knighthood and warfare. But the more significant influence of *The Black Knight* is seen by the fact that Master Kane, Calvin's trainer and a commoner, loves Sarah and she him. The film must therefore resolve the issue of how they can be married and overcome the class barrier. In *The Black Knight* John earns his title and is thus elevated to Linnet's class so that he becomes an acceptable suitor; here it is accomplished by the fact that Arthur, in order to reclaim the love and trust of his subjects, opens the tournament to all (commoners included), and by the fact that Sarah—the heroine and the Black Knight—has, as Arthur avers, "earned the right" to choose her own husband. Thus both films share the propagandistic role of reinforcing the demo-cratic principle over the autocratic, though the 1995 production is updated to challenge the passive role of women and to suggest that they are not chattel. As we have seen, however, the effort to champion Yankee democracy and Equal Opportunity can also be traced back to the liberal Democratic strains of the Will Rogers version.

In fact, the film largely follows the model of the 1931 version by invoking elements of the romantic comedy. When Belasco is exposed as a criminal and traitor, he is merely banished. Moreover, Merlin arranges Calvin's moment of return to his own time to occur *before* Calvin's strike out that began the film—thus allowing Calvin to live the American myth of the second chance. His newly-acquired confidence (which mirrors Arthur's) allows him to hit a homer with a bat that, symbolically, has "Excalibur" inscribed on it.[26] When he reaches home base, Calvin finds Katey awaiting him and also sees Arthur, who is dressed in contemporary denim and blue jeans, sitting in the stands. The reunion of the lovers in the concluding frame thus continues the tradition of the Rogers and Crosby versions, accomplished by coupling the device of time travel with the principle of transmigration. As in *The Natural* (1984), the act of hitting the home run allows the sports hero to erase time, complete the fantasy, and begin anew. The past is revised. Time travel can be used as a way of eradicating time; in Jay Gatsby's quest to achieve the grail that is Daisy, linear time doesn't exist at all. Gatsby's story does not include a realization of the myth of the second chance; he is a failed time traveler.

MONTY PYTHON AND THE HOLY GRAIL (1975)

> The boys all took a flier at the Holy Grail now and then. It was a several-years' cruise. They always put in the long absence snooping around . . . though none of them had any idea where the Holy Grail really was, and I don't think any of them actually expected to find it, or would have known what to do with it if he *had* run across it. . . . Every year expeditions went out holy grail-ing, and next year relief expeditions went out to hunt for *them*.
> —Mark Twain, *A Connecticut Yankee in King Arthur's Court*,
> Chapter 9, "Beginnings of Civilization"

> My first thought was, he lied in every word,
>   That hoary cripple, with malicious eye
>   Askance to watch the working of his lie
> On mine, and mouth scarce able to afford
> Suppression of the glee, that pursed and scored
>   Its edge, at one more victim gained thereby.
>   —Robert Browning, 'Childe Roland
>   to the Dark Tower Came'

We believe that Twain's dismissive spoof of "holy grailing" in *Connecticut Yankee* is probably the distant intertext for *Monty Python and the Holy Grail*. (See illustration 4.) In his *Connecticut Yankee* Twain imagined, for example, that the knights of Camelot could ride about wearing sandwich boards, a highly humorous incongruity that finds a nightmarish double in the medieval paintings of Hieronymus Bosch. Jacques Lacan (in the 1949 essay, "The Mirror Stage") saw in Bosch visual analogies to his theory of the condition of the human unconscious, the unconscious for him being an analogy to the heuretical method by which all texts—both private (dreams) and public (texts)—are generated: The unconscious is a text generator. The heuretics of Mark Twain and the Monty Python group are not vastly different, for in the work of the latter—both in its original, televised incarnation as *Monty Python's Flying Circus* (1969–1974) and in its feature films—we see a similar use of the Middle Ages as a vehicle to generate humorous effects out of—absurdist? nonsensical?—incongruity. If we imagine *Connecticut Yankee* as the relay, then the two authorial entities—Mark Twain and Monty Python—have much in common in their use of the discursive site known as "the Middle Ages," just as the Monty Python group's own configuration was both British and American (Terry Gilliam).

The "Holy Grail" in Gilliam and Jones's directorial team effort functions rather like British director Alfred Hitchcock's famed "MacGuffin," an object the desire for which initiates the plot but finally is insignificant to it and was of no real consequence to begin with.[27] Of course, unlike Hitchcock's films, *Monty Python and The Holy Grail* is not plotted at all, for plot is a feature of narrative poesis and the film contains no narrative as such; Gilliam has observed that the film is not really a feature film at all but an assemblage of "short sketches" and gags.[28] We would argue, however, that the film does have a unity, although it is unconventional, with "title pages" that signal a new sequence. Its unity is encyclopedic, that is, it is organized topically, as in, for instance, "The Adventures of Sir Galahad" and "The Story of Sir Robin." Sir Robin, however, is not a character in the received Arthurian legend, but the imposition of this legendary figure into the proceedings is a minor illustration of how the film is a dense assemblage of heterogeneous elements and allusions: Films and film genres (an allusion in the opening credits to the films of Ingmar Bergman; animation, documentary, musical, and slapstick comedy), self-reflexivity ("Scene 24"), and fairy tales ("The Three Billy Goats Gruff"). In short, it is an attempt to subvert any logics of signification. Eco might say that the film thrives on "its glorious incoherence," echoed in Terry Gilliam's own retrospective observation that the film has a "mad energy."

This film abounds with dislocatable moments; in fact, it is a veritable feast for the cult audience the Monty Python Group has acquired. We would like to examine only one of these moments in order to illustrate our points about the heuristic principle that informs its composition. "The Bridge of Death" scene draws upon several codes for its invention and meaning. Here, King Arthur (Graham Chapman) leads four of his knights to this adventure: Sir Bedivere (Terry Jones), Sir Lancelot (John Cleese), Sir Robin (Eric Idle) and Sir Galahad (Michael Palin). The sketch begins with a self-reflexive remark when one of the knights says, "Look, there's the old man from scene 24" who, it turns out, is the keeper of the Bridge of Death (Terry Gilliam). Three questions will be asked of

4. From left: Terry Jones as Sir Bedivere, Graham Chapman as King Arthur, John Cleese as Sir Lancelot, and Eric Idle as Sir Robin in *Monty Python and the Holy Grail*. Photo courtesy of The Museum of Modern Art/Film Stills Archive.

anyone wishing to cross the bridge, and should he respond incorrectly he will be "cast into the gorge of eternal peril." The keeper, remarkably like the "hoary cripple" at the opening of Browning's poem that serves as our epigraph, announces: "Whoever cross the bridge of death must answer me these questions three, 'ere the other side he see." Lancelot is the first to try and succeed, largely because the questions are so easy: "What is your name?"; "What is your quest?"; and "What is your favorite color?" Sir Robin, initially reluctant to try the test, is encouraged by the ease with which Lancelot is allowed to pass, so he eagerly steps forward to cross the bridge. The first two questions are the same as those that were posed to Lancelot, but the third question to him is "What is the capitol of Assyria?" "I don't know that!" he exclaims and he is immediately jettisoned into a bellowing chasm. The keeper chuckles malignantly to himself. Next is Galahad, to whom the keeper of the bridge poses the same questions he had asked Lancelot: Galahad responds accurately to the first two but when he avers that his favorite color is blue (as Lancelot had answered), he becomes flustered and stutters, "No, yellow" but this is enough to trip him up and he too is cast into the gorge. At last Arthur and Bedivere approach the bridge and Arthur answers the first two questions about his name and quest. The third question, however, is "What is the air speed velocity of an unladen swallow?" to which the king responds with a counter-question: "What do you mean? African or European swallow?" The tables have been turned on the crafty bridge-keeper, who exclaims: "What? I don't know that!" after which he is himself jettisoned into the pit. Bedivere, impressed by Arthur's ability to befuddle the keeper asks, "How do you know so much about swallows?" to which the king replies coolly, "You have to know these things when you're a king, you know." The two cross the bridge, an "Intermission" is flashed upon the screen, but the film then resumes immediately—another self-reflexive point intended to add humor.

This entire scene takes just three minutes and thirty-eight seconds, yet it is extremely dense because of the number of discursive codes it employs. For instance, the "Bridge of Death" that Lancelot crosses successfully and with great courage is reminiscent of an episode found in several medieval romances (among them Chrétien's *Lancelot*) in which the knight must cross a perilous sword-bridge, using nothing but his hands, in order to rescue Guinevere, who has been abducted and taken into a sort of Celt otherworld by Meleagant. A more obvious code, however, is that of the folktale "The Three Billy Goats Gruff," especially with the wicked keeper who demands authority over his bridge but who is vanquished at the end. Its structure is tripartite, of course, with the three questions, and this episode also relies upon science and geography, when the anachronistic "technical warfare" between Arthur and the bridge keeper commences in the form of information about swallows. As we have suggested above and in our epigraph, Browning's poem "'Childe Roland to the Dark Tower Came'" might well serve as one of the intertexts for the bridge-keeper sketch.

In his review of *Jabberwocky* (1977), the first solo directorial effort of Terry Gilliam (1940–   ), Richard Corliss placed Gilliam in a "tradition of Americans who make films in England," a tradition which included directors Richard Lester (*A Hard Day's Night, Help!*), Joseph Losey (*The Servant*), and screenwriter William Rose (who later, back in the United States, won an Academy Award for his screenplay for *Guess Who's Coming to Dinner?*). On the basis of the "spirited jape" *The Holy Grail* and its follow-up, *Jabberwocky*, Corliss claimed that Gilliam had "surrendered" himself to "the British sense of humor, that odd combination of Oxbridgian wit and music-hall vulgarity." He observed about *Jabberwocky* that its humor consisted of "arcane references to the chivalric code [that] rub up against bawdy gags about knickers and knockers" ("Pretty Ugly" 73). While we agree with Corliss in his identification of the source of the humor as incongruity, we disagree with him when he says that it is a peculiarly British invention. What Corliss is identifying as an "odd combination" can be more precisely identified as a "density" of heterogeneous discursive codes that we have called intertextual collage. Moreover, we suggest the "odd combination" cannot always be immediately comprehended as funny, as the sequence in the film that consists of Arthur's dismembering the Black Knight reveals: Is it funny or horrible? Or both funny and horrible? (A more infamous illustration is the sketch concerning Mr. Creosote in *The Meaning of Life* (1983), who explodes from over-eating, a scene that finds its dark double in the 1995 film *Seven* in the image of an obese man dead from gluttony.)

The performance model we are both using and advocating is really a method of inventing a way to talk about how individual filmmakers have used the various discursive codes available to them as members of human culture. We must emphasize that we are not saying that the invention process that the film represents is a random one. We acknowledge that each film represents a process of invention operating within a system of constraints, these constraints being both highly individualized (idiosyncratic) and institutional (the general logic that allows inscription). We argue that much of the oddness of *Jabberwocky* that Corliss's review identifies can also be attributed to *The Holy Grail*, revealing how both films grew out of the encounter between pure chance (the inventive principle) on the one hand, and Gilliam's (or the Monty Python group's) obsessions (constraints) on the other. The action of chance within these (determinate) constraints no doubt helps explain the process of creativity in general: Chance provides the grain of sand that irritates the oyster enough to make the pearl. Chance is the co-author of all artworks. We take this operation of chance and constraint—which should not be necessarily understood as a dialectical synthesis—to be central to the Monty Python group's creative method (for example), hence the group's apparent affinities to Surrealistic practices. We conclude that *The Holy Grail* is not a purely intentional object, as the commentary by the film's directors, Terry Gilliam and Terry Jones, on the "audio commentary" track on the Voyager Criterion laser disc version of the film would attest. The film is, in part, also a found object. In retrospect, we can see that Gregory L. Ulmer's discussion of *chora* and *Geschlecht* that governed our understanding of the remake, is also a way of pointing out how individual invention or creation happens within a system of constraints, both private and social.

Indeed, in the etymology of the theatrical use of the word "gag" one can see in its use the room for an individualized, spontaneous invention within an otherwise prescripted process. The OED provides a definition of "gag" as "expressions, remarks, etc. not occurring in the written piece but interpolated or substituted by the actor." The word would seem to have originated in the mining industry, where a gag was a makeshift piece of timber used as a prop or stay to support the walls of a shaft, a temporary support until a stronger piece of timber could be used. Through the process of metaphorical elaboration, one meaning of gag referred to an object used to prop open the mouth, and in certain circumstances to even stop it up or seal it (as in a legal "gag order"). In its theatrical use, however, the word is used to name a moment of individual spontaneity and creativity within a preexisting written piece. The specific problem for the gag writer is how to introduce novelty (the "bit") into the larger, stereotyped unit of the comic "sketch." *Monty Python and the Holy Grail* represents the Monty Python group's solution to the specific problem of how to translate the format of their television show, that consisted of short sketches and gags, into a feature film. The solution was to gather the sketches under the rubric "quest," although even this particular use of narrative poesis is eventually stopped—or "gagged."

Twain's attitude toward "holy grailing" was probably influenced by Tennyson, although Twain never cited, nor would he have cited, Tennyson's *Idylls* as influencing *Connecticut Yankee*. Tennyson himself was reluctant to compose an idyll using the grail material contained in his medieval source, Malory, because of its Catholicism in general and because of its emphasis upon serving God by adhering to a monastic ideal. Instead, Tennyson espouses a Protestant view, one that stresses the importance of balancing the active and contemplative lives. He composed his grail idyll reluctantly, and only at the urging of the royal family. His son, Hallam Tennyson, quotes from the poet's diary: "I doubt whether the 'San Graal' would have been written but for my endeavor, and the Queen's wish, and that of the Crown Princess" (*Alfred, Lord Tennyson: A Memoir,* II 65). *Monty Python and The Holy Grail* might never have been made had it not been for the money "put up by various rock groups and record companies—among them Led Zeppelin, Pink Floyd, and Charisma Records," in addition to the fact that the film was made as an attempt to keep the Monty Python troupe together after *Monty Python's Flying Circus* ended its run on television in the fall of 1974 (Jack Mathews, *The Battle of Brazil* 9).

As we mentioned earlier, the quest for the holy grail merely serves the function, namely, to draw a number of heterogeneous stories and sketches together. There is no causal-chronological logic linking the episodes—the quest is a red herring—only a contrived device, "The Book of the Film," that binds the various episodes together by showing a hand turning the pages of an (ancient) book, a device that might well have been lifted from the opening of Disney's

The Sword in the Stone (1963), a film we discuss in chapter 4. Besides being a linking device it also represents what Eco would call a "stereotyped iconographical unit," culled from Hollywood epics and "costume dramas." The film's episodic, open-ended nature, in addition to its frequent citation of other films and film genres, as well as its disjunctions, ruptures, non sequiturs, and disconnected images ultimately make it as equally compelling an example of the principle of "the cult film as intertextual collage " as Eco's chosen model, *Casablanca.*

NOTES

1. John L. Fell, in *Film and the Narrative Tradition*, examines Méliès's (et al.) formal contributions to the invention of the narratological language of the cinema, for example, "dissolves" to achieve a passage of time and change of location, and "double exposures" to suggest physical transformations occurring in characters, and so on (203–226). But we are more interested in Méliès's contribution to the content of film, e.g., fantasy, melodrama, and spectacle (212). We have profited from Katherine Singer Kovács, "George Méliès and the *Féerie*" in John L. Fell, ed., *Film Before Griffith* (Berkeley: University of California Press, 1983): 244–257.

2. We follow David Ketterer's work regarding how Twain consistently employed science fiction devices in his work. Ketterer discusses Twain and science fiction in *New Worlds for Old: The Apocalyptic Imagination in Science Fiction*; see also his collection, *The Science Fiction of Mark Twain* (Hamden, CT: Archon Books, 1989).

3. In an interview for *Film Comment* (July/August 1995), when asked at what stage in his creative development did he eschew "realism or naturalism as an ideal," Boorman responded, "Very early, because when I was making documentaries I found it profoundly unsatisfactory" (55).

4. Including the made-for-television version of 1978 (see note 6), Twain's *Connecticut Yankee* has been filmed six times. In contrast, *Hamlet*, including silent film versions, has been filmed at least eight times as a motion picture (this latter figure is probably quite low, because it does not take into account all of the foreign film versions). Nonetheless, we know of no particular title, excluding those by Shakespeare, that has been filmed as often as Twain's novel.

5. Of course, *chora* and *Geschlecht* are difficult and elusive terms, and our discussion necessarily omits Ulmer's long discussion of the concepts (*Heuretics* 71–74). We understand *chora* as the "space" allowed or made available for individual creation within a system of allowances and constraints—*Geschlecht*—both idiosyncratic and social

6. We have chosen not to discuss the 1978 made-for-television adaptation of the novel that was part of WQED/National Educational Television's Emmy Award-winning series, "Once Upon a Classic." This version, approximately one-hour long, was set in the frame year Twain himself set it, though given the time constraints the elaboration was quite truncated.

7. This widely known and cited essay first appeared in *SubStance* 47 (1985): 3-12, and was later reprinted in *Travels in Hyperreality: Essays*. Trans. William Weaver. (San Diego: Harcourt Brace, 1986).

8. William Goldman's book was published in 1983 though excepts were appearing earlier; Eco's essay originally was presented as a paper at a conference in Toronto, Canada on June 18, 1984. We suppose that it is possible to argue that

Goldman's book influenced Eco, but we strongly suspect that it is an example of the convergence of ideas rather than one of mimetic influence.

9. Several scholars have pointed out that Twain was the first writer to confront the paradoxes of actual time travel and that he was not merely employing a version of Washington Irving's "Rip Van Winkle" device, in which the protagonist merely falls asleep and awakens years later. Philip Klass writes, "All backward-in-time stories come from . . . *A Connecticut Yankee*. . . . there was no such story before" ("An Innocent in Time" 23). In addition to Klass's article, see the Introduction to David Ketterer, ed., *The Science Fiction of Mark Twain* (xiii–xxx) and William J. Collins, "Hank Morgan in the Garden of Forking Paths: *A Connecticut Yankee in King Arthur's Court* as Alternative History." *Modern Fiction Studies* 32:1 (Spring 1986): 109–114.

10. The Philip Klass named as the author of this essay is not to be confused with Philip J. Klass, author of several books intended to debunk UFOs. The Philip Klass who authored this article also has written science fiction under the pseudonym William Tenn, and taught writing at The Pennsylvania State University beginning in the late 1960s. Apparently author David Morrell was Klass's student, for Morrell's first book, *First Blood* (1972), was dedicated to "Philip Klass and William Tenn."

11. By "Fortean" we mean a work influenced by the thought and research of American writer Charles Fort (1874–1932). Fort, a student of the paranormal and strange and unusual phenomena, postulated the utterly paranoid idea that "We are property," meaning that the earth and its inhabitants are the playthings of some advanced and apparently ludic creatures from outer space. Several noted works of science fiction are known to have been influenced by Fortean ideas, the most often-cited being Eric Frank Russell's paranoid *Sinister Barrier* (1943). We are not aware of any criticism that has been written on Kubrick's film that asserts that it is a Fortean film, and for this reason are astonished. Fort's assertion that "We are property" is the unstated premise of *2001: A Space Odyssey*, as it is of Arthur C. Clarke's story that served as the film's ostensible source, "The Sentinel" (1951). A contemporary Fortean, John Keel, has titled one of his books exploring the strange and unusual *Disneyland of the Gods*, an illustration of the way the Disney experience has become a (postmodern) vehicle to promote Fortean ideas.

12. In "Dianoia/Paranoia: Dick's Double 'Impostor'," Neil Easterbrook conveniently provides a list of rhetorical tropes that "are conventionally grouped under the rubric of 'the double.'" He lists (20) inversion, reversibility, ironic reinscription, false dichotomies, and paralogy. Topoi associated with the double "includes twins, phantoms, clones, *Doppelgängers*, ghosts, alter egos, double agents, androids, and simulacra; its signature modalities include duplicity, duality, simulation, dissimulation, verisimilitude, parallelism, and metonymic substitution" (24). Easterbrook's essay is in Samuel J. Umland, ed., *Philip K. Dick: Contemporary Critical Interpretations* (Westport: Greenwood Press, 1995): 19–41.

13. Vallee might well have cited William Morris's *The Earthly Paradise* (1868–70), which contains the story of Ogier the Dane and several other stories that use a form of the time travel device. *The Earthly Paradise* uses a narrative frame device that harkens back to Chaucer and Boccaccio. The "wanderers" are fourteenth-century Norwegians who have fled their pestilence-ridden home. They hope to find the "earthly paradise," and after more than thirty years of travel they arrive at a city located in the Adriatic Sea, inhabited by descendants of the ancient Greeks, whose members are referred to as the "elders." In addition to this frame, Morris's work includes several stories of mortals who are transported to other realms and other times, among these tales are "Ogier the Dane" and "The Land East of the Sun and West of the Moon." In the face of it, Morris is apparently employing the "lost world" motif, and so the wanderers' encounter with them is not precisely a result of time

travel, only implicitly. The text that Twain may have plundered, Max Adeler's "Professor Baffin's Adventures" (1880), also a lost world tale, is likely to have in turn been heavily influenced by Morris's serial poem of a decade earlier. In any case, neither Morris nor Adeler used a timeslip like Twain.

14. The idea of plural worlds, or ontological pluralism, has also been explored by American philosophers, not just American science fiction writers. C. I. Lewis's *Mind and the World Order* (1929) is a key document in this line of thinking; Lewis was a pivotal figure in the line of developers of systems of modal logic, a genealogy that runs from the Aristotle of *De Interpretatione* through Leibniz to Lewis and (in the present day) Saul Kripke and David Lewis. Modal logic is the logic of possible worlds, an exploration of much science fiction.

15. See, for example, the "Afterword" by Edmund Reiss to the Signet paperback edition of the novel (321–331); David Ketterer, in *New Worlds for Old*; and also Donald L. Hoffman, "Mark's Merlin: Magic vs. Technology in *A Connecticut Yankee in King Arthur's Court*, in Sally Slocum, ed., *Popular Arthurian Traditions*, 46–55.

16. Katz reports that Dickson left Edison's employ in 1895 "and worked briefly with [Major Woodville] Latham on the development of the Panopticon" (*Encyclopedia* 338). Latham himself was the inventor of the "Latham Loop," "still fundamental to the threading of modern projectors" (*Encyclopedia* 693).

17. Eddie DeLange (1904–1949) was a bandleader in the 1930s and also a lyricist in the 1930s and 1940s, and it is possible that Miles Davis and band recorded "Darn That Dream" as a sort of tribute after DeLange's untimely death on July 13, 1949. DeLange, together with Dick Charles and Larry Marks, wrote "Along the Navajo Trail" that was a big hit for Bing Crosby and the Andrews Sisters in 1945. Jimmy Van Heusen (1913–1990) was placed under contract to Paramount in 1940, where he began his long collaboration with Johnny Burke. Van Heusen and Burke went on to write songs for sixteen Bing Crosby films.

18. Two articles in Eric Smoodin, ed., *Disney Discourse: Producing the Magic Kingdom* (New York: Routledge, 1994) examine the business history of the Disney organization: Douglas Gomery, "Disney's Business History: A Reinterpretation" (71–86) and Jon Lewis, "Disney After Disney: Family Business and the Business of Family" (87–105).

19. In retrospect, the formation of Touchstone Pictures under Miller's leadership is an indication of just how well the Disney organization is attuned to *Geschlecht*. Jackson's chronology reveals that virtually all of the Disney organizations releases after 1985 were by Touchstone Pictures. Another subsidiary, Hollywood Pictures, was formed in 1990. Disney Pictures releases were reserved primarily for animated feature films, which of course were associated with Disney since the late 1930s. Our point is that the formation of Touchstone Pictures gave the Disney organization a means to avoid releasing "sanitized" or bowdlerized material at the same time allowing the name Disney to remain without taint.

20. In fact, it was the Disney organization itself which was in fact responsible for this change. We will discuss *The Sword in the Stone* (1963) in chapter 4 as a form of integrative propaganda. While it is also a children's film, the source is the first book of T. H. White's *The Once and Future King*, "The Sword in the Stone" (1938), the only book of that volume geared for young audiences.

21. Adrian Bailey, writing in *Walt Disney's World of Fantasy*, claims that the inspiration for "Main Street, U.S.A.," the entrance to Disneyland, came from Walt Disney's memories of Marceline, Missouri, where his family moved in 1906 and lived until about 1910. Apparently Disney had a sentimental attachment to the town; Bailey writes that "the happy memories of a childhood in Marceline remained with him always. When, some fifty years later, Walt added a Main Street to Disneyland, it

was Marceline that provided the inspiration" (23). Disney would have lived there from about age five to age nine.

22. The two plot formulae Attebury identifies correspond to a remarkable degree to what John Clute calls the "Edisonade" and "Robinsonade." The Edisonade was discussed in connection with the 1931 *A Connecticut Yankee*. The original model for the Robinsonade, of course, is Defoe's *Robinson Crusoe* (1719), which is a romance "of solitary survival in such inimical terrains as desert islands (or planets)–and also supplies much of thematic and symbolic buttressing that allows so many of these stories to be understood as allegories of mankind's search for the meaning of life." The powerful thematic of the Robinsonade, he argues, is its "convincing celebration of the power of pragmatic Reason, and its depiction of the triumph, alone, over great odds, of the entrepreneur who commands that rational Faculty" (*The Encyclopedia of Science Fiction* 1017).

23. Ron Moody's Merlin is actually quite memorable. He is outfitted in a deep purple robe with make-up that accentuates his blackened eyes and corpse-like pallor, all of which is topped off with a Kewpie Doll curl. Moody was to reprise the Merlin role, albeit in a much different fashion, sixteen years later, when Disney remade the film as *A Kid in King Arthur's Court*.

24. We have found scant information about the director of *Oddball*, Russ Mayberry. Before directing *Oddball*, he had directed just one other feature, a low-budget biker film titled *The Jesus Trip* (1971). Christopher Wicking and Tise Vahimagi indicate that he directed installments of many television series, originally billed as Russell I. B. Mayberry. As Russ Mayberry he directed episodes of *Bewitched, The Monkees, Marcus Welby, M.D., McCloud*, and *The Rockford Files*, in addition to other television series. They observe that his career has mainly been devoted to "the mean streets of the Universal crime beat," but that "even here, the comedy is not far away" (180). See Mayberry's entry in Wicking and Vahimagi's *The American Vein* (New York: E.P. Dutton, 1979).

25. Note that, just as in the 1989 remake, the language used in the film is contemporary English—not trendy English. We note this in regard to the 1989 remake as well.

26. Excalibur, Arthur's sword, had been neglected by the king because of his grief over Guinevere's death. Arthur's renewed interest in ruling Camelot is thus signaled when, during the rescue of Katey, he wields the famous sword once more. The sword is a symbol of Arthur's virility, and of his kingdom. Likewise, the bat Excalibur serves as a symbol of Calvin's new-found confidence that allows him to hit a home run. A similar use of Excalibur as a symbol of a regained self-confidence and even courage can be found in *Kids of the Round Table*, a Canadian production directed by Robert Tinnell. The film debuted at the 1995 Cannes Film Festival and starred Johnny Morina as Alex, a young boy who is chased into the woods by some neighborhood bullies; in the woods, he manages to come across Excalibur—and shortly after that Merlin (Malcolm McDowell). The film also featured Michael Ironside as an inept villain and Canadian pop star Rene Simard as one of his bumbling henchmen. The film is yet another illustration of the principle of intertextual collage.

27. Donald Spoto, in *The Dark Side of Genius*, writes that the MacGuffin "simply gets the story going. In the case of *The 39 Steps*, the MacGuffin is a secret formula—the specifications for a line of fighter planes. But it is to *prevent* the secret from being known—rather than to reveal it—that the adventure-chase is precipitated; thus the formula, which at first seems crucial, is immediately reduced in significance" (160). He also calls it "red-herring element" (160).

28. We take these remarks from the audio commentary track (Analog Track 2) of the Criterion laser disc *Monty Python and the Holy Grail*. Voyager, 1992.

3

The Arthurian Legend
as Hollywood Melodrama

No wonder then that these have been the years of conformity and
depression. A stench of fear has come out of every pore of American life, and we suffer from a collective failure of nerve.
—Norman Mailer, *The White Negro* (1957)

As Lao-Tzu says somewhere in the *Tao Te Ching*, "Law" and
"Justice" become important when love and trust have collapsed.
—Morris Berman, *Coming to Our Senses* (1989)

A conventional view of the Hollywood melodrama is conveniently provided by
Thomas Schatz, who observes in his study *Hollywood Genres*, "Generally
speaking, 'melodrama' was applied to popular romances that depicted a virtuous
individual (usually a woman) or couple (usually lovers) victimized by repressive
and inequitable social circumstances, particularly those involving marriage,
occupation, and the nuclear family" (222). He goes on to observe, about 1950s
Hollywood melodramas in particular, that "No other genre films [of that decade]
projected so complex and paradoxical a view of America, at once celebrating and
severely questioning the basic values and attitudes of the mass audience" (223).
Although we agree with this assessment, we also accept the observation made by
Jackie Byars, in *All That Hollywood Allows: Re-reading Gender in 1950s
Melodrama*:

Melodrama, as a mode, pervades many genres and through them presents a way to
refuse the recognition of a world drained of transcendence. . . . Usurping the place of
religious education, melodrama has operated since [the middle of the nineteenth
century] as a site for struggles over . . . fundamental values. Melodrama became for
the Western world the ritual through which social order is purged and sets of ethical
imperatives are clarified. (11)[1]

We therefore suggest that, although it may seem slightly strange that Hollywood's first motion picture based on Malory's *Morte* would be in 1953,[2] the first of the so-called "Eisenhower years," the legend provided a vehicle with which Hollywood filmmakers could address social behaviors and address ethical imperatives with the sanctimoniousness of the pulpit.

Two suppositions must be stated at the outset to account for such improbable serendipities as the above sketch implies. One is that we must never dispute William Goldman's observation, stated in *Adventures in the Screen Trade*, that "Movies are a gold-rush business" (xi). There was considerable interest in the Arthurian legend because M-G-M decided to make a movie based on it, and several other studios followed suit. It is that simple, and that banal.

The other explanation requires that we contextualize the emergence of the first film, *Knights of the Round Table*, in the United States of the 1950s. We could cite several factors, primarily the one now historically bound under the umbrella "McCarthyism," a cluster of political agendas and practices, as well as cultural symptoms. But the dimension of McCarthyism most relevant to our study of the films is its emphasis on loyalty and loyalty oaths, providing the concept that draws together several films that otherwise are apparently unrelated beyond their source material. Other factors are certainly important and will be discussed in relation to the individual films.

Knights of the Round Table (1954)

A work of considerable significance in our discussion of Arthurian legend and Hollywood melodrama is Richard Thorpe's *Knights of the Round Table* (1954). This film stars Mel Ferrer as Arthur and Robert Taylor as Lancelot, and it features Ava Gardner, whose portrayal of Guinevere remains a stellar one. (See illustration 5.) *Knights of the Round Table* is a key film because its focus on the famous love triangle illustrates how the legend is so amenable to the melodramatic form. Its influence is apparent in a film released four decades later, *First Knight* (1995), which also conforms to the formal conventions of melodrama; but *Excalibur* (1981), more dynamic, ambitious, and inclusive in its use of the legend's elements is also indebted to it. The 1953 film credits Sir Thomas Malory for its source of inspiration and, indeed, it does follow the rough outline suggested by that work. For our purposes, *Knights of the Round Table* serves as a touchstone film against which to measure other treatments, and not simply because it was the first to attempt to film Malory. Despite its failings, and these are several, *Knights of the Round Table* was an ambitious production that sought to preserve the inviolate core of the legend, that is, its tragic grandeur. As we show in this chapter and in ensuing chapters, its influence is considerable on all following productions, and for this it merits a detailed discussion.

5. Guinevere (Ava Gardner) and Lancelot (Robert Taylor) are alarmed by a commotion outside of Lancelot's chamber in the 1954 film, *Knights of the Round Table*. Photo courtesy of The Museum of Modern Art/Film Stills Archive.

The film's director, Richard Thorpe (1896–1991), entered the film industry in the early 1920s as an actor, but then began directing films in 1923. Eventually, he was hired by M-G-M in 1935 and directed many features for that studio. There, according to Ephraim Katz, he established himself as a "prolific, technically proficient filmmaker" who "proved himself to be a reliable director of all genres" (*The Film Encyclopedia* 1133).[3] By the time he retired in 1967, Thorpe had directed "well over one hundred features" during his long career (Dixon, *The "B" Directors* 471–72). Not a director who is ever likely to be championed by the *auteur* school of critics, Thorpe nonetheless remains a director of some interest and in retrospect was an apt candidate to direct the film. He had considerable Hollywood experience and no doubt had sufficiently internalized the studio system's values.

Thorpe thus served as an ideal choice to direct a picture that is simultaneously a costume drama or period picture, a melodrama, and an example of Hollywood image management at a time when Hollywood, in its troubled history, desperately sought it. Previously, Thorpe had directed the M-G-M box office success, *Ivanhoe* (1952), which also starred Robert Taylor and Felix Aylmer (the latter cast as Merlin in *Knights of the Round Table*). *Ivanhoe* is certainly one of M-G-M's most spectacular historical epics; no doubt M-G-M wanted *Ivanhoe*'s results repeated with *Knights of the Round Table*, the first instance of Hollywood attempting to translate Malory to the screen.

In many ways the choice to film the legend was a prudent decision given Hollywood's preoccupation at the time with religious themes; it thus explains why the grail quest intrudes on the plot so insistently yet is merely appended to it: It is not essential to the story and properly cannot even be called a subplot, as it does not develop in any coherent sense. As Gerald Mast has argued, films with religious themes were an excellent choice for Hollywood image boosting in the years following World War II (the age of alleged Communist, i.e., "atheist," infiltration)[4]—more of the "Hollywood Babylon" syndrome.

Such films were a subtle alternative to blatant propagandizing, as we shall see with the overtly propagandistic film *The Black Knight* (1954). Warner Brothers had released *The Miracle of Our Lady of Fatima* in 1952, about the miracles which occur in a small Portuguese village. Three years later, in 1955, the same studio was to release the lackluster epic *The Silver Chalice*, about a freed Greek slave (Paul Newman's first screen role) who is asked to design the stand on which will sit the cup used by Jesus at the Last Supper. Cecil B. DeMille's *Samson and Delilah*, also a mixture of (biblical) epic and Hollywood melodrama, had been released in 1949; and DeMille, just a few years later, was to direct *The Ten Commandments*, which was released in 1956. We will review DeMille's film as a model epic in chapter 5, devoted to *Excalibur*. *Knights of the Round Table* thus represented a splendid opportunity to blend the action-packed, Technicolor thrills of a period film adventure with the moralizing of a particularly Tennysonian kind combined with its gratuitous, intrusive allusions to an apocryphal holy relic.

Knights of the Round Table begins with the fledgling Arthur's bid for and his eventual rise to power with the help of Merlin (Felix Aylmer) and that of the idealistic Lancelot. The film then concentrates on Arthur's love for Guinevere and her tragic involvement with Lancelot, after which it portrays the king's demise as he battles the evil Mordred, who is forcefully played by Stanley Baker. At the same time, the story occasionally alludes to the grail quest with Perceval (Gabriel Woolf) as its hero, and it concludes with a penitent Lancelot receiving divine reassurance that his son, Galahad, will eventually achieve the quest, although Lancelot himself has been denied a vision of the holy cup.

Despite this loose "Malorian outline," however, *Knights of the Round Table* features prominently the love triangle while ignoring other elements associated with the story. Moreover, it freely conflates or alters characters and events in order to adapt the legend to the tight constraints dictated by the filmic medium, and it draws upon the contributions of writers other than Malory (primarily Tennyson and White) to do so.

As stated, this film's success demonstrated how easily the Arthurian story lends itself to the formal requirements of melodrama, and its focus on the love triangle of Arthur, Lancelot, and Guinevere appears as an influence on a number of other films we will discuss later in this chapter. But by its ability to compress and conflate the legend, to make it conform to the requirements of the film medium, *Knights of the Round Table* serves as a precursor to *Excalibur* as well, a film that also claims—deceptively—to be an adaptation of Malory. This is remarkable since, as we shall see in chapter 5, *Excalibur* is more than melodrama; it has features of the Hollywood epic. *Knights of the Round Table* served as a model for later filmmakers on how to alter freely character roles and relationships; it also offered a means by which they could explore which components of the legend were expendable and which were essential to guarantee contemporary box office success.

The film credits Malory at the outset, and it begins with an abbreviated version of his opening book. The young Arthur, with the help of Merlin, attempts to claim the sword in the stone, which will signal his right to succeed Uther as sovereign of England and restore internal peace, a condition vital to the realm's security. As in Malory's work, Arthur's right to the throne is contested by petty rulers who point to his illegitimacy, but the film begins its pattern of conflating characters and their functions to conform to the time constraints required of film when Morgan and her "consort" Mordred serve as Arthur's greatest initial (and final) obstacle. It is indeed a bold stroke to wed Morgan le Fay (Anne Crawford) and Mordred so that Arthur's two great enemies are truly united against him. Moreover, by making Mordred Morgan's husband, the film removes the most objectionable aspect of the legend and the taint against Arthur, for as we know, in Malory's work Mordred is Arthur's incestuous son born of his liaison with Morgause. And while Malory's Morgan serves as a disruptive force early in Malory's narrative, her role in Arthur's final demise is negligible; in fact, hearkening back to a much earlier tradition, she is one of the three lamenting queens aboard the vessel that carries the moribund king off to Avalon, where he will be healed.[5]

Another notable opponent in the film is Mark, identified here, however, as "King of the Picts," who works in collusion with "Cornish pirates." With a few others, these characters oppose Arthur's right to rule even though he alone can remove the sword from the stone; but the man who would be king is determined to use any means necessary to unite the realm under his guidance.

To counter the stiff resistance Arthur meets at the outset, the film introduces in the second scene an idealistic Lancelot, the world's greatest knight, who is engaged upon a quest to find and serve Arthur. Just how Lancelot has heard of Arthur is unclear, since the latter is as yet an unestablished leader—he has not won the crown, and the film makes it clear that it is unlikely that he could have done so without Lancelot's help. Yet Lancelot wanders far and wide in search of him. This is a detail that shows the film's reliance not on Malory's version of the story but more probably on that of his epigone, T. H. White. In Part 3 of *The Once and Future King* titled "The Ill-Made Knight" (first published separately, however, in 1940), White emphasizes Lancelot's love of Arthur, or rather his passionate enthusiasm for the *idea* of Arthur, from his boyhood to his arrival at the elder king's court. Although in the film there is no discernible age difference between Arthur and Lancelot, *Knights of the Round Table* does borrow from White's version Lancelot's obsession with an Arthur he has never seen in order to explain the continual enmity between Lancelot and Mordred and to emphasize the tragedy of the love triangle. In other words, it is the stuff Hollywood melodramas are made of.

It is instructive to note that in order to augment Arthur's sense of betrayal later, the film establishes the friendship and mutual respect between Arthur and Lancelot before it even introduces Guinevere. In the third scene, Lancelot single-handedly fights off some of Mordred's men sent to ambush Arthur as he rides to the Ring of Stones, where he will plead his case to the council that will convene there. Arthur happens upon the skirmish and comes to Lancelot's assistance, since he sees that the latter is woefully outnumbered. Not knowing that his assistant is the very person he seeks, Lancelot is angered that by helping him Arthur has diminished his glory and demands recompense by challenging the king to a sword fight. Each is a worthy match for the other, of course, and each conducts himself in accord with the highest dictates of chivalric courtesy, so that predictably, the fight ends in a draw. When Lancelot learns the identity of this person he has just challenged, he is so chagrined with himself that he shatters his sword; and when Arthur discovers Lancelot's admiration for him, he is so touched that he magnanimously gives his own sword to the knight.

This auspicious beginning initiates a period of what would now be recognized as rather intense male bonding. Lancelot is instrumental in aiding Arthur as he struggles to claim the throne. At Christmas, while they await the end of winter in order to engage Mordred's forces, Arthur presents to Lancelot a ring with an inscription that reads: "Friend shall I be and call me not other. This is a pledging 'twixt brother and brother." But this promising friendship is immediately threatened. After Mordred and his constituents are defeated by Arthur's army and by Merlin's superior strategy, Lancelot is angered by Arthur's ready forgiveness of the rebels and, refusing to pay homage to him, leaves his court in an act of self-banishment.

Lancelot is right, of course, in his suspicions of Mordred, and much of the remainder of the film revolves around Morgan and Mordred's efforts to undermine Arthur's power. Near the film's conclusion, the moribund Arthur admits that Lancelot was right about Mordred and implores him to dispatch the treacherous knight before he can conquer England and do irreparable damage to it. Lancelot willingly complies and eradicates the threat to the land. Before he does so, however, he carries out Arthur's other dying wishes—to throw his beloved sword into the sea and to tell Guinevere, now dwelling as a penitent nun—that the king forgives her and loves her still. Lancelot does so, with each of these acts taking place (bathetically) in about thirty seconds. The film ends with the afore-mentioned vision of the holy grail, in which Perceval and Lancelot receive the heavenly tidings that Galahad will achieve the grail.

The love triangle here is one of the heart, not of the body, a radical departure from Malory's text, despite occasional efforts to argue to the contrary.[6] None-theless, its effect is as devastating as if actual adultery had been committed between Lancelot and Guinevere. As we have seen, the film establishes at the outset the love and esteem between Lancelot and Arthur. It also avers that Arthur has known and loved Guinevere from childhood, a detail that serves, once again, to heighten the effects of betrayal later on. (This, of course, is not in its ostensible source.) Arthur's coronation and his wedding occur on the same day; he thus realizes two dreams at once. On that day also Lancelot returns to court after his angry departure and self-imposed exile to pledge anew his dedication to the king.

One significant event, which allows the tragic plot to unfold, occurs during this self-imposed exile: Lancelot meets and rescues Guinevere without knowing who she is. We witness a fatal attraction, of sorts, though neither is aware of its consequences at the time. While wandering in search of adventure, Lancelot comes upon a tree that bears the arms of disgraced knights who have been sent away on foot by a scurrilous and unchivalric knight, known simply as the Green Knight. This able but unscrupulous knight victimizes unwitting opponents: When he defeats them, he abducts their ladies, hangs the losers' armor upon a tree, and dishonors them further by sending them off, sans lady, armor, or horse.[7] Lancelot is scandalized by this practice, and he requests permission from the current captive lady to serve as her champion. To this she willingly complies, and Lancelot defeats the Green Knight, after which he sends him to Arthur's court, a motif that is always intended to regenerate a barbaric but potentially worthy knight.

The lady Lancelot liberates is Guinevere, but neither he nor she is willing to reveal his or her identity, which might have prevented the seed of love from taking root. When Guinevere asks the knight his name, he refuses to tell her, responding: "There is shame upon my name," an obvious indicator of the guilt he feels for having abandoned Arthur, his first love. Guinevere is incredulous when he says this, but she, too, evades a direct response when Lancelot asks her where she plans to go now that she is free. She coyly replies, "To the wedding of King Arthur and Princess Guinevere at Camelot," which is apparently the means by which Lancelot learns of the king's impending marriage, news that pricks his conscience and prompts him to return to court in order to be reconciled with him.

This encounter between Lancelot and Guinevere, in which neither unmasks, is also a standard practice in the world of Malorian romance. Upon occasion, there is a reason for withholding one's identity—take, for instance, Gareth, who comes to court incognito because he wishes to prove his worth and earn his place as a knight rather than relying on his family (Gawain is his brother and Arthur is his uncle). More often, however, the use of disguise or lack of disclosure in Malory's work results in disaster, especially when Lancelot engages in this practice. We will remember, for instance, the near-mortal wound Lancelot suffers at the Tournament of Winchester: He enters it incognito, and as a result Sir Bors does not recognize him and nearly kills him. The most memorable example of disaster that springs from witholding one's identity, however, is that of the brothers Balin and Balan, which ends in mutual fratricide. This first encounter between Lancelot and Guinevere in the film, then, despite its putative innocence, is an ominous beginning for the two whose passion for each other will prove disastrous for their beloved king, friend, and husband.

Thus, three key events occur on one day: Arthur's coronation, his wedding, and Lancelot's return to court and subsequent reconciliation with his king. The Round Table is established, and the knights pledge an oath that smacks of Tennysonian values; in fact, along with an occasional snippet from Malory's *Morte*, several phrases are lifted directly from the oath required by Tennyson's Arthur as the king himself recounts it in the "Guinevere" idyll.[8]

This reconciliation frustrates Mordred and Morgan, who know that as long as Arthur and the puissant Lancelot are friends, peace will reign and they cannot hope to overthrow the king. Here the film begins to emphasize almost exclusively the love triangle—Mordred and Morgan see that Lancelot and Guinevere are hopelessly in love, as does the wise Merlin. Because the latter overhears their plot to create an enmity between Arthur and Lancelot by exposing this attraction, he implores Guinevere, for the sake of the kingdom, to send Lancelot away. Somewhat indignant at the suggestion that she would consciously carry on an extra-marital affair, Guinevere nonetheless agrees to comply with Merlin's exhortation.

A somewhat contrived subplot to the love triangle is the inclusion of a young woman, Elaine of Astolat (Maureen Swanson), whose first sight of Lancelot—in the first scene that featured him—results in something of a schoolgirl crush on the knight. She is reintroduced when her brother, Perceval, brings her to the queen and asks that she be made a lady-in-waiting. Elaine's crush has, meanwhile, turned into an obsession; knowing this, Guinevere pleads with Lancelot to marry the young Elaine and leave the court. In a key scene she admits to Lancelot that she knows he is in love with her but implores him to marry Elaine for the good of the realm. Lancelot also recognizes the need to repress his growing love for the queen and agrees to do so.

It is worthwhile to note here that the creation of Elaine's character and her function is one of the film's radical departures from its acknowledged source, Malory's *Morte*, and betrays the fact that the film relies upon other contributors to the legend. It owes more to Tennyson and T. H. White, in fact but transforms even their works in respect to this figure in order to serve the needs of a compressed filmic version that features the love triangle. In Malory's work there is Elaine of Castle Carbonek, with whom Lancelot is tricked into sleeping so that he can sire Galahad. This way, both father and mother of the "true grail knight" will be of grail lineage. This is the Elaine of the grail family who comes to court and makes Guinevere extremely jealous. There is another Elaine, however, known as the Fair Maid of Astolat. It is she who, in another incident, dies of unrequited love for Lancelot and, in a macabre final episode, wills that her corpse be sent on a boat to Camelot, evidently as a last testimony of her love (or as a last reproach of the knight?). As we know, Lancelot does not marry in Malory's work—he remains faithful to his first love, Guinevere, even when, at their final meeting, she urges him to take a wife and forget her.

In his version of the legend, Tennyson omits the grail Elaine and features only the Fair Maid of Astolat, who dies of love for Lancelot. He makes much of the age difference between the two. It is T. H. White after Tennyson who conflates the two Elaines for the sake of logic and economy: The grail maiden who conceives and gives birth to Galahad also dies of love for Lancelot. *Knights of the Round Table* takes the fair maid of Astolat and makes her the sister of Perceval of Astolat, the pious young knight who searches for the grail throughout the film while also serving Arthur, thus connecting her with the grail cause. It is necessary to do this, since the entire grail history and quest are severely truncated in the film—mentioned only in the background by way of Perceval's occasional reports of his success or failure while on this quest—in order to make her the worthy mother of Galahad.

Here also, in an unprecedented event, Lancelot marries Elaine and they set up housekeeping in the north, where Lancelot has exiled himself in order to serve his king by fighting the rebellious Picts—the excuse he uses in order to leave the court and thus avoid Guinevere. When Elaine dies giving birth to Galahad, she dies fulfilled, meekly. It is appropriate to note here that the entire film is informed by a Victorian psychology of character and motivation, but nowhere is it more apparent than in the figure of Elaine. She is passive, selfless, and long suffering, so chaste as to be virtually sexless (to contrast with the role of Guinevere as a *femme fatale*, the other Victorian female prototype), and she dies willingly while giving birth to a son. Likewise, the fact that there is no actual adultery in this work—a clear bowdlerization of Malory—though there is plenty of guilt for just thinking of it, also suggests a Victorian psychology. This observation is not intended to indicate that "Victorian" suggests a time long past, nor is it meant in any pejorative way; on the contrary, we share much and owe much to our Victorian ancestors, the first true moderns. Other Victorian qualities include contrived elements of plot, with a heavy emphasis upon coincidence to forward the action and lead to the tragic end. Any reader familiar with a Thomas Hardy novel will immediately recognize this device. In the film it can be seen, for instance, when Lancelot, in need of his sword, finds it has been sent out for repair, and when he accidentally drops the ring Arthur had given him, which is later mistakenly read as a sign of his faithlessness.

Although Elaine strives to be the perfect wife to Lancelot and he attempts to be a good husband, the marriage cannot obliterate Guinevere's place in Lancelot's heart. Nor can the queen forget Lancelot. In a touching scene Guinevere fondles a coin the knight had given her as a gift and laments to her husband that she is an unworthy wife, thereby revealing her guilt for sinning in her heart if not with her body. Arthur is at first puzzled by Guinevere's self-effacing utterance, but when she drops the token, he recognizes it and understands, all at once, the source of her pain. As he retrieves the coin and returns it to her, Arthur says of Lancelot: "I love him also, Guinevere."

Meanwhile, Lancelot also expresses the guilt prompted by his illicit feelings for the queen. He tells Perceval that he himself is unfit to search for the grail because he is a "sinner," though Perceval, who engages in a kind of hero worship of his big-brother-in-law, is incredulous, not knowing, of course, the knight's private desires. The love between the two is impossible to eradicate, and when, after poisoning Merlin, Morgan and Mordred, in the true spirit of a Victorian parlor melodrama, contrive to create Lancelot's return to court, the passion between the two is a time bomb waiting to explode.

As in Malory's narrative, Lancelot (now, conveniently, a widower in the film) finds himself once again at Camelot, where he is wary of his love for the queen and of its potential disruptive force if brought to fruition. Thus, he tries to mask his love by paying attention to other ladies: He wears the scarf of another as a token at a tournament, and at a banquet he engages in a wager in order to win a kiss from the Lady Vivien. These ruses, however, prove too much for Guinevere, rousing her jealousy as they do in Malory's work, and her inability to control her passion precipitates the slander and strife that, at last, signal the end of Arthur's order.

In an interesting role reversal, it is Guinevere who by stealth of night goes to Lancelot's chamber. He is repairing a whip, pinches the finger on which he wears the ring Arthur had given him so long ago, and thus removes it. In Malory's work, we will remember, the queen had sent for Lancelot to visit her chamber in Arthur's absence, but melodrama reigns in this scene as she makes a tempestuous and desperate entrance into Lancelot's room. This is the trap set by

Morgan and her consort, who send Agravaine and his cronies to discover the pair in compromising circumstances.

Lancelot is alarmed by the queen's entrance, reminding her that her very presence in his private chamber constitutes high treason. But the woman prevails over the queen here, and Guinevere presses him for answers to personal questions: Why has he hurt her? Humiliated and shamed her? Has his love turned to contempt? In a desperate effort to save their honor, Lancelot denies his love for her, claiming that "it is not in my nature to love or honor." However, as she begins to leave, it is too late. There is a knock at the door. Lancelot searches for a weapon (as in Malory, he has none handy, though for a different reason) and attempts to arm himself by removing his cloak; Guinevere sees that he has been secretly wearing the scarf she gave him when they first met, and she then understands that he loves her still: "Then it was I who had too little faith," she says, and the two kiss. Unlike in the *Morte*, where actual adultery certainly does occur—though not necessarily on this occasion, Malory is quick to inform us—in the film this kiss is the sole extent of their betrayal of Arthur, but it is enough to create havoc in the kingdom. Lancelot knows the consequences of having been discovered in a compromising situation, and so he defeats the knights who surprise them and takes Guinevere into his protective custody.

In a contrived episode, one worthy of Hollywood melodrama, Mordred shows Arthur Lancelot's quarters and the ring the latter had given Lancelot, inadvertently dropped when he was surprised by visitors. Arthur is convinced that the removal of the ring signaled Lancelot's betrayal of him, or of the pledge "'twixt brother and brother," and thus sets a trial to sentence the two putative "adulterers" even in their absence. It is important to note that it is Mordred, and not Gawain (as in Malory's text), who attempts to goad the king into rash legal acts against his wife and best knight. A trial ensues and the knights of the Round Table are asked to vote on the innocence or guilt of the pair. Lancelot, however, interrupts the proceedings to defend himself and the queen.

In a moving scene he reminds Arthur of their friendship. He then ack-nowledges his love for Guinevere, but he champions and, the film suggests, is even credited with the actual creation of the doctrine of courtly love, which operates on the principle of endless repression and delay, and he can then assert their innocence. Lancelot's speech also reveals the degree to which Victorian (e.g., Tennysonian) values have governed this filmic version of the legend and underscores the degree to which *Knights of the Round Table* diverges from its ostensible source. For Lancelot in the *Morte* can make no such claim as that urged by Lancelot in the film: "A man and a woman may love each other all their lives with no evil between them. I dare to say such love is good for by denial and suffering the heart is purified." Such is likewise the claim made by Tennyson's Arthur in the "Guinevere" idyll when he claims to have charged the knights "to live sweet lives in purest chastity,/To love one maiden only, cleave to her,/And worship her by noble deeds,/Until they won her; for indeed I knew/Of no more subtle master under heaven/Than is the maiden passion for a maid,/Not only to keep down the base in man,/But teach high thought, and amiable words/And courtliness, and the desire of fame,/And love of truth, and all that makes a man" (ll. 471–480).[9]

Lancelot's dignified treatise in the film makes Arthur relent, and the king then refuses to mete out the prescribed punishment for adultery—namely, beheading for Lancelot and burning at the stake for the queen. Instead, although they have been found guilty, Arthur reduces the sentence: Banishment for Lancelot, the convent for his queen. Saddened, Lancelot accepts the sentence and leaves, but Mordred is angered, insisting that the king is weak and has betrayed justice for his own personal satisfaction. This is the rallying point he uses to wage civil war against Arthur.

The king, who desires peace because he has England's welfare in mind, meets his death at the usurper's hands under circumstances that follow Malory closely. A truce is called and terms are made, but an adder appears and one of the knights in Arthur's entourage raises his sword to kill it. Because each side is distrustful of the other, this begins the battle in which Arthur meets his death. But the film departs from Malory when Mordred survives the battle and, as noted, the dying Arthur must dispatch Lancelot to slay the traitor, after which the hero hears the divine voice announcing that his son will achieve the grail. Nonetheless, the emphasis in *Knights of the Round Table* is not on a complete retelling of Malory, and the grail material is decidedly superfluous to the story. The film clearly conforms to the dictates of melodrama, featuring prominently the love triangle and infusing it with the ethos of the 1950s—one that is closely allied with the moral tone typical of Victorian didactic literature as well.

Sword of Lancelot (1963)

A film that rivals *Knights of the Round Table* in quality and importance is the 1963 release of *Sword of Lancelot* (in Britain it appeared under the title *Lancelot and Guinevere*). It was produced and directed by independent filmmaker Cornel Wilde (1915–1989) who also cast himself as Lancelot, opposite his wife and business partner Jean Wallace (1923–1990), whose portrayal of Guinevere remains, along with the earlier performance by Ava Gardner, the most convincing and compelling. (See illustration 6.) Brian Aherne plays the role of King Arthur, and it is worth noting at the outset of our discussion that these actors were definitely "mature" for their parts: Wilde was forty-eight years old, Wallace was forty, and Aherne sixty-one when the film was released.[10] This is not to say that the main players in *Knights of the Round Table* were young: Robert Taylor was forty-two years old, Mel Ferrer was thirty-six, while Ava Gardner was thirty-one. What is significant about this is that the actresses cast as Guinevere in later efforts tend to be much younger. Moreover, it is instructive to note that as we shall see, major criticism of the 1995 version *First Knight* involved negative responses to Sean Connery as Arthur (sixty-four when the film was released) and of Richard Gere, who was forty-five. Such arbitrary and capricious critical standards reflect the increasing preoccupation with youth in our culture (as discussed in chapter 2), not any textual stricture that would prevent mature actors from portraying these characters realistically.

Sword of Lancelot won significant acclaim in the United States as well as abroad; according to Kevin Harty, it won "the Gold Prize in an Italian film festival and was critically well received" (*Cinema Arthuriana* 13). Although it is most decidedly a melodrama, *Sword of Lancelot* is striking because in contrast to its forerunner, *Knights of the Round Table*, it is audacious in its presentation of events and in its *ethos*. For instance, the illicit love between Lancelot and Guinevere is explicit: The film leaves absolutely no doubt that the love is adulterous, portraying one scene in which the lovers are in bed nude. Equally bold is the fact that in this film Guinevere is the aggressor—she is an obsessive character and as such a classic *femme fatale* who is crafty and relentless in her pursuit of Lancelot until his resolve fails him and he becomes enmeshed in a torrid affair with her. Finally, although it stops short of stating explicitly that Mordred is an incestuous son of Arthur, *Sword of Lancelot* does portray the villain as the king's illegitimate offspring and heir hopeful, something that its predecessors— melodramas and others—refused to do. Although it remains undeniably indebted to 1950s melodrama in its structure, the film's informing vision and ethos belongs to the 1960s and not to an earlier decade. It diverges from the received legend as it was interpreted by *Knights of the Round Table*, but it does so, as we shall see, in ways that make it fascinating from a psychological and aesthetic perspective.

Wilde's Lancelot has a heavy accent and is extremely concerned with his grooming, in order to stress his sex appeal and courtliness. Gawain had observed the knight with white lather on his body, and he thus feared that Lancelot had the plague. Actually, the knight was busy washing himself with an invention Merlin had given him: Soap. We are then immediately plunged into the melodrama when a messenger arrives from King Leodogran of Cameliard (John Longden). From his arrival, we learn that Arthur has requested the hand of Leodogran's daughter (Guinevere) in marriage, but the latter now sends a refusal of the request because he doubts whether Arthur is the rightful ruler of Britain and the legitimate heir to Uther. Thus, Leodogran suggests that the matter be settled by trial by combat. Arthur should send a champion to rival Leodogran's, and in a battle to the death, Arthur's claim to the throne and to Guinevere can be decided.

It must be noted here that this is unquestionably derived from Tennyson's contribution to the legend, although he uses Leodogran's doubts for a different purpose. The same skepticism about Arthur's parentage and right to rule occurs in Tennyson's opening idyll "The Coming of the King" so that he can introduce the dual accounts of Arthur's birth—the ordinary one, recounted to Leodogran by Bedivere, and the mythic coming, told to him by Bellicent, which elevates Arthur to a supernatural status. Not until he receives a *somnium coeleste* does

6. Jean Wallace (right, as Guinevere), about to become Brian Aherne's (King Arthur's) reluctant bride as Cornel Wilde (Lancelot) stands by, in *Sword of Lancelot* (1963). Cornel Wilde and Jean Wallace had been married for several years; they were also business partners, producing this film, among others. Photo courtesy of The Museum of Modern Art/Film Stills Archive.

Leodogran finally dismiss his doubts and grant Arthur's request to marry his daughter. In the film, there is a grizzly scene in which Lancelot, Arthur's chosen champion, convinces Leodogran by means of a trial by combat: with his sword he slices the latter's champion's head in half. Such an attitude by Leodogran cannot be found in Malory, where he responds to Arthur's request by saying, "That is to me the best tydynges that ever I herde, that so worthy a kyng of prouesse and noblesse wol wedde my doug[h]ter" (60). He then gives Arthur the gift of the Round Table.

As in *Knights of the Round Table*, then, the friendship between Arthur and Lancelot is established long before the arrival of Guinevere, who completes the triangle; but whereas in that film Lancelot merely rescues the queen from the Green Knight, who has abducted her en route to her own wedding, in this film Lancelot actually endangers his own life by winning her in combat for the king. It seems likely that in so doing, *Sword of Lancelot* transposes to this story key elements of the Tristram myth, originally a separate romance later grafted onto the Arthurian legend proper. This augments its tragic end and also infuses the film with an overtly romantic ideology, one that is inherent in the Tristram and Iseult story in that the happiness of the lovers, referred to by Guinevere as their "freedom," is at odds with the dictates of society.[11]

We will remember that in most versions of the Tristram myth, regardless of whether it is in the prose or in the more idealized poetic tradition, King Mark of Cornwall sends his nephew Tristram to win for him Iseult of Ireland, famed for her beauty. Tristram complies with this wish, even though he had previously met and fallen in love with Iseult. In several versions this love is either caused by or at least intensified by the accidental consumption of a love potion. Tristram places a higher premium on his honor than on his personal happiness (or else denial of his desire affords him some form of satisfaction that must remain occult), and it is this denial that precipitates the tragedy. He allows Iseult to marry Mark, even though on the voyage from Ireland to Cornwall, when the potion was consumed, he had become Iseult's lover. This is similar to what occurs between Lancelot and Guinevere in *Sword of Lancelot*, and one must look to the Tristram story for its inspiration, since there is no precedent for it between Lancelot and Guinevere. Another way that this film transposes elements from the Tristram legend occurs when Lancelot introduces Iseult to the wonders of soap in a highly suggestive bathing scene: The knight refers to the soap as a "love philtre" (we will recall that earlier Gawain had thought him ill with plague when he saw Lancelot's body lathered with the same substance). Once again, we have an allusion to the Tristram and Iseult myth, and the fact that Gawain mistakes the soap for illness is suggestive also of the connection between love and sickness that prevails in western notions of romantic passion and, in the case of Tristram and Iseult, even results in death. Thus, it is the called the *liebestod*, or the "love-death."

Lancelot wins Guinevere for Arthur, and en route to Camelot for the wedding they are attacked by the king's enemy, in this case thugs hired by

Mordred, who wants to prevent the royal marriage to protect Mordred's claim to the throne. It is noteworthy that a similar instance appears in *Knights of the Round Table,* and that it is also presented in the other melodramas discussed in this chapter: *Camelot* and *First Knight.* Here, however, Guinevere is no helpless maiden abducted by a knight and held in a tower; instead, she herself joins in the slaughter when she stabs a knight who is about to kill Lancelot. At this early juncture in the film, she acknowledges (covertly, at least) her love for Lancelot, although he responds by denying his feelings in favor of his code of honor. (Interestingly, we will see how this episode served as a precursor to one in *First Knight,* where Guinevere shoots a knight with a crossbow in a similar kidnapping or murder attempt.) We also see her aggressiveness and her courage in this scene, a departure from traditional portrayals of her as passive and helpless.

Despite their obvious mutual attraction, Lancelot's denial of his feelings for Guinevere continues, and one memorable scene in the film is when he is designated to escort her down the aisle at her wedding. As they begin their slow and tortured walk to the altar, Guinevere pleads with the knight to abort her impending union with Arthur but Lancelot, prompted by his code of honor and his duty to his king, is still determined to deny his love.

The dialogue in this scene, and Jean Wallace's superb depiction of Guinevere as a character bordering on madness in her desperation, makes it a memorable melodramatic moment in the film. It is worth reproducing the strained verbal exchange, as each struggles to maintain self-control. The melodramatic splendor of the dialogue in this sequence makes it memorable:

Guinevere:	Lancelot, save me.
Lancelot:	From what, my lady?
Guinevere:	From myself. From this.
Lancelot:	This is what you wanted, to be queen of all Britain.
Guinevere:	What my head wanted, not my heart.
Lancelot:	The king loves you.
Guinevere:	Say the word and I'll stop all this by swooning in your arms.
Lancelot:	There is no word.
Guinevere:	Say that you wish it were you waiting there for me. Before it's too late.
Lancelot:	It's too late now your majesty.

Lancelot delivers Guinevere to Arthur, and the marriage continues, to the delight of a doting Arthur who is, of course, oblivious to the sublimated passion between his "child" bride and his favorite knight.[12]

Although Guinevere marries Arthur, she continues to pursue Lancelot and, at last, seduces him. She comes upon Lancelot reading a scroll in her private garden. When she inquires about the text that has him so engrossed, he responds that it is the "Odes of Horace," the stoicism of which he finds instructive. Undaunted, Guinevere asks the knight to teach her how to write "I love you" in Latin, averring that she should like to surprise her "dear Arthur" with her knowledge of Latin. But when Lancelot scratches it in the dirt for her and recites it out loud, she coyly pretends he has actually said the desired phrase to her and the two kiss passionately. An obsessed character, Guinevere moans repeatedly "I love you" to the knight, and it is clear that Lancelot's defenses were at last worn down on that afternoon in the garden, whilst Arthur was away on a hunting expedition.

Eventually, of course, the entire court (save Arthur) is aware of this illicit liaison, which also creates a conflict for Lancelot and makes him miserable. One of the film's strengths is its use and depiction of a minor character, Sir Lamorak (Archie Duncan), who here is portrayed as a robust, earthy, and entirely engaging friend of Lancelot. Knowing that Lancelot faces danger by the rumors of his affair with the queen, Lamorak finds his depressed friend in the same garden and convinces him that the two should leave the court and return to their native France to fight the invading Gauls. In this way, he argues, Lancelot can forget his love for the queen. Lancelot complies, but Guinevere has overheard their plans and hurls angry accusations at her lover: She should have known better than to trust a Frenchman—what is he afraid of? To which Lancelot responds that there are some things all men are afraid of, among them being burned alive in front of a bunch of shopkeepers—the penalty for adultery. He knows that Mordred (Michael Meacham), Arthur's illegitimate son, is watching their every move and waiting to set a trap, but Guinevere remains impetuous and determined to continue the affair. Thus, she implores him to come to her chamber that night, at least for one last tryst, and although he refuses to promise, she is confident he will do as she bids.

The unsuspecting queen tries to shuffle Arthur off to bed with a double dose of sleeping drops and a word of reassurance after he tells her there is "pain in his heart." Evidently believing that the cause of his weariness and trepidation results from court matters, or perhaps not caring about the source, she tells him he will feel better in the morning. (We learn that he is "pained" because he has been persuaded by Mordred to set a trap for the lovers.) As she leaves Arthur's chamber, the queen unlatches the gate to her private quarters and awaits Lancelot's arrival. She and Lancelot make love for what he believes will be the last time, after which he whispers,"This is how I want to remember you. After loving."[13] As he leaves her chambers, however, Mordred appears—with Arthur behind him—along with several knights and announces that "the trap is sprung." Lancelot escapes, but the queen is imprisoned and sentenced to be burned at the stake.

Brian Aherne's moment to shine as Arthur occurs when he portrays the king bordering on madness because he is torn between his duty as king (to suffer the execution of his adulterous queen) and his personal desire to save his wife, whom he so clearly adores. In an agonized moment, he asks Merlin whether he has made the right decision to sacrifice his wife in order to prove to his subjects that he is judicious, thereby preserving the hard-won peace of the kingdom. Merlin, who can sympathize with Arthur's dilemma, cannot comfort him by imploring him to reverse his decision. Fortunately, Lancelot resolves the crisis when he and his loyal followers rescue Guinevere in the nick of time. But just before Lancelot does so, the film works in another key plot development. When he had escaped Mordred's trap, Lancelot had unwittingly slain Gawain's brother, Gareth, who was unarmed; this serves as an impetus for Gawain's hatred of the knight and his obsessive desire for revenge. Because his vendetta against Lancelot knows no bounds, Gawain (George Baker) urges Arthur to lay siege to Joyous Garde, where Lancelot has taken Guinevere, and he refuses to be reconciled with him.

This enmity is what makes Lancelot miserable. Loathe to raise his hand against his king—who has him besieged—or against Gawain, who issues a challenge by way of daily insults, Lancelot cannot resolve the conflict in his heart created by these divided loyalties. Guinevere urges him to buy their freedom by dispensing with these two knights, which would also prevent more men from dying on the lovers' behalf. A proud and impetuous queen, she now despises Arthur because he was willing to allow her to be burned at the stake in front of peasants, and she obviously feels no hesitation in asking Lancelot to kill the king so that she and the knight may be free of her ties to him.[14] Although Lancelot is at first mortified by such a suggestion, he does agree to end Gawain's harassment of him by accepting his challenge.

When he defeats Gawain, Lancelot refuses to kill him but instead sends him to Arthur with a message, one that sues for peace, unbeknownst to Guinevere. Arthur replies that he will end the siege if Lancelot will exile himself in Brittany and if Guinevere will enter a convent, the worst possible punishment if one takes into account the queen's passionate nature and her fierce love for Lancelot. When Guinevere learns of this agreement she naturally feels betrayed by the latter. Lancelot persuades her that she should comply: Arthur had not insisted that she take vows, and Lancelot promises to come and take her away from the convent when the crisis is over and he can safely leave Brittany.

Lancelot's absence allows for Mordred to split the kingdom and incite a civil war, and Gawain seeks the knight in Brittany in order to be reconciled with him and to implore Lancelot to return to England to stop the wicked usurper (who has already killed Arthur). Gawain also reports that Merlin is now deceased and that Vivien (whom Mordred had earlier enlisted to help him spy on the lovers) drank poison when Mordred no longer needed her. Moreover, Gawain reports that Mordred burned the convent where Guinevere was confined, but that the queen escaped. Lancelot hastily returns to Britain with Gawain and defeats Mordred by virtue, once again, of his superior military strategy. As in the 1954 film, *Knights of the Round Table*, this final battle deviates from Malory and features Lancelot and Mordred, not Arthur and his incestuous son. The same holds true for *First Knight*, as we shall see, where Arthur is slain by Malagant and Lancelot must dispense with him immediately after, although there is no Mordred, of course, in that film.

The closing scene of *Sword of Lancelot* features a final encounter between Lancelot and Guinevere. True to his word, the knight arrives at the convent meaning to take his beloved away, now that Arthur is dead and Mordred is no longer a menace. But when Lancelot sees Guinevere, the knight is shocked into the realization that the former queen has indeed taken vows, for she is dressed in the habit of a nun. Guinevere explains that after having spent a year in the convent, she has experienced a transformation. She avers that she has seen the "light" and tries to persuade Lancelot that he will see it also. At first he is incredulous, but at last the knight accepts Guinevere's vows and her decision, averring that he will, somehow, find strength.[15]

What might appear to be a contrived ending will be familiar enough to Arthurians who know their Malory (or their William Morris). For in that text, the two do have a final meeting, and a poignant one at that, in which Guinevere repents of her sin and sends Lancelot away without a final kiss. The irony here and in the film is powerful—free to marry, the queen refuses to do so. Yet somehow this conclusion is convincing: An obsessive character throughout the film, the queen has clearly sublimated her passion and tranferred her loyalty from Lancelot to Christ. And Lancelot's self-reliance and stoic resolve hearken back to what he was before he became entangled with the queen. He knows he has the inner strength to survive the greatest adversity.

Sword of Lancelot focuses on the love triangle of Arthur, Lancelot, and Guinevere to the near exclusion of the other components common to the legend. For instance, it only hints at the history of Arthur's parentage (in Leodogran's refusal to acknowledge him as Uther's rightful heir) and omits the grail quest entirely. Because of the focus on this and the lovers' betrayal of Arthur, the film does bear similarities to 1950s melodramas. And its final message of renunciation, which advocates the denial of personal happiness in order to serve a higher ideal, hearkens back to classical Hollywood films such as *Casablanca* and ultimately to a Victorian (i.e., Tennysonian) view of duty and desire. Still, *Sword of Lancelot* celebrates the passion between the lovers, portrays it explicitly, and refuses to shy away from Mordred's relationship to Arthur. Thus, it offers an innovative use of the legend, unlike the earlier films that employed the Arthurian mythos. Perhaps this is why *Sword of Lancelot* appears to have as much in common with, say, *Excalibur*, as it does with *Knights of the Round Table*. In some ways, it serves as a worthy forerunner of *Camelot*, a film that was released four years later, in 1967.

Camelot (1967)

Alan Jay Lerner and Frederick Loewe's *Camelot* made its Broadway premiere the month before Eisenhower left office and three weeks after Kennedy won the presidency. The film adaptation of *Camelot* was released between *In the Heat of the Night* (August 1967) and *Guess Who's Coming to Dinner* (December 1967), two films that overtly address race. (Both films won Academy Awards that year, as did *Camelot*, though *In the Heat of the Night* won Best Picture of the Year.)

If the 1950s were, broadly speaking, concerned with loyalty and loyalty oaths, the 1960s were more concerned with race, and the films released in those decades tend to reflect this trend—except for anachronisms such as *Camelot*, a film properly belonging to the 1950s but released in the late 1960s.

Released in October 1967, and directed by Joshua Logan—a Broadway theater director known for his sensitive direction of 1950s Hollywood melodramas such as *Picnic* and *Bus Stop* (both released in 1956)—*Camelot* was the final film over which Jack L. Warner controlled the production. It is certainly one of the best-known and most popular of the films that employ the Arthurian legend.[16] Yet *Camelot* remains difficult to assess, in part because of its complicated lineage. It is based on the successful Broadway musical of 1960, in turn inspired by White's *The Once and Future King* (published as a novel in 1958).[17] But each of these works is, of course, distinctly different one from the other, since the conventions that govern narrative are not the same as those of a Broadway play, nor can one expect a film to conform to the formal requirements of either narrative or play. The problem is exacerbated further by the fact that when viewed as a musical *qua* musical, *Camelot* is very old-fashioned, adhering to the operetta form, in which the songs do not advance the story but are instead reflections or expressions of the characters' emotions and inner turmoil. This pattern is traditional when compared to more innovative Hollywood musicals such as *Showboat*, in which the songs are used to develop and forward the plot. But if we examine the film's treatment of the Arthurian material, it clearly does conform to the dictates of melodrama, while also sharing with *Sword of Lancelot* a frankness in its portrayal of illicit love. It even goes one step beyond the former in that it follows Malory and White in portraying Mordred, who is played superbly by David Hemmings, not only as Arthur's illegitimate son but also as the result of an incestuous union. Even though Mordred is an opposing presence to Arthur and his ideals in the film, his role in bringing about the *final* catastrophe is minimized drastically. Instead, as we shall discuss in more detail, the film departs from its literary antecedent, White's novel, and stresses instead the love triangle as the most destructive element. In placing the guilt squarely on the shoulders of the illicit lovers, Lancelot and Guinevere, the film shares more with the Tennysonian tradition than with White's work.

Its focus on the love triangle and betrayal, along with its omission of other elements—Arthur's parentage and rise to power and the grail quest—qualify *Camelot* as a melodrama. In fact, even those who give the nod to the film as a musical understand that its success depends on more than catchy tunes and dazzling costumes. The *Variety Movie Guide*, for instance, asserts, "What gives *Camelot* special value is a central dramatic conflict that throbs with human anguish and compassion. . . . The focus is kept on three mentally-tortured people, the cuckolded king, the cheating queen, the confused knight" (90). In other words, the melodramatic features are the compelling dimension of the film; without them, it would be the most expensive community theater production ever made. *Camelot* stars Richard Harris as Arthur, Vanessa Redgrave as Guinevere, and Franco Nero as Lancelot.[18]

The film employs a frame device and opens near the end of the action—Lancelot's stronghold, Joyous Garde, has been reluctantly besieged by Arthur. Moreover, Mordred (David Hemmings) has split the king's ranks and is preparing to war against him, although Arthur mentions this as only a future complication of the more pressing battle with Lancelot. On the eve of this battle, Arthur recalls via flashback the events that comprise the story proper; we are returned to the opening scene only after the melodrama has been remembered, and Arthur has a final meeting in the forest near Lancelot's castle with his knight and renegade queen turned nun. Here, Lancelot and Guinevere both express regret for the trouble they have caused and wish to make reparation, but Arthur asserts it is too late. His men, he laments, no longer desire justice but revenge, and the old dark days have returned to haunt them. He knows that they must now "ride the tide of events," and that, paused on the eve of his final battle, "The charade will soon begin." Lancelot asks Arthur, "Is there nothing to be done?" Arthur can only reply, "There's nothing to be done, but to play out the game and leave the decisions to God."

On the eve of battle and filled with the despair of failure that the love triangle has interfered with his efforts to improve humanity's condition, Arthur is cheered quite unexpectedly when a young page, one Tom of Warwick (Gary Marsh), who in White's novel also wears the Malory family bearings on his surcoat, still believes in his ideals. Arthur sends the boy away from the battle and orders him to tell the stories he knows of Camelot, which he fears is fast becoming a faded ideal. Renewed by the hope that if even one young boy can still believe in his dream, a manic Arthur willingly prepares to engage in the battle that he knows he may lose. There are some crucial differences between the film's conclusion and that of *The Once and Future King* that reveal the degree to which this film complies with the melodramatic formula discussed in this chapter.

While both the novel and the film end of a note of hope, and do so for the same reason, *Camelot* concludes just before Arthur's forces will engage Lancelot's. In White's work, the novel ends on the eve of the battle in which Arthur will fight the mocking Mordred, who has attempted to take the king's realm and his wife during his absence. In both the film and the novel, it is as though Arthur himself is cognizant of his own impending doom and that of his realm. Arthur knows he is an actor in a game larger than any of its players; thus, though Mordred may attempt to usurp his power, the king knows the script dictated by the tyranny of tradition and can take solace in the thought that young Tom of Warwick will perpetuate his ideal via the written word. Thus, the film version follows the example of White's novel, despite the fact that the former concludes with an event that occurs before the conclusion of *The Once and Future King*, in that it uses metafictional commentary to imply an optimism that results from a belief in the power of education and in the transmission of culture through storytelling to restore and perhaps make permanent the utopian ideal lost by the love triangle.

It is significant that *Camelot* concludes just prior to the battle of Joyous Garde in which Arthur and his forces will fight Lancelot and his men, ostensibly to restore the king's honor, but really to satisfy the lust for revenge that Arthur's men feel. By doing so, the film underscores the love triangle and points the accusing finger at this melodramatic element of the legend. It omits White's conclusion, in which Arthur must prepare for battle against Mordred, one that stresses instead the incestuous liaison of Arthur and Morgause as a main reason for the tragedy. Such an emphasis runs contrary to White's conception and interpretation of the story and its events. His biographer, Sylvia Townsend Warner, includes an excerpt from a letter that White wrote while he was composing the novel: "You know, the real reason why Arthur came to a bad end was because he had slept with his sister. It is a perfect Aristotelian tragedy and it was the offspring of this union who finally killed him. Morgause (the sister) is really more important in the doom than Guenever is, both through being associated with the Cornwall feud and through the incest theme (for her son Mordred finally brings the doom" (*T. H. White* 130). Moreover, as the discursive commentary at the end of book two says of the story, "It is the tragedy, the Aristotelian and comprehensive tragedy, of sin coming home to roost. That is why we have to take note of the parentage of Arthur's son Mordred, and to remember, when the time comes, that the king had slept with his own sister. He did not know he was doing so, and perhaps it may have been due to her, but it seems, in tragedy, that innocence is not enough" (*The Once and Future King* 312). Hollywood melodrama, however, does not use Aristotelian tragedy as its model, and *Camelot* thus ends with the battle of Joyous Garde in order to implicate the destructive power of guilty love—not King Arthur's but rather that of his wife for his most puissant knight and treasured friend, Lancelot.

First Knight (1995)

The last film we should like to examine as melodrama has been erroneously and injuriously compared with both *Camelot* and *Excalibur. First Knight*, directed by Jerry Zucker (*Ghost*), debuted in July 1995. This film conforms to the dictates of Hollywood melodrama in that it focuses almost exclusively on the love triangle: There is no portrayal of Arthur's early career (in fact, he is well advanced in years when the film opens), no grail quest, and the villain (Malagant) is no illegitimate or incestuous son, although he is imagined as a renegade knight of Arthur's Round Table. *First Knight* instead presents a very pristine version of the legend's central conflict—the illicit desire between the two characters whom Arthur loves most—and the ensuing destruction that results from their passion.

Although in its emphasis upon the love triangle and betrayal it conforms to melodrama as does *Camelot*, the similarities to it stop there. As we shall see, in its treatment of the legend, *First Knight* has much more in common, curiously, with the 1954 *Knights of the Round Table* than it does with either of the films released in the 1960s, *Camelot* and *Sword of Lancelot*. Yet, oddly, upon its release there were critics who disparaged the film because it was not a remake of *Camelot*, while others compared it unfavorably with *Excalibur*.[19]

It is worth mentioning in passing here that John Boorman's efforts in *Excalibur* were much maligned for several years after that film was released, primarily by academics who cried foul because in their view it failed to follow closely enough its putative source, Malory's *Morte*. We must point out, however, that despite this initial reaction, *Excalibur* has since been embraced by academics: The film is widely discussed, even featured in courses on the legend, and distinguished scholars, many of them Arthurians, have acknowledged its merits. Germane to our discussion of negative criticism of *First Knight* is that even a film as artful as *Excalibur* met with initial hostility for reasons we will discuss in our ensuing examination of each of these cinematic efforts.

Although *First Knight* received negative reviews by some of its syndicated critics, it was highly lauded by others. No doubt the controversial nature of the film stems from the difficulties encountered by *any* work of art that attempts to revitalize a legend with a weight of tradition as pronounced as the Arthurian material. This problem became intensified for filmmakers because with the release of strong films like *Excalibur* we can detect not only an established *literary* tradition but perhaps also an emerging cinematic one as well. One of three objections to *First Knight* exemplifies this response: It is not Malory, it is not *Camelot*, and it is not *Excalibur*. This criticism can and should be disregarded, since the film is in no way to be understood as a remake of these earlier films.

First Knight has also been berated for its lack of verisimilitude, a fate that has befallen a plethora of other films that have activated the Arthurian legend or chosen a historical subject. The primary basis for this complaint seems to be focused on its costuming, its armor, or its architecture. This charge also seems ungrounded, since the very nature of the Arthurian legend defies allegiance to a particular historical period, except for the fact that its inception is medieval.[20] It was and always will be as James Douglas Merriman avers, "not historical," and as a romance it is and always was set in an idealized past that never existed, save in the imaginative literature of nearly any given period. Moreover, the legend's longevity must be explained, in large part, by its mythopoeic nature: its adaptability. As for its verisimilitude—that is of no more consequence than sets and costumes on the theatrical stage.

The final repeated objection to the film also introduces us to a discussion of its merits: The actors who play the lead roles are either too old or too weak to be cast in such demanding part. The resistance exhibited in contemporary criticism to casting Sean Connery as Arthur and Richard Gere as Lancelot is very curious indeed when one considers that they are not the first "mature" actors to play these roles. Connery was sixty-four years old and Gere forty-five, but as we discussed earlier in this chapter, both *Knights of the Round Table* and *Sword of Lancelot* employed mature actors in these roles, as well as in the role of Guinevere, without incurring charges by critics of irreverence. At issue is irreverence, or rather, an ill-formed concept of "realism," for what putative signified does the age of these players violate? We conclude that this critical reservation is merely a resurgence of what literary historians call "neo-classicism," a belief that certain subjects may receive only a certain kind of treatment.

First Knight opens with a controversial portrayal of a Lancelot who has been labeled a soldier of fortune, but who is really closer to a poolroom hustler or street huckster. Despite the pragmatic use of his knightly prowess, Lancelot is of "noble" stock, and this will eventually prevail in his character.[21] He wanders aimlessly and earns his livelihood by persuading unsuspecting opponents that he can be beat at swordplay, only to dazzle the crowd at the last minute with his superior skill and bravado. He is a lone wolf, too, who shuns society and cannot stay in one place for long. Moreover, Lancelot reveals himself to be not only a knight errant but also a would-be erring knight when, after his daring rescue of Guinevere, he attempts to seduce her using not-so-chivalric manners and means: He urges a kiss upon her, and when she slaps him, he replies undaunted, "I can tell when a woman wants me." This Guinevere (Julia Ormond) is not so easily won; Ormond's portrayal of her bears the imprint of such strong queens as Morris's in his "Defence of Guenevere," but even more to that of the Guinevere played by Jean Wallace in *Sword of Lancelot.* In that film Guinevere had stabbed a knight who had been part of an ambush party when she was being escorted by Lancelot to Camelot, where she would wed Arthur. In so doing, she saved Lancelot's life. Likewise, the Guinevere played by Ormond in *First Knight* aids Lancelot when she uses a crossbow to kill a knight—one who also was a member of the party sent to ambush her as she was en route to marry Arthur. This Guinevere also plays a form of soccer and rules a kingdom.

Despite several efforts to win Guinevere, Lancelot's growing desire is not consummated, even though Guinevere begins to feel an attraction for him: It finds expression only in a parting kiss, when a redeemed Lancelot takes his leave of the queen. Nonetheless, Arthur witnesses this moment of intimacy and recognizes the restrained passion in it, and his ensuing jealousy prompts a vendetta against his wife and his "first knight." He insists on a public trial for them, which distracts him, renders his kingdom vulnerable to the attack of Malagant, and brings about his own death. Thus, *First Knight* shares a family resemblance with *Knights of the Round Table* in its insistence on the lack of actual adultery between Lancelot and Guinevere, even though this love triangle is the heart of the story. This bowdlerized treatment of the adulterous relationship is perplexing unless one considers it is Hollywood's conservative response to sexual license after the advent of AIDS: There has been a noticeable shift toward depictions of monogamous characters or else portrayals of the dangers of extramarital dalliances. This serves as an example of the film industry's own internal censorship, which can be seen in earlier films such as *Fatal Attraction* (1987) and *Licence to Kill* (1989), the latter film depicting a monogamous James Bond in contrast to his promiscuous behavior in earlier films of the series.

First Knight's most interesting innovation thus involves its portrayal of Lancelot as a maverick who earns his lucre by suckering opponents and professes to believe in nothing but hap. "Left or right, it makes no difference. It's all a matter of chance," he tells Arthur when their first interview concludes and he is prepared to depart (*First Knight* novelization 99): He also pursues a woman whom he knows to be promised to another man. And yet we must recognize that this is the unredeemed Lancelot, a tortured soul who has suffered a personal tragedy (witnessing the murder of his family by "pagan warlords") and who thus does not value his own life. Eventually Lancelot becomes a true knight of Arthur's Round Table (though his motive for accepting the offer is to be near Guinevere, and not because he immediately ascribes to its ideals). A transformed character, Lancelot shows that he is unselfish, willing to die in the service of others and also for an ideal.

The turning point occurs not when he becomes a knight but when in Arthur's service he participates in the liberation of peasants whom he believes, like his own family, have sought sanctuary in a church that has been intentionally set on fire. Although he was unable to help his loved ones as a child, in this uncanny *déjà vu* Lancelot experiences a spiritual rejuvenation when the peasants are freed unharmed. He is then able to embrace Arthur's ideal: "In serving each other we become free." This inscription is engraved on a brazier that encircles the Round Table, which itself consists of twelve knights and the king, the perfect apostolic number. Arthur says, "This is the heart of Camelot. Not these stones, these timbers, these palaces, these towers. Burn all this and Camelot lives on, because it lives in us. Camelot is a belief that we hold in our hearts" (98). The fact that the Round Table consists of twelve knights who profess the code of selflessness and service to others suggests that it serves as a replacement for the absent grail quest as a spiritual ideal in its motto and in employing the perfect apostolic number. It is also well to remember that despite Lancelot's knight errantry, he is also, in Malory, at least, an erring knight—he impregnates Elaine (who has his illegitimate child) and sleeps with the wife of his best friend and liege. Thus, in the narrative tradition Lancelot, too, must repent of his erring ways—as does Lancelot in *First Knight*.

Another innovation may be seen in the conception of Arthur as a master military strategist without Merlin assisting him, and as a character who is much older than either Lancelot or Guinevere. He has seen the incarnation of his youthful dream in the establishing of Camelot—both the city itself and what it represents—and has, apparently, achieved this because of his single-minded pursuit of his ideal. An aged king at the opening of the film, Arthur longs for the warmth and pleasure of marital bliss (and also an heir). Because he has established the Round Table on solid principles and has himself adhered to these virtues, Arthur remains invulnerable until he succumbs to what can only be recognized as a "Momism"—the domestic distraction that ensues from his marriage to Guinevere.

Philip Wylie is probably still remembered for coining the word "Momism" in his 1942 book of social criticism, *Generation of Vipers*, which enjoyed such success that in 1950 the American Library Association honored it by naming it one of the most influential nonfiction books of the first half of the twentieth century. In Wylie's view, Momism, a seductive and destructive use of feminine power, developed in the nineteenth century when women were made the social center and moral guardian of the home. Wylie averred that the feminine mystique that held such sway over men undermined national security, which was then threatened by communism and a refusal to believe in the necessity of military preparation. It is important to recognize that *First Knight* is informed by the decades-old American political commonplaces associated with Momism.

Arthur's January love for Guinevere "weakens" and distracts him from his important military and political duties—duties at which he has excelled most of his life—thus making his kingdom vulnerable to the opportunistic Malagant (Ben Cross), a veritable anti-Christ who, himself a renegade knight of the Round Table, serves as a rebellious and Luciferic foil to Arthur and his ideals. "A man who fears nothing is a man who loves nothing," Arthur confides to Lancelot (99), and Malagant recognizes that the way to defeat the king is to take advantage of his love for Guinevere. Thus, he tries to abduct Guinevere twice, succeeding the second time, although Lancelot also succeeds in rescuing her again, and finally Malagant invades Camelot, after which he kills Arthur during the public trial of Lancelot and Guinevere upon which the king, prompted by his wounded pride, had insisted.

Malagant is a familiar villain, if not also a compelling one. He functions as Lancelot's unredeemed double in the film, since both espouse the principle of self-interest and *laissez-faire* economics. Lancelot cannot live with himself as such, however, and eventually he does not permit Malagant to live with it either, slaying him after Arthur's murder. Himself a former knight of the Round Table, Malagant, masquerading as a lawgiver, pursues his own dreams of power. For instance, he attempts a not-so-friendly takeover of Leonesse when Guinevere's father, its ruler, dies. He commits an act of terrorism to persuade Guinevere to relinquish her claim to Leonesse when he burns one of its villages and proclaims, "Know that I am the law" (27). And when Arthur attempts a reconciliation with Malagant, the latter again asserts that he is on the side of law and order: "Lawlessness is a disease that infects all it touches" (124).

Moreover, whereas Arthur's tactic is to rule by commanding loyalty through a shared set of ideals and by setting a virtuous example, establishing a sort of benevolent autocracy, Malagant instills fear in his followers and engages in gratuitous brutality (he believes in tyranny). An example of this can be seen when Malagant forces his henchman Ralf to confess falsely to the accusation that he had torn Guinevere's dress. After extracting this false confession from him, Malagant breaks Ralf's nose. He then turns to Guinevere and says: "This is what Arthur doesn't understand. Men don't want brotherhood, they want leadership" (155).

Finally, he declares to the king and to the citizens of Camelot: "Did you truly believe that Camelot was a land of brotherhood? I will tell you the truth, Arthur. Camelot is a land of wealth and privilege, protected by a highly trained professional army. No need to be ashamed of that. The strong rule the weak. That's how your God made the world, although you will tell it differently" (267). Himself a tyrant, Malagant nonetheless promises Camelot's citizens "freedom from Arthur's tyrannical dream, freedom from Arthur's tyrannical God" (268), but his argument is defeated by Arthur's willingness to make the supreme sacrifice— that of his own life—so that the ideal of Camelot can survive. He renounces Malagant and his demands and urges his subjects to fight Malagant of Gore to the end, thus supplying them with the motivation to take up arms and defeat the invaders.

As villain, Malagant serves to construct the Manichaean universe of the film; the apparently apolitical Lancelot finds himself caught in a struggle between the forces of light and the forces of darkness. Michael Rogin has observed in the work of Philip Wylie that Wylie links both women's "absence and their presence to boundary invasion, body destruction, and apocalypse," fears that seem to apply rather well to the universe imagined in *First Knight* (*Ronald Reagan, the Movie* 245). Indeed, the film's opening sequence—the sacking and burning of a peasant village by Malagant's forces—is a graphic display of Malagant's willful disregard for boundaries that continues for much of the film. In cold war films we see fears about boundary transgressions and obliterations, an analogy to which can be found in the boundary disputes and skirmishes of postmodernism. Rogin observes:

Cold war films present themselves as defending private life from Communism. Like domestic ideology, however, these movies promote the takeover of the private by the falsely private. They politicize privacy in the name of protecting it and thereby wipe it out. Domestic and cold war ideologies not only dissolve the private into the public; they also do the reverse. They depoliticize politics by blaming subversion on personal influence. That influence, in cold war cinema, is female. The films subordinate political consciousness to sexual unconsciousness. They inadvertently locate the need to make boundaries to protect identity in the fear of being swallowed not so much by Communism as by the mother. (245)

Camelot's apocalypse is prevented when Lancelot chooses to side with the forces of light, he vanquishes Malagant, and happiness ensues. Yet we observe that the boundary transgressions of the malignant Malagant virtually coincide with the announcement of Guinevere's impending marriage to Arthur, revealing how Guinevere's arrival at Camelot is linked to the collapse of boundaries and borders.

Perhaps the strangest aspect of *First Knight* lies in its conclusion. Arthur is provided a Viking burial—sent out on the water in a raft that is torched by flaming arrows while his loyal subjects, as well as Lancelot and Guinevere, look on mournfully. This scene bears at least a superficial resemblance to the conclusion of *Excalibur*, only here there is no hope of a supernatural return. Arthur is dead, definitely dead, though his dream is transferred, as is his sword and his wife, to Lancelot. That Guinevere is present at the end pushes the legend to its limit—she is not in a nunnery doing penance for her sin—in fact, we are encouraged to believe that she may marry Lancelot and rule the kingdom with him, with Arthur's blessing. We suspect that some of the critical condemnation of the film is a result of its being rather oddly old-fashioned, not only in its use of the Viking burial—a stereotyped iconographical unit from late 1950s and early 1960s "period" pictures—but also because it drew from political commonplaces that emerged out of the 1930s and 1940s (e.g., Momism).

First Knight focuses on the tragedy of an ill-conceived passion, divided loyalties, and conflicting emotions; the melodramatic component of the legend appears to have a timeless appeal, although it can be interpreted very differently by individual filmmakers. Even though *Knights of the Round Table* and *First Knight* portray a passionate love that is never consummated, its effect on Arthur's kingdom remains the same as that which occurs in the melodramas that depict the love as an adulterous one, *Sword of Lancelot* and *Camelot*. That the legend's melodrama is retold and reinterpreted by Hollywood is indicative of its popularity and thus stands as testimony to one of the reasons why Arthur and his *entourage* remain so compelling. For it is to Hollywood, and not to academia, that we must look to explain the legend's continued popularity. The institution of Hollywood, like that of higher education, is an archive that stores the cultural memory.

NOTES

1. Byars has drawn heavily from Peter Brooks's *The Melodramatic Imagination* in that she agrees with Brooks that the melodrama has become the modern mode "for constructing moral identity" (11). Brooks argues that since the mid-nineteenth century, "the arts have been constructed on, and over, the void, postulating meanings and symbolic systems which have no certain justification because they are backed by no theology and no universally accepted social code" (quoted in Byars 11). Following Brooks's lead, she argues that "the arts are integral to the production of a cohesive social code" or "'moral universe'" (11).

2. We refer here to *Knights of the Round Table*, which was released late in 1953, although the New York premiere did not occur until January 7, 1954.

3. Richard Thorpe is perhaps most noted as the director of Elvis Presley's *Jailhouse Rock* (1957), but also *Tarzan's New York Adventure* (1942), a precursor of John Boorman's 1985 film *Emerald Forest*; Boorman began directing features in 1965 and, interestingly enough, it was a "rock film," *Catch Us If You Can*, at the time Thorpe's career was coming to an end. Years later, in 1981, Boorman was to direct a

film using the Arthurian legend, *Excalibur*. Their careers thus converge in a most interesting way.

4. See Mast's *A Short History of the Movies* (Indianapolis: Bobbs-Merrill, 1976), 327–28. See also Robert B. Ray, *A Certain Tendency in the Hollywood Cinema, 1930–1980* (Princeton: Princeton University Press, 1985), 129–152.

5. In his article, "The First and Last Love: Morgan le Fay and Arthur," Ray Thompson discusses early texts that portray a positive and loving relationship between Morgan and Arthur. See *The Arthurian Revival: Essays on Form, Tradition, and Transformation* , Debra N. Mancoff, ed. (NY: Garland, 1992) 230-48.

6. See, for instance, Beverly Kennedy's defense of Lancelot in her study, *Knighthood in the Morte Darthur*, Arthurian Studies xi, Cambridge: D.S. Brewer, 1985. In her second chapter, "A Typology of Knighthood," she asserts boldly of Lancelot: "if he is to be the hero of the *Morte Darthur*, and he clearly is the hero of Malory's work, he must be his queen's true, i.e. chaste love, in intention, whether or not he is able in practice to be perfect" (94). How one can be chaste "in intention" but "adulterous" in practice is a true puzzle to these readers, especially when we consider that despite his nobility Lancelot is, in Malory's work, also very much an erring knight. He sleeps with his king's wife (more than once) and impregnates a virgin whom he does not then marry.

7. This represents yet another conflation, that of the Green Knight of *Sir Gawain and the Green Knight* fame, but it might also be indebted to Malory's portrayal of Sir Tarquine, a sadistic knight who shames others by stripping and beating them, after which he throws them in prison.

8. See the code of the Round Table knights in Tennyson's "Guinevere" ll. 464–480 and in Malory's work on pp. 75–76. In the film the knights say: "I will fear God, honor the King and defend this realm with honor and with might." The king vows: "With God's good grace I will hold myself true to this fellowship of knights. In the name of each man here I vow in God's name to do battle against all evil doers, but never in any wrong cause, nor do any outrage. I will defend the helpless and protect all women, and be merciful to all men. I will honor my word. And I will not commit treason nor slander. I will be true in friendship and faithful in love. All this I do swear on the hold of my sword." And Merlin extracts the same oath from the knights.

9. The best that Malory can do in defense of the love between Lancelot and Guinevere is to point out that it is at least a faithful and lasting one, as opposed to the brief affairs indicative of love in his own day. This treatise on love may be found as a discursive statement at the opening of "The Knight of the Cart" episode in Vinaver's edition of Malory (649). The most incisive and helpful article on this subject to date is Donald L. Hoffman's "The Ogre and the Virgin: Varieties of Sexual Experience in Malory's *Morte Darthur*," in *Arthurian Interpretations* 1:1 (Fall 1986): 19–25.

10. Aherne thought enough of the film to mention it in his autobiography, *A Proper Job*, published in 1969. He calls Cornel Wilde "a very remarkable fellow who not only finds his own material and puts his own money into pictures, but . . . directs them, and plays the starring roles—and very good pictures they are too" (348). Writing in 1968, Andrew Sarris, in the canonical *The American Cinema*, claims that "Wilde is still too bland as both actor and director to be given major consideration, but he does reveal a modestly likable personality in over its head with themes oversized for the talent and skill available" (225).

11. Denis de Rougemont's groundbreaking work, *Love in the Western World* (1940) has a comprehensive summary of the features of the Tristram myth that we found to be quite valuable.

12. There is a similarity between Arthur's nervousness here about whether his age might be an impediment to Guinevere's love for him, just as Sean Connery later also expresses insecurity. Here, Arthur refers to her as the 'poor child' or the 'child'

twice in reference to the ambush she had suffered en route, thus underscoring the age difference.

13. The atmosphere of sexual abandon that develops between Lancelot and Guinevere is rather remarkably prefigured by Cornel Wilde and Jean Wallace's first film together, the stylish film noir classic *The Big Combo*, released eight years earlier, in 1955. As Carl Macek observes in Alain Silver and Elizabeth Ward, eds., *Film Noir: An Encyclopedic Reference to the American Style*, "The relationship between Susan Lowell (Jean Wallace) and [mob financier] Mr. Brown (Richard Conte) is a blending of fatalistic deference combined with a feeling of raw sexual abandon." He goes on to say, "Despite her sense of guilt, Susan resigns herself to this situation [with Mr. Brown] because of her own sexual dependence on Brown" (29). Interestingly, Cornel Wilde played Leonard Diamond in the film, a zealous detective who strives to expose Mr. Brown as a mob financier and, in the process, take Susan Lowell away from him. The implied sexual jealousy of Diamond, as well as his implicit desire to steal Brown's moll away from him (by legally sanctioned means) can hardly be missed. Wilde and Wallace were married in 1951, but divorced in 1981. Jean Wallace's portrayal of Guinevere is thus intertextually connected to Susan Lowell, not the least being her obsessive sexual nature, in this case, for Lancelot.

14. This scene had been portrayed in E. A. Robinson's "Lancelot" (1920). Saddened that so many knights are losing their lives because of their adulterous love, Lancelot's grief only angers Guinevere, who argues that he should put an end to the slaughter by slaying Arthur and Gawain: "Why carve a compost of a multitude,/ When only two, discriminately dispatched,/Would sum the end of what you know is ending / And leave to you the scorch of no more blood / Upon your blistered soul?" (133) Likewise, the pithy and robust portrayal of Sir Lamorak in this film is similar to his depiction by Robinson in his "Merlin" (1917).

15. It is possible to argue that *Sword of Lancelot* is a late expression of a curious form of 1950s melodrama called a "male weepie." Thomas Schatz, in his *Hollywood Genres*, mentions films such as *The Cobweb* (1955) and *Bigger Than Life* (1956) and calls them examples of straightforward male "weepies," films which examine "the plight of the middle-class husband-lover-father. Each of these [aforementioned] melodramas is a sustained indictment of the social pressures which have reduced the well-meaning patriarch to a confused, helpless victim of his own good intentions" (239). Such is the plight of Lancelot, seduced and then abandoned by Guinevere, in this film a *femme fatale* and thus a victim of his own good intentions.

16. According to Adam White, *The Billboard Book of Gold & Platinum Records*, the original soundtrack to the film *Camelot*, released in October, 1967, was certified "gold" (over 500,000 copies sold) on September 17, 1968, and certified "platinum" (over one million copies sold) October 13, 1986, nineteen years after its initial release. We think this sort of positivistic data may be indicative of its popularity over the years. In contrast, the original cast album of *Camelot* was certified "gold" on February 9, 1962, but has never been certified "platinum" (as of 1990).

17. The play toured in 1959, playing in several major Eastern cities, before it premiered on Broadway in December, 1960, to rather good reviews.

18. Despite Joshua Logan's impassioned defense of the film in his autobiography, *Movie Stars, Real People, and Me*, Vanessa Redgrave (who, according to Logan, was called a "tall Communist dame" by Jack Warner [189]) was a startling choice for the actress to play Guinevere, given that Julie Andrews, who played Guinevere in the Broadway play and was actually a singer, would have been more logical. Logan may have avoided Julie Andrews because she had played the asexual Victorian governess Mary Poppins in the 1964 Disney film (for which Andrews won an Academy Award as Best Actress); he avers that she was "never a dangerous Guenevere" (183). Incidentally, T. H. White developed a friendship with

Julie Andrews during the development of the play *Camelot*, which would also make her a more logical choice as well. Logan provides an extended defense for his casting of *Camelot*, probably as a result of the film doing rather poorly at the box-office.

19. See, for instance, "This 'Camelot' Remake Doesn't Sing," written by Jay Boyar of the *Orlando Sentinel*, reprinted in the Friday, July 25, 1995 morning edition of the *Omaha World-Herald*, or Jerry Giles's review, "Sorry, Camelot It's Not," in *Newsweek*, July 10, 1995: 56. See also Todd McCarthy's review in *Variety* (June 26–July 9, 1995): 78 & 85; and the review by Andy Pewelczak in *Films in Review* (September/October 1995): 56–57.

20. In her review of *First Knight*, Yardena Arar, of *The Los Angeles Daily News* (rpt. in *The Sunday World-Herald Entertainment Section,* July 16, 1995: 2) observes that *First Knight* "is the third medieval epic to be released in as many months—"Rob Roy" and "Braveheart" came out in spring—but Zucker said he is used to going up against similarly themed movies." This observation contains two inaccuracies typical of the negative responses to *First Knight*: First, that it is tied to a particular historical period, and second, that *Rob Roy* is medieval, when it is based upon the life of an eighteenth-century Scots hero. Zucker himself argues that he was working with legend, and thus making what he called a "fantasy," while the other two films were "historical dramas." The issue of "historical accuracy" or verisimilitude might indeed be raised in discussions of *Rob Roy* and *Braveheart*, but the issue is irrelevant to *First Knight*. Again, in what "historical" period is it most properly set?

21. The novelization of *First Knight* (by Elizabeth Chadwick) makes clear that although Arthur's knights may doubt Lancelot's nobility because of his enigmatic past and because of the rumor that "he fights for money," (198) Arthur recognizes his true worth. Moreover, we learn that the reason for his derring-do and cavalier attitude springs from a tragedy that befell him when he was nineteen and witnessed the murder of his pregnant wife, Elaine, as well as that of his parents and three sisters. We are told pointedly, "His father had been lord of the manor, ruler of a small, contented domain, and Lancelot his newlywed heir, on that fateful day" (185). This motif of the unknown who comes to court and is viewed suspiciously by most of the knights, but who ultimately proves to be noble—in birth and in deeds—should be familiar to those acquainted with Malory's tales of Gareth and Beaumains.

4

The Arthurian Legend
as Forms of Propaganda

I . . . used the Arthurian period merely as a peg to hang the picture
on.

                                                    —E. A. Robinson

Richard Slotkin, in his book *Gunfighter Nation*, calls Anthony Mann's *El Cid*
(1961) "the first of the Kennedy-era epics" to draw on "the *Camelot* imagery that
came to invest the New Frontier" (305). This is because

Heston's El Cid is a larger-than-life abstraction of chivalric honor whose early
speeches and battles are highly stylized to suggest embodiment of an archaic
nobility. Like the gunfighter, whose legendary reputation becomes a code he must
live by . . . El Cid has power because he becomes the mythic embodiment of his
people's aspirations. His chivalry is demonstrated by his sacrifice of love for the
sake of honor. This medieval code is given a modern and liberal inflection, however,
by El Cid's insistence that his personal honor requires him to act as the "champion"
of national values . . . against the private and selfish considerations of rival contenders for the throne. (305–6)

   Certainly Arthurian films do not concern themselves with the Spanish
Christian kingdom in the time of the Moors in particular, but the ideological
features of Mann's *El Cid* that Slotkin identifies are not a feature of "Kennedy-era
epics" alone; they are in fact features of—what shall we call them?—late
Truman-era epics of the early 1950s. Two films from almost a decade earlier, and
with release dates less than two months apart, reveal such a similarity: *The
Story of Robin Hood* (June 1952) and *Ivanhoe* (August 1952). These two films
were released during the summer preceding the 1952 presidential election and
contain all the features Slotkin urges are characteristic of "Kennedy-era epics."[1]
We can refer not only to these 1952 films but also to later films, such as *King*

Richard and the Crusaders (August 1954), *The Black Shield of Falworth* (October 1954), *Prince Valiant* (April 1954), but also to *The Black Knight* (October 1954) all of which were released within six months of each other. (Again, Hollywood is a lemming business. The situation we describe here is similar to the summer of 1995, when "period" pictures *Braveheart*, *Rob Roy*, and *First Knight* were all released within a three-month period.) We must never forget Hollywood's self-appointed role as a defender of American values, especially during an age when it was alleged that Communists had infiltrated the film industry. Our point is not to refute Slotkin—and we do not—but to suggest that all the above-mentioned films, including those putative "Arthurian films" of the early 1950s, partake of the same American political commonplaces as Slotkin identifies in *El Cid*, an epic from the early 1960s, but clearly informed by historical films of the early 1950s.

Of the Hollywood films that draw from the Arthurian legend in this early 1950s period, perhaps the most overtly propagandistic is *The Black Knight*, released in late October 1954 and directed by Tay Garnett. (We briefly sketched Garnett's career in chapter 2, in connection with the 1949 *A Connecticut Yankee in King Arthur's Court*.)

The Black Knight (1954)

Slotkin's sketch of the main features of *El Cid* applies, *mutatis mutandis*, to Richard Thorpe's *Ivanhoe*, but also to *The Black Knight*. Indeed, *The Black Knight* begins with at least a superficial allusion to *Ivanhoe*, namely, the brief opening sequence that features a roving troubadour. *Ivanhoe* begins with Robert Taylor on horseback, riding along strumming a dulcimer as he searches for the imprisoned King Richard. *The Black Knight* begins with a troubadour (Elton Hayes) on horseback, riding and strumming along as well, even though he then vanishes from the film.

For convenience, we can quickly summarize the main action and cast of characters of *The Black Knight*. The essential characters are John, a blacksmith (Alan Ladd), Sir Ontzlake (Andre Morrell), Sir Palamides (Peter Cushing) and his "servant," Bernard (Bill Brandon), King Mark (Patrick Troughton), and King Arthur (Anthony Bushell). We suggest that the above are essential characters, although an assortment of other "names" pepper the plot but ultimately prove insignificant to the cold war paranoid scenario that is the heart of the film. Indeed, none of the major Arthurian characters has any significant role; all are peripheral to the main action. There is a Guinevere (Jean Lodge), an Earl of Yeonil (Harry Andrews), a Lady Linnet (Patricia Medina), and a Sir Hal (Basil Appleby), but the core action consists of the fatherless John becoming recruited by Sir Ontzlake—an older knight who acts as an analogue of an FBI agent recruiting domestic spies—to serve as an undercover counterintelligence agent.

Sir Ontzlake, who observed the brief expression of love between John and Linnet, plays upon John's desire for Linnet in his effort to recruit him. He avers that "knighthood is a flower to be plucked," that he himself had his knighthood bestowed upon him because of his valor and service to his country. He admits to John: "Some are born to knighthood. I was not." He encourages John to aspire to a similar goal so that he may eradicate the barrier of social class between himself and his love, the Lady Linnet. Sir Ontzlake encourages John further by remarking of the sword John has just forged: "You made it, now let it make you." He also encourages John in a way that appeals to his patriotism: "There comes a time in every man's life when he must fight for what he wants most," be that freedom or love, presumably. Finally, Sir Ontzlake utters one of the great paranoid sentiments of any film: "There is treason all about us, and it must be stamped out before all of us—you, I, and King Arthur himself—are overwhelmed." As a recruiter, Sir Ontzlake's rhetoric neatly and happily combines the personal and patriotic missions for John. Sir Ontzlake's recruitment mission, as one might expect, is successful.

The Black Knight is an interesting expression of cold war paranoia, "a situation in which," William Epstein writes, "betrayal and patriotism are mutually reciprocal and virtually indistinguishable" ("Counter-Intelligence: Cold War Criticism and Eighteenth-Century Studies" 77). In order for us to reveal more precisely the way in which *The Black Knight* is informed by the paranoid situation of the cold war period, it might be profitable to compare the film to a Warner Brothers western, *Springfield Rifle*, starring Gary Cooper and directed by Andre de Toth, released precisely two years earlier (October 1952). Like Alan Ladd, Gary Cooper had been a popular Hollywood star for many years, and the two had played in a number of similar roles, both starring in some of the notable westerns of the early 1950s. In 1952, the same year as *Springfield Rifle*, Gary Cooper had starred in *High Noon*, and in 1953, a year before *The Black Knight*, Alan Ladd had starred in *Shane*. Time has shown that the two westerns were the stronger films, but the films the actors made as immediate follow-ups to the westerns have been virtually forgotten. Remarkably, the two ignored films have a number of features in common.

Film critic John H. Lenihan has observed that *Springfield Rifle* used "subversion against a subversive enemy even at the risk of sacrificing home and family" (*Showdown* 37). Lenihan, conveniently, has summarized the main features of the action, as follows:

The film's hero, Major Lex Kearny (Gary Cooper), poses as a traitor in an attempt to infiltrate and destroy a gang that is stealing horses from the Union army during the Civil War. The mastermind of the thievery is a high-ranking Union officer, a living example of treason in high places. Kearny's charade as a traitor creates domestic tension when his wife demands an explanation of his suspicious behavior. . . . In the end, Kearny's devotedness to a job that threatened his personal happiness receives due recognition in a military ceremony complete with a flag waving in the background and a proud family looking on. (37)

It is important to note that *Springfield Rifle* differs significantly from pre-World War II Warner Brothers westerns such as *Dodge City* (1939), *Virginia City* (1940), or *They Died with Their Boots On* (1941)—all of which starred Errol Flynn—in that this 1952 film, as Lenihan notes, "promoted a patriotism based less on idealism and good will than on the dirty but necessary aspects of winning the war. Heroism involved performing unusually violent and underhanded deeds that especially dismayed the fair sex" (*Showdown* 38). In contrast to the aforementioned pre–World War II westerns starring the gallant and chivalric Errol Flynn, both Cooper and Ladd are engaged in wars involving spies, counterintelligence, and enemies from within, insidious threats which demanded tactics far from "fighting fair," tactics that demanded fighting "fire with fire": Because collaboration is a form of counterintelligence used by the enemy, it must also be used against the enemy. It is ironic that the gallant chivalry of the Flynn westerns is not promoted in a film such as *The Black Knight*, a film in which it would be expected these values might well appear. Robert B. Ray identifies this irony as a "discrepancy between intent and effect" characteristic of post-World War II films, and observes that "the rise of the western . . . reflected an emerging American awareness that the passage of time might have discredited certain values and attitudes previously assumed immutable" (*A Certain Tendency of the Hollywood Cinema* 169).

Lenihan's discussion of *Springfield Rifle* provides an interesting set of features with which to explore *The Black Knight*. In *Springfield Rifle*, Major Kearny willingly engages in a charade in order to become an undercover agent, as does John in *The Black Knight*. Major Kearny employs such tactics in order to ferret out the traitor who is selling horses to the enemy. In *The Black Knight*, John goes undercover in order to identify and expose King Arthur's enemies, who are disguising themselves as Viking raiders and thus are posing a threat to his realm. In both films the threat seems to be external, but in fact the real enemy is internal, the traitors from within, who must be found out and destroyed. In *Springfield Rifle*, it turns out that the traitor is a high-ranking military officer; in *The Black Knight*, the traitors are among the king's closest advisors (Sir Palamides and King Mark). Whereas King Mark is traditionally deceitful and treacherous—at least in the medieval prose tradition—it must be remembered that Palamides is, on the whole, honorable, although a Saracen. He is a character capable of being transformed (as he eventually becomes a Christian). The reason that a *minor* Arthurian character is activated is probably to express a xenophobic attitude toward foreigners.

The Black Knight acknowledges class distinctions while creating a rags-to-riches fantasy in which virtue reigns supreme and inherited privilege is seen as effete.[2] The commoner John is stigmatized by an unfortunate coincidence, being seen by the woman he desires but who is of a higher class, the Lady Linnet, in the ruins of the castle of the Earl of Yeonil, her father, after a "Viking" raid, which leads Linnet to believe John is one of the "Viking" raiders and hence a traitor. John, of course, is unjustly accused, having returned to the castle in order to lend a helping hand to the lord who had moments earlier banished him when he caught John and Linnet in an embrace. Thus John was prompted by honor and loyalty even after being dismissed by the earl, though Linnet confuses his loyalty for treachery (an extratextual effect of the cold war paranoid analytical situation mentioned above). In *Springfield Rifle*, Major Kearny must willingly dupe his wife and son in order not to jeopardize his mission, whereas John, because of his pledge to Sir Ontzlake, must suffer the insults of Sir Palamides while his true love, Linnet, looks on in justified scorn. He can do nothing to defend himself, thus honoring the vow made in his verbal agreement with Sir Ontzlake. We emphasize this vow in order to reveal why John cannot act: Should he act otherwise, he will "blow" his cover. In fact, John masquerades in two ways: as an undercover agent acting on behalf of Sir Ontzlake and also by masking his true identity by the disguise of "The Black Knight."

Lenihan is right to observe that these undercover tactics of 1950s cold war films are "dirty" and "underhanded," yet John is justified in doing them because the high-ranking enemy infiltrator, Sir Palamides, has already instituted a crafty counterintelligence plan via his dumb and mute "servant," Bernard, on the one hand, and by having a collaborator (collaboration being a particular form of counterintelligence) in Sir Mark, who has the ear of King Arthur. John's and Sir Ontzlake's dubious underhanded tactics are thus justified, as the enemy is both within (Sir Palamides and King Mark), but also without (the "Viking" raiders).

The preposterousness of the named enemy—the "Vikings"—must not over-shadow the fact that the name allows us to derive the true nature of the enemy, the way in which the film connects to an ideology and thus can rightfully be called propaganda. We must note that the role of the "Viking" invaders is some-times filled by Sir Palamides' and King Mark's forces. Thus, while there are indeed Viking *invaders* (the outside enemy) there are also Viking *impostors* (the inside enemy), thus suggesting the Protean nature of the malignant enemy in this and other cold war films.[3] The simulative powers of the enemy thus are like the powers of the "monster," which is, by definition, a master simulator.

Sir Palamides is a Saracen, as is his putative servant Bernard. His collaborator, King Mark, is eventually revealed to be a pagan; King Mark admits to Palamides that he is a false Christian, that he was baptized only to "deceive Arthur." He avers, "The high priest at Stonehenge knows my plans." Paganism and orientalism (as in "infidel") are yoked together in opposition to King Arthur, the defender of Christendom.[4] Thus, the paganism of King Mark—who orders Linnet and all the Christian monks who do not renounce Christianity to be sacrificed at Stonehenge—and the aforementioned orientalism of Sir Palamides suggest the real nature of the ideological enemy, communism (as in its metonymy, atheism). In a rather remarkable scene, King Arthur orders Stone-henge and its "evil practice" to be destroyed, and the viewer watches in awe as the historic stones topple to the ground. Presumably, the communist stronghold has been razed (though the issue of how Stonehenge was resurrected is left unexplained). Edward Herman and Noam Chomsky have argued in *Manufacturing*

Consent that anti-communism is America's "national religion" (29–35) and the film's pitting of Christian religion against a religion that is yoked to the enemy reveals the imbrication of this commonplace into the logic of the film.

In addition to its anti-communist dimensions, *The Black Knight* also reveals Hollywood's propensity to draw on certain stereotyped villains, the most obvious one in this case being the imposing figure of Bernard, Sir Palamides' "servant." Ian Cameron, in *Adventure in the Movies*, relates an anecdote told by director Richard Brooks, who began as a writer in Hollywood in the early 1940s. Brooks's story is about his early experience as a writer in Hollywood, in particular his experience with a producer whose idea for a new feature film was to place three of the studio's star actors in a desert setting. Each time Brooks would pitch a story to the producer, he was asked, "Where are the riffs?" or "Who are the heavies?" meaning, "the fellows in the white sheets on horses" (*Adventure* 33). Sir Palamides and Bernard are the "riffs" or the "heavies" in *The Black Knight*. For instance, in true melodramatic fashion, Bernard, naked to the waist and looking vaguely oriental, is ordered to enter the Lady Linnet's chamber, where he is instructed to use whatever means necessary—the implication can hardly be missed—to "make her talk." Bernard's smirk and malicious grin suggests the perverse pleasure he receives in carrying out this order from Sir Palamides, and he takes to it with great relish. Indeed, he would have had "his way" with Linnet had it not been for the timely arrival of John, dressed in his guise as "The Black Knight," who rescues her and vanquishes Bernard. (See illustration 7.)

Sir Palamides is *the* pagan knight in Malory's work, and an oddity because of this. He competes with Sir Tristram for the love of King Mark's wife, Iseult, but he is never successful in winning her, although he often distinguishes himself in jousts. His temper sometimes leads him to ill-manners and to a violation of the chivalric code, but at last he is baptized. We see nothing of the nobility of character in *The Black Knight* version of Sir Palamides, nor is he interested in winning a lady's love. Instead, he is the evil collaborator with King Mark, presumably because both are pagans. His orientalism is emphasized by his exotic and feminine appearance (he wears rings, bracelets, and huge looped earrings). For Bernard, however, there is no medieval antecedent, and from the details of his character and function in *The Black Knight* emerges a commentary, or a warning against the tacit racial implications of competing religions. First of all, like the spy he is, Bernard has a "cover": Sir Palamides claims that he is a mute, but John swears that on the night of the Viking raid of Yeonil's castle he had heard Bernard utter an elated cry as he murdered Yeonil's wife, thus disproving that he is a mute, but also shockingly revealing the savagery of murdering an innocent (white) woman and enjoying it. The domestic threat is unmistakable here—if you don't want your house to be overrun and innocent women killed, you had better guard against letting them in the door.

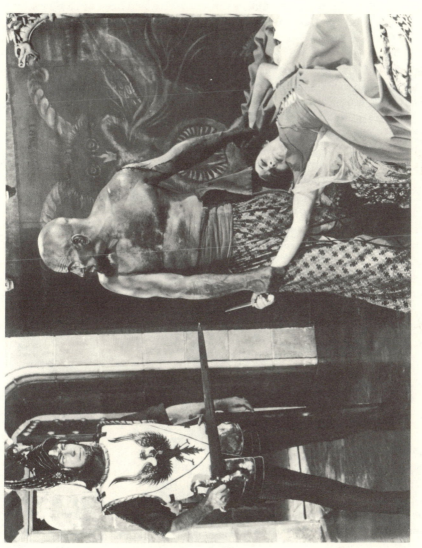

7. Alan Ladd (left) as the title character comes to the rescue of Linnet (Patricia Medina) before the dastardly Bernard (Bill Brandon) has his way with her, in *The Black Knight* (1954). Photo courtesy of The Museum of Modern Art/Film Stills Archive.

Moreover, after the "Viking" raid by the "Northern invaders," the Earl of Yeonil becomes senile, incapable of caring for himself. He is incoherent, hallucinates (he believes his dead wife is alive), and must be cared for by his daughter, Linnet. The resemblance of this subplot to a similar one in *Gone with the Wind* (1939) is rather striking: Yeonil is very much like Scarlett O'Hara's father, who suffers from senility, talks to his dead wife, and must be cared for by Scarlett. Ostensibly his sickness was brought on by a fall from a horse, but it is clear that it really results from the grief and loss of his wife, as well as being precipitated by the Yankee occupation of the South and the threat to an antebellum ideal by the Union soldiers who ravage Tara. *The Black Knight* thus connects with *Gone with the Wind* in a highly suggestive way.

The Black Knight activates only the trappings of the Arthurian legend—its cast of characters and its society—in order to infuse it with its own propagandistic aims. But this should not be surprising; that the *Matter of Britain* was from its inception open to such political manipulation is evident in the texts of the many writers—among them Geoffrey of Monmouth, Thomas Malory, Alfred, Lord Tennyson, and T. H. White—who have used it for social commentary. We must not forget that this abuse of the legend is in part what caused its decline during the Renaissance and the Reformation. It is not, then, such a radical departure to see films such as *The Black Knight* use the legend to comment on social and political tensions, but it is unusual to use the legend exclusively for this purpose. *The Black Knight* is only one of several films that employ the legend for such propagandistic ends. The invocation of an ahistorical and idealized past lends itself to such uses, and we suggest that this is how films that use the legend connect to westerns and romantic genres.[5]

Siege of the Saxons (1963)

Remarkably, *The Black Knight* was loosely remade by Columbia a mere nine years later under the title *Siege of the Saxons* (1963). Directed by Nathan Hertz Juran (1907–   ) the remake draws heavily from the plot of the earlier film and even uses footage from it. *Siege of the Saxons* also recycles the armor and shield Alan Ladd wore in *The Black Knight*. In fact, even after several viewings of both, one is likely to confuse elements of the two. To be sure, there are differences, but both contain the traitor from within who is one of the king's closest allies, and both contain pagan rites associated with Stonehenge. Although the point hardly matters, we argue that *Siege of the Saxons* is a more engaging film than *The Black Knight*, certainly more entertaining, if only because it disguises its propagandistic ends under the guise of escapist entertainment. As such, Nathan Hertz Juran was the ideal choice for director as he had specialized in fantasy films since the time he turned to directing in the early 1950s. Previously he had served as a highly successful art director for many motion pictures, winning the Academy Award for Best Art Direction in John Ford's *How Green Was My Valley* (1941).

Wheeler Dixon has noticed that as a director Juran "had two careers: one as Nathan Juran, whose films are mainstream and often rather dull; the other as Nathan Hertz, whose films are cheap, hysterical, and fascinating" (*The "B" Directors* 272). Nathan Hertz films include *The Brain from Planet Arous* (1958), with John Agar, and *Attack of the Fifty-Foot Woman* (1958) with Allison Hayes. (The latter was remade in 1993 starring Daryl Hannah.) Dixon views these latter two as the "bizarre, tacky, yet thoroughly transcendental" films that Nathan Hertz directed (*"B" Directors* 273). *Siege of the Saxons*, however, is a Nathan Juran film, and thus, for Dixon, it is merely "entertaining" (273). In any case, Juran's output as director consisted of films in the Mélièsian cinematic tradition.

Juran had directed several films for Columbia in the late 1950s, and while we must stress that we have no evidence to prove our claim, we strongly suspect that Columbia wanted to capitalize on the popular interest in the Arthurian legend as result of the success of the Broadway musical *Camelot* (1960). As a result, Columbia remade one the Arthurian film it already in its catalogue, *The Black Knight*. *Siege of the Saxons* was released in Britain with the title *King Arthur and the Siege of the Saxons* in August 1963, no doubt to exploit the commercial popularity of the Arthurian legend as a result of the Broadway smash *Camelot*—much like *Sword of Lancelot* and *The Sword in the Stone*, both released the same year. Indeed, as a result of the popularity of the musical Camelot, the 1954 *Knights of the Round Table* was rereleased in 1962.[6]

The protagonist of *Siege of the Saxons*, Robert Marshall (Ronald Lewis), like John of the earlier film, is not a nobleman by birth—indeed, he calls himself a thief—but a commoner whose dedication and faithfulness to King Arthur and his daughter, Katherine (Janette Scott),[7] eventually leads to their marriage in a rags-to-riches fantasy similar to that of *The Black Knight*:

> *Kate*:   I love *you*.
> *Robert*: No, Kate. Marriage to a commoner is the one luxury a
>   queen cannot afford.
> *Kate*:   Robert Marshall, in reward for services rendered to the
>   crown, we hereby proclaim thee Baron of Cornwall. . . .
>   Now will you marry me?
> *Robert*: I don't know, Kate. How do I know you're not just
>   marrying me for my possessions?
> *Kate*:   Guards! Guards!
> *Robert*: Ah, Kate. When you put it that way . . . How could any
>   man say no?
> *Kate*:   Robert, if you really *don't* want to marry . . .
>   [They kiss.]

Replacing Sir Palamides as the traitor within is Edmund of Cornwall (Ronald Howard), the king's champion, who is collaborating with the Saxons (the outside enemy) to overthrow a King Arthur (Mark Dignam) ailing from a bad heart. In place of Bernard, the servant of Sir Palamides, is a character referred to only as "The Limping Man" (Jerome Willis), a sadistic psychopath dressed in black leather whose characteristic feature is, as one might expect from his designation, a robotic limp. (He is the hired assassin of Edmund.) Unlike *The Black Knight*, *Siege of the Saxons* has a Merlin figure (though absent through much of the film) who knows the secret of Excalibur and recognizes the rightful heir of King Arthur, Arthur's daughter Katherine.

Like John in *The Black Knight*, Robert's loyalty to the king is questioned. In *The Black Knight*, John storms a castle, presumably Camelot, where he has trailed the "Viking" invaders and, gaining entrance, sets upon Bernard—who had moments earlier been in disguise—after which he denounces him to a startled court. King Arthur, however, is swayed by the eloquence of Sir Palamides, but because it is the Feast of the Pentecost, the king grants John a boon and gives him three months to prove his innocence.

In *Siege of the Saxons*, Robert, who had earlier proved his mettle to the king by admitting to Arthur that he is a thief, is sent ahead by the king to Edmund's castle, where, it turns out, "The Limping Man" is lying in wait to assassinate King Arthur. "The Limping Man" knocks Robert unconscious and, using a crossbow, makes an attempt on Arthur's life. He misses his target, however, the arrow striking Arthur in the shoulder. (The arrow's fortunate miss is a common device in westerns.) The unwitting Robert learns of the attempt only after he gains consciousness. Although Robert is innocent, like John, he must flee for his life and, like John in *The Black Knight*, prove his innocence on penalty of his life. These similarities are revealing, as they show how the underlying cold war commonplaces remain intact through the translation: The real enemy cannot be distinguished from a false one (loyalty and betrayal being virtually indistinguishable), the enemy has sophisticated counterintelligence tactics in place, and traitors exist in the highest levels of government, as Senator Joe McCarthy had claimed little more than a decade earlier.

Much of the film is devoted to the tempestuous relationship that develops between Robert and Katherine. Through Robert Marshall's steadfast dedication to the king and his rightful heir, Katherine, the enemy is vanquished and, as in *The Black Knight*, the personal and political outcome is a happy one. As in a Shakespearean comedy—*The Taming of the Shrew* comes to mind because its heroine lends her name and her independent spirit to *Siege's* Katherine—matrimony is the reward for the long-suffering hero. Domestic happiness prevails and socio-political order is restored as well.

Shakespeare popularized this model that writers of Arthurian romance so frequently use. Before the bard put pen to paper, medieval writers employed this courtly ideal in which the remote, cold, and seemingly unattainable lady nonetheless inspires a suitor, usually a young man or one whose noble identity has been concealed, to valorous acts that benefit all. His motive may be selfish and personal, but the results are altruistic. Certainly this is the case with the two episodes Malory incorporated into his work, those of Gareth and Beaumains, in which two young unknowns, verbally abused by a torrent of savage remarks from the ladies they serve, are in the end rewarded with wealth, recognition, and marriage. Shakespeare made this model attractive when he created a heroine with the irresistible appeal of Kate; he also emphasizes the need for a harmonious political order. Tennyson used the courtly ideal in his Arthurian idyll, "Gareth and Lynette" (modified slightly from Malory's work), and he also stresses the connection between domestic happiness and political order.

The Black Knight and Siege of the Saxons stand as testimony to the survival of this courtly model, as do countless other Hollywood films. As John G. Cawelti observes in Adventure, Mystery, and Romance, a typical feature of the adventure formula is the hero's reward through the favor "of one or more attractive young ladies" (and one might add wealthy as well) and notes the erotic interest "served by attendant damsels" (40). That the hero really may be of low birth (e.g., John in The Black Knight and Robert in Siege) represents a modification of the formula intended to suit the sensibilities of a twentieth-century American audience, one that values the democratic ideal and the myth of endless possibilities for anyone who is willing to work steadfastly toward a given goal. Once again, we see the degree to which Hollywood films serve as a mythic register of culture. The motif of the courtly lover has been around for centuries; it should not be surprising, then, that it appears in these films in a modified form.

The Sword in the Stone (1963)

> No amount of disdain can disguise our complicity in the promulgation of the Disney experience, and the anatomy of pleasure that it exposes, even when it adopts the inverted, derisive form posited by the cultural elite.
> —Neville Wakefield, Postmodernism (101)

We have argued that both The Black Knight and its remake Siege of the Saxons drew upon the "enemy in our midst" theme that was common in Hollywood films of the 1950s and that this common theme suggests the two films' underlying purpose as agitprop. Our argument relied largely on our readers' faith in what was meant by our use of the term propaganda. There were a number of underlying and unquestioned premises in our use of the word (strategically omitted during the discussion), among them that propaganda is a largely unconscious, subliminal operation that is nonetheless effective, and that this unconscious operation, in turn, effectively leads to behavioral changes in the individual. These omissions allow us at this point to raise a number of questions about the nature of propaganda, and whether The Sword in the Stone should be considered propaganda at all.

At this point, we must make a distinction between propaganda of the agitational or *agitprop* sort and the integrative propaganda that might be found in a film such as Disney's *The Sword in the Stone* (1963), an animated feature that has the same putative source text as the Broadway musical *Camelot*, T. H. White's *The Once and Future King*. To be more accurate, both films use only certain books of White's novel; *Camelot*, as we saw in the previous chapter, primarily adapts books three and four, while *The Sword in the Stone* draws from the first book.

The Sword in the Stone is not *agitprop* like *The Black Knight* and *Siege of the Saxons*. A standard view assumes that, because it is a Disney film, it should be considered the sort of propaganda that Jacques Ellul calls the propaganda of integration, by which he means propaganda which promotes a political quietism, conformity, and passivity. It is this integrative form of propaganda that Herman and Chomsky argue, in *Manufacturing Consent*, is the type deployed by the American mass media, the purpose of which is "to inculcate individuals with the values, beliefs, and codes of behavior that will integrate them into the institutional structures of the larger society" (1). The function of propaganda for Herman and Chomsky is a virtual restatement of Ellul's original formulation about integrative propaganda. In *Propaganda* Ellul states that the

propaganda of integration . . . aims at making the individual participate in his society in every way. It is a long-term propaganda, a self-reproducing propaganda that seeks to obtain stable behavior, to adapt the individual to his everyday life, to reshape his thoughts and behavior in terms of the permanent social setting. We see that this propaganda is . . . extensive and complex. . . . It must be permanent, for the individual can no longer be left to himself. (75)

He goes on to say that the propaganda of integration "is much more subtle and complex than agitation propaganda. It seeks not a temporary excitement but a total molding of the person in depth" (76). At the outset of the argument he says that integrative propaganda "did not exist before the twentieth century" (74).

Konrad Kellen, in his "Introduction" to Ellul's *Propaganda*, explains this last assertion by stating that for Ellul the status of the individual in the twentieth century is like that of an epigone who has been "cast out of the disintegrating microgroups of the past, such as family, church, or village" into a mass society, and as a result is "thrown back upon his own inadequate resources, his isolation, his loneliness, his ineffectuality" (*Propaganda* vi). To extrapolate, in such an isolated and deracinated condition the abandoned, helpless individual is without sufficient internal resources so as to be malleable, that is, vulnerable to the propagandistic manipulation by the various educational prostheses of the State, primarily the media. In short, Ellul's critique, while never explicitly citing the work of the Frankfurt School, falls well within the parameters of that School's debate about the nature of authentic existence. The point is, the work of Disney would fall within the category of an inauthentic "mass culture," a degraded form of experience for which the Frankfurt School expressed a noted distaste. Neville Wakefield calls this line of inquiry "the old-fashioned ideological critique" that demands in its critical formulation "the terms of misrepresentation and falsification." If indeed Disney has been a primary contributor to the formation of postmodernism, then "who," Wakefield asks, "is being misrepresented and what is being falsified" in the "kingdom of the imaginary" promulgated by Walt Disney? (*Postmodernism* 100–101). The question *should* be asked, for thé critique of inauthentic experience has an underpinning that is thoroughly paranoid. Why? Because it depends upon a theory about human psychology theory that is both possessional and dissociative.

The critique depends upon a possessional and dissociative model because, as stated earlier, it presumes that the lone, isolated individual in the twentieth century is like a prematurely abandoned infant, without sufficient internal resources to fend off the false, invasive thoughts of the alien meme. The Marxist critique of postmodernism is paranoid in this sense. If Heideggerian Being has the same sense as Lukácsian totality—Lucien Goldmann's thesis in *Lukács and Heidegger*—then the forgetfulness of Being (a dis-memberment) has the same sense as the Marxian theory of reification. If abstracted in Althusserian terms, then the "representation of the imaginary relationship of individuals to their real condition of existence," becomes ideology, or "false consciousness."[8] Psychologically speaking, false consciousness corresponds to being possessed with the Other's thoughts: The alien meme, masqueraded as Self, has usurped the Self's own thought and presents itself as Self. Marxist ideological critique is thus amenable to a possessional/dissociative psychology, betraying certain affinities to strains of gnostic and orphic thought as well. According to Wakefield, the American "culture industry," so despised by the denizens of Frankfurt, "was a view of American mass culture as manipulation—as a process of degrading, de-historicising and defiling 'real' human needs by providing them only with 'false', 'disneyfied' solutions" (*Postmodernism* 100), a position that certainly informs Fredric Jameson's widely disseminated treatise on postmodernism.

Should we, then, consider *The Sword in the Stone* as integrative propaganda? This would mean that we are relying, in our critique, on the terms of misrepresentation and falsification that simply are not applicable in this case. Wakefield's (and, and we shall see, Jean Baudrillard's) point is that it is really not possible, or even relevant, to approach the animated features of Disney asking questions about whether they are true or false representations of reality. In the era of postmodernism, Wakefield observes, the

coordinates of value that had served to elevate the critique above its subject seem to have imploded in our age of hyperreality: as the subject itself, in this case the whole of American society, has become dispersed in, and ultimately indistinguishable from, its various representations. To attempt to claim that Disney somehow exists apart from this orbit of representation is clearly untenable. (101)

Of course, there are no implications in this line of inquiry that would deny the power of Disney as a force in American culture. When Russell Banks, for

example, was asked to discuss "the movie that changed his life," he cited
Disney's *Bambi* (1942). Banks writes:

The story of *Bambi*, subtitled in Felix Salten's book "A Life in the Woods," is both
simple and amazingly complete. From birth to death, it describes and proscribes the
territory of a male life in a sequence that follows exactly the Victorian and modern
middle-class view of that life properly lived. It's a rigorous, wholly believable, moral
story. . . . *Bambi* makes all the stops on the life-circuit, and does so in a rigorously
structured, comprehensive, and rhythmically patterned way, as precise and inclusive
as a Catholic mass or a cycle of myths. Which, of course, makes it feel universal. . . .
Bambi may be agitprop, but it's agitprop of a very high order. ("*Bambi*: A Boy's
Story" 79)

Like Banks, we have doubts about whether the film qualifies as *agitprop* at
all, and with him our immediate inclination is to say that because *Bambi* is
imaginary it must therefore be false. Yet this is troubling. Jean Baudrillard
observes that "the Disneyland imaginary is neither true nor false" (*Simulations*
25), provoking the rather unsettling question that underlies this entire
discussion: How do we recognize anything as ideology? Paul de Man wrote that
"what we call ideology is precisely the confusion of linguistic with natural
reality," an insight that captures the essence of the dilemma (*The Resistance to
Theory* 11). We may possess false beliefs about our own beliefs, and have no
way of knowing it. Baudrillard says that ideology "only corresponds to a betrayal
of reality by signs; simulation corresponds to a short-circuit of reality and its
reduplication by signs. It is always the aim of ideological analysis to restore the
objective process; it is always a false problem to want to restore the truth behind
the simulacrum" (*Simulations* 48). Given this insight, Wakefield suggests that
it is appropriate to reject the "antonymical oppositions of real and imaginary,
truth and falsity that sustain the imperial dismissal of whole areas of culture as
being in some way self-evidently inauthentic"—that is, blatantly propagandistic
(101). Baudrillard's point is that a simulation is not a mere reflection of the
objective world, as through the lens of a camera, but is rather already an
imaginative, subjective expression of the world, like the projection of a
phantasmagoria.[9] If, as a Disney animated feature, *Bambi* (or *The Sword in the
Stone*) is not propaganda but rather a simulacrum, then what is it a simulation
of?

At this point, perhaps we should review the film itself. Interestingly,
Richard Schickel, writing in *The Disney Version* (1968) called *The Sword in the
Stone* one of the "least well known of Disney's animated films" (197) and then
proceeds to ignore the film in an otherwise important study (his was the first
critical study to follow Walt Disney's death in 1966). In fact, Schickel's sole
observation about the film is in connection with the character of the owl,
Archimedes, a figure which he argues is derived from Jiminy Cricket of Disney's
earlier *Pinocchio* (1940), one of those "wee" creatures which "showed Disney and
his people a convenient way to brighten and lighten any story they feared might

grow too serious or unpleasant for audiences" (197). The film goes unremarked in Bob Thomas's study, *Walt Disney: An American Original* (1976) as well, but is briefly mentioned in Kathy Merlock Jackson's *Walt Disney: A Bio-Bibliography* (1993). Jackson observes that *The Sword in the Stone* "was the last animated feature that Walt Disney would live to see his studio release" (64). In addition, she indicates that *The Sword in the Stone* was rereleased only twice in the thirty years that separates her study from the film's initial premiere on Christmas Day 1963: In 1972 (when Warner Brothers' *Camelot* was also rereleased) and in 1983. In contrast, *Bambi* was rereleased six times through 1988, *Pinocchio* seven times through 1992, and *One Hundred and One Dalmatians* (1961) four times through 1991. (Disney tended to rerelease his films about every seven years, a practice he started by the successful rerelease of *Snow White and the Seven Dwarfs* in 1944—seven years after its initial release. In fact, when *Snow White* was released in 1987 for its fiftieth anniversary celebration, it was (re)appearing in theaters for the seventh time. In contrast, *The Sword in the Stone* was rereleased only twice in twenty years.) We therefore conclude that Schickel's observation still stands, that indeed *The Sword in the Stone* remains relatively obscure when compared with other Disney's feature-length animated films. It is rarely invoked in the same breath as the "classic" Disney animated films such as *Snow White and the Seven Dwarfs* (1937), *Pinocchio*, or *Fantasia* (1940).

Our research has revealed that it is unclear to what extent Walt Disney did in fact oversee the production of *The Sword in the Stone*. Bob Thomas details the extreme care and "total control of the script process" (340) Disney spent on the production of *Mary Poppins* (1964); he concludes that most of Disney's talents and energies were focused on this particular project during the period from 1960–1964 (*Walt Disney* 336–345.) Perhaps following Thomas's lead on this period of Disney's life, Marc Eliot, in his controversial 1993 biography, *Walt Disney: Hollywood's Dark Prince*, claims that Disney

became obsessed with *Mary Poppins* the way he hadn't been with any film, animated or live-action, since *The Three Caballeros* [1944]. He worked on *Poppins* day and night for months, moving into his office at the studio as he had so often done in the old days. He demanded everything to the smallest detail be executed exactly as he wanted, no matter how much time or money it consumed, until he was satisfied. (281)

Despite the fact that Disney maintained tight artistic control over all facets of his studios' productions, Eliot notes that Disney had little to do with the production of *Dumbo*, for instance, "the bulk of which was completed in the summer of 1941, before he returned from South America" (175). We conclude that while Disney was certainly involved in the preproduction process of *The Sword in the Stone*—approval of the script, for instance—the film is largely reflects the devoted work of its writer, Bill Peet, and its director, Wolfgang ("Woolie") Reitherman, the latter being one of "The Nine Old Men" who were the essential core of Disney's animating team.10 Bill Peet had joined the studio in October 1937, about the time *Snow White* was being completed, and was to remain with the studio for the next twenty-seven years.

According to John Culhane, Woolie Reitherman "became the first person in Disney Studio history to get overall directorial credit for a feature"—for *The Sword in the Stone* ("The Last of the Nine Old Men"15). Reitherman was born in Munich, Germany on June 26, 1909. He moved with his parents to Kansas City when he was one year old. Later, they moved to Sierra Madre, California. After high school, Reitherman attended Pasadena Junior College for two years, and at the age of twenty-three he began to attend the Disney Art School that had opened its doors on November 15, 1932. In 1933 he was hired by Disney and began work at the Hyperion studio. All in all, he worked on twenty of Disney's animated features. Culhane reports that Reitherman "had being flying since the twenties ("Last" 11), and after Pearl Harbor was bombed on December 7, 1941, when Reitherman was thirty-two, he enlisted in the air force as a pilot. After the war

Lieutenant Colonel Reitherman's qualities as a leader of men were quickly put to use by Disney, who made him a directing animator on all the cartoon features up to *Sleeping Beauty* (1959), for which he directed the climactic sequence in which Prince Phillip battles the dragon and hacks his way through a forest of thorns to wake the Princess with a kiss. (15)

He was co-director of *One Hundred and One Dalmatians* (1961). When Walt Disney died in 1966 during the production of *The Jungle Book* (1967), it was Reitherman who took over the production and saw it completed and that it met its scheduled release. He then became the producer of the studio's entire animated feature output. Woolie Reitherman finished several other features after Disney's death as well: *The Aristocats* (1971), *Robin Hood* (1973), and *The Rescuers* (1977). His last feature, on which he was co-producer, was *The Fox and the Hound* (1981). At his retirement, Reitherman had spent his entire creative life— almost fifty years—working for Disney and Disney Studios. He was killed in an automobile accident in May, 1985.

The Sword in the Stone drew on the veteran talents of five of the Nine Old Men: With Reitherman as director, the directing animators were Frank Thomas, Milt Kahl, Ollie Johnston, and John Lounsbery. The character design was handled by Milt Kahl and Bill Peet, the art direction by Ken Anderson. (Among the character animators was Eric Larson, who had been with Disney the longest of any of the Nine Old Men.) The story was written and designed by Bill Peet. (Peet was to leave Disney Studios in 1965 as a result of creative disputes over *The Jungle Book*; afterwards, he wrote and illustrated children's books, a practice he'd begun before he left the studio.) In their massive study of the art of Disney animation, Frank Thomas and Ollie Johnston refer to Peet as "the talented, pungent, irascible humorist from Indiana" (*The Illusion of Life* 376). In addition to writing and sketching the story for *The Sword in the Stone*, Peet also performed the same tasks for the animated feature that preceded it, *One Hundred and One Dalmatians*. Thomas and Johnston write:

Bill Peet always had a strong, overall concept of the story material that integrated the humor in both the characters and the situation. Rather than spot gags, his integrity drove him to search out an idea that lifted the situation out of the commonplace, and still left the door open to further development in this new direction. Yet after conceiving all this in his mind, he could reject the entire notion if it did not work with the other parts of the story. (377)

In his autobiography, Peet avers that it was he who suggested to Walt Disney that an animated feature should be made from T. H. White's *The Sword in the Stone* (*Bill Peet: An Autobiography* 168). White's work had been published in the United States in 1938 with some fanfare, having been singled out by the American Book Club as one of its featured selections (Sylvia Townsend Warner, *T. H. White* 104–05). The English edition of *The Sword in the Stone* was published in August, 1938, the month of the Munich Crisis. T. H. White's notebooks, however, indicate that the Disney organization became interested in *The Sword in the Stone* almost immediately following its publication: By May, 1939 White records that he had "tried to settle [the] Disney contract" (Warner, *T. H. White* 124). Of course, it is not clear that Disney and White arrived at terms over the option of the work, so it may well have languished for over twenty years before Bill Peet revitalized it again around 1961, most likely after the success of *Camelot* on Broadway. It makes sense, however, that Disney would be interested in doing such a film; he had settled on Julie Andrews for the role of Mary Poppins as a result of seeing her in *Camelot*. At any rate, Peet relates that Disney wanted Peet to write a screenplay before work on story boards began. Peet says that he found during the process of adaptation that

The Sword in the Stone was complicated, with the Arthurian legend woven into a mixture of other legends and myths. Getting a more direct story line called for a lot of sifting and sorting. Walt questioned the first version of my screenplay, pointing out that it should have had more substance. So I made an all-out effort to give it more substance by enlarging on the more dramatic aspects of the story. (*Autobiography* 169)

It is unclear what Peet means by "substance," but we suspect that Disney's hesitations led to Wart becoming a variation of the standard Disney inventor hero: He is taught to use his "wits" to outsmart all his physically larger and hence more powerful opponents—the Pike and the Hawk, for instance. Neville Wakefield, on whose work we have drawn heavily in this discussion, argues that Disney's films fall into two categories, and that from his film work Disney drew the "blueprint" for his theme parks (106). The first category, of which *Snow White and the Seven Dwarfs* (1937) and *Sleeping Beauty* (1959) are examples, "are tales of death, rebirth, suspended animation, and miraculous redemption," and these themes "find their corollary in the Disneyland experience" (106). The other category, represented by the early Disney animated shorts such as the "Alice" series of the 1920s and the later feature-length films *Alice in Wonderland* (1951) and *Mary Poppins* (1964), "involves the grafting of real actors into imaginary landscapes." All these films can be read "as in some way exploring the genre established by Lewis Carroll" (107). Certainly the Disney theme parks in some sense derived by extrapolation of Lewis Carroll's "Alice" works, in that Disney devised a way to allow park visitors literally to walk into cartoonland. We argue that *The Sword in the Stone* falls into the latter, Carrollian category.

In writing the screenplay to *The Sword in the Stone*, Bill Peet reveals that he patterned the figure of Merlin after Walt Disney—"Walt the wizard"— admitting that in his drawings of Merlin, he "even borrowed Walt's nose" (*Autobiography* 168–169). Referring to Walt Disney as a wizard links him to our previous discussion in chapter 2 and our discussion of the "wizard" figure that encompasses Thomas A. Edison, Baum's Wizard of Oz (perhaps modeled after Edison), and the Hank Morgan/Martin figure and his double, Merlin, from *A Connecticut Yankee at King Arthur's Court*. What Peet suggests, intentionally or not, is a way of reading *The Sword in the Stone* that allows us to see the film as a model of the entire Disney experience, the experience of the theme parks and that of all the films in general.

At this point we must backtrack a little. According to Bob Thomas, the idea for Disneyland, the first of the Disney theme parks, originally imagined as "Mickey Mouse Park," dates back to August 1948 (*Walt Disney* 225). Disneyland remained only an idea for several years, until December 1952, when Disney formed WED Enterprises, "a personal corporation" that he "needed . . . to help him create Disneyland" but which he also used to fund his purchase of the Zorro stories for television (*Walt Disney* 252). In the meantime, Disney had agreed to produce a television special, broadcast on Christmas Day 1950, the first of many Christmas Day specials to follow (Jackson, *Bio-Bibliography* 47). Beginning on October 27, 1954 the first weekly "Disneyland" television show aired on ABC, a program Disney had agreed to do because ABC had agreed to invest heavily in Disneyland, providing him with the much needed capital (*Bio-Bibliography* 50). As Jackson observes, Disney's venture into television "was calculated to nourish another of his projects that he regarded as more important: the establishment of a theme park called Disneyland" (48). The television series "would serve to popularize Disneyland" (50). In other words, Disney was a shrewd "master of mass media" and "tapped the potential of one mass medium to popularize material in another" (59). She writes:

As he served as host of his "Disneyland" television show, his face and homespun voice became familiar nationwide. His portrait graced the covers of numerous popular magazines, among them *The Saturday Evening Post*. In this magazine, beginning on November 1, 1956, there also appeared eight installments from Disney's first biography, *The Story of Walt Disney*, affectionately told by his first-born daughter Diane to Pete Martin. (*Bio-Bibliography* 59)

Peet's admission that he modeled Merlin on Disney should not, therefore, be surprising, given that by 1956, the name Walt Disney was metonymically associated with the American holidays of Thanksgiving and Christmas: He was a living legend, a larger-than-life figure. Yet *The Sword in the Stone* is not the only one of Disney's animations that contain this element of self-figuration.

Jack Zipes, although he largely proceeds with the presuppositions of the standard ideological critique, makes an otherwise very important observation about Disney's relationship with the fairy tale. He states that

it is noteworthy that Disney's very first endeavors in animation (not considering the advertising commercials he made) were the fairy tale adaptations that he produced with Ub Iwerks in Kansas City in 1922–23. . . . To a certain degree, Disney identified so closely with the fairy tales he appropriated that it is no wonder his name virtually became synonymous with the genre of the fairy tale itself. ("Breaking the Disney Spell" 28).

Zipes shows that in the early history of animation, the early animators before Disney "literally drew themselves into the pictures and often appeared as characters in the films." (We might add that this is also true of the films of film pioneer Georges Méliès, who acted in his own films and often used himself as the subject for visual tricks.) This was not without precedent before Disney began his career as an animator. Donald Crafton, in *Before Mickey: The Animated Film 1898–1928*, remarks that

the early animated film was the location of a process found elsewhere in cinema but nowhere else in such concentration: self-figuration, the tendency of the filmmaker to interject himself into his film. . . . Part of the animation game consisted of developing mythologies that gave the animator some sort of special status. Usually these were very flattering, for he was pictured as (or implied to be) a demigod, a purveyor of life itself. (qtd. in Zipes 28)

We are struck by the remarkable correspondence between Crafton's observations about early animators' tendency for self-figuration and the Wizard of Oz, who in the 1939 film projected himself as an over-sized demigod—an image of himself in his own figurative phantasmagoria. We therefore suspect that it is more than a serendipity that Peet referred to Walt Disney as "Walt the wizard." (Baum's first Oz novel, *The Wonderful Wizard of Oz*, was published in 1900. Was his model for the wizard Edison or a composite of early animators, or both? As we noted in chapter 2, by the late nineteenth century Edison was known as "The Wizard of Menlo Park," and Baum's wizard is technologically adept.) Zipes goes on to say that "it might be considered somewhat one-dimensional to examine all of Disney's films as self-figurations, or embodiments of the chief designer's wishes and beliefs," but in fact he then shows precisely how Disney's early animated features are elaborate exercises in self-figuration (28–29). His discussion of Disney's *Puss in Boots* (1922) is particularly revealing, as he shows that the film's hero, unlike that of Perrault's source text, "is the enterprising young man, the entrepreneur, who uses technology to his advantage" (33). In the source text, it is the cat who displays the admirable qualities attributed to the young man in the Disney version. In Perrault's story, the youngest of three sons of a poor miller is given only a cat as his inheritance. A witless simpleton, he imagines he will starve with such a useless legacy but the cat, by use of his own wits and inventiveness, creates an illusory figure, "The Marquis of Carabas," out of this impoverished master, and through several cunning strategies, manages to marry his master to the king's daughter. Among Disney's revisions, Zipes notes the insertion of a sequence in which the hero and Puss (in the film changed to a feminine feline) go to the movies and see a film starring "Rudolph Vaselino as a bullfighter" (32). Zipes explains that it is through this "technological medium of the movies that Puss's mind is stimulated." Puss also uses a "hypnotic machine" to help out the hero (33). Again, there is the association of the movies with technological adeptness.

The hero of *The Sword in the Stone* is a young man who, through his mentor Merlin, learns *how* to be enterprising—to use "brain over brawn," "wits," and ingenuity—and overcome all obstacles, including, we might add, overcoming the cruelty of a brutal foster brother (Kay) and the punishments of a cold, militaristic, and humorless foster father (Sir Ector). His spirit is triumphant—though he has the help of the wizard Merlin. We note that the young Arthur's parentage is left an enigma—he is without a past, simply a twelve year-old boy—nor does he know who Merlin is when he first meets him.

We can also discern the film's emphasis on learning the value of enterprise and drive by noting its transformations of its source. In White's work, Merlin transforms Wart into a fish, a bird, an ant, a wild goose, and then a badger, respectively, so that Wart may acquire by analogy the requisite knowledge of certain social and political systems he will need when he becomes king. From these experiences Wart eventually discovers in turn the evils of tyranny, fascism, and complacency, and finally recognizes the importance of tolerance, harmony, and passive resistance to aggression. In the Disney version, however, the social and political applications of these lessons are removed.

Instead, Merlin insists that the Wart should learn that his own capacities for self-reliance, ingenuity, and wit must be developed in order to triumph over those obstacles that are inevitably a part of life. "Brain over brawn" is the lesson Wart must grasp from his near-fatal encounter when he—having been transformed by Merlin into a small fish—is pursued by a larger one and he must rely not on Merlin's help but on his own instincts and alacrity to survive. From the squirrel experience Wart learns that love, "greater than gravity," is the "most powerful force on earth," a lesson that intimates Wart's distant (adult) future as betrayed husband and king—with which this film remains otherwise unconcerned. There were several ways in which an adult audience could have brought a knowledge of the love triangle to the film: The Broadway play *Camelot*, the 1954 *Knights of the Round Table* that was rereleased in 1962, *Sword of Lancelot*, released earlier in 1963, or from White's own *Once and*

Future King (1958)—not to mention a myriad of other possible sources as well. When Merlin transforms Wart into a sparrow the mage must intervene, however, because his protégé falls into the clutches of Madam Mim, who takes "delight in the gruesome and grim." The antithesis of Merlin, Madam Mim challenges the wizard to a "duel" in which they use their protean skills to outwit each other as various forms of predator and prey. The inclusion of Madam Mim reveals that degree to which Bill Peet at least knew the original serial publication of White's work, not the version of *The Sword in the Stone* that eventually appeared as the first book of *The Once and Future King* (1958). According to biographer Sylvia Townsend Warner, White later cut out the "pastiche of Madam Mim" for book publication (*T. H. White* 100). Through his superior wit and inventiveness Merlin vanquishes Madam Mim even though she breaks all of the rules that she herself had insisted upon before they began. The Wart is dazzled by his master's ability to think and act quickly, and Merlin avers that this struggle was worth it provided that Wart learned from his observation. Wart, now a quick study, dutifully recites the dictum that "Knowledge and wisdom is the real power."

That Wart should divine the importance of self-reliance and initiative makes sense considering the fact that his prior education had consisted of menial drudgery for Sir Ector; in this way his life is similar to Cinderella's. As mentioned previously, his foster father Ector only supplied discipline and instruction in jousting; Merlin must finally fill the void of true mentor-parent. T. H. White used the legend as a means to explore the political struggles of his own time, to expose the evils of war, and to speculate on its causes; the Disney version is unconcerned with politics and morality. "Do you want to be all muscle and no brain?"; "You can't always trust in luck"; "You're on your own, lad, I can't solve that problem"; "How do you ever expect to amount to anything without an education?"; Merlin utters these and like admonishments repeatedly in the film. Their pervasiveness underscores the film's emphasis on self-reliance, wit, drive, and initiative as the keys to success.

However, we must not lose sight of the way the film employs features of the work of Lewis Carroll, *Alice's Adventures in Wonderland* (1865) (this also the name both of one of Disneyland's amusements and one of Disney's full-length animated features) and *Through the Looking-Glass* (1871). For when Wart literally "drops in" on Merlin in his hut—leaving the brutish reality of Kay's world behind—he also drops into a magic kingdom, where normal laws of proportion, size, and mass are suspended. The world is suddenly replete with animate, anthropomorphized objects like an impertinent sugar bowl and a friendly, walking chair. Wart, himself a cartoon character, drops into a world that is even more of a cartoon, as it were, in which Merlin/Disney rules wonderland. When Merlin packs up, his possessions can, by his incantation, defy the logic of size and mass and obediently load themselves into a small travel bag—books, furniture and all. When Sir Ector banishes Wart to the kitchen, Merlin rescues him from his toils by enchanting the pots and pans and begins a sort of "assembly line" in which the dishes wash themselves. He transforms himself into fish and enters the water world of the moat, and later transforms himself and Wart into squirrels in the world of the forest. With Merlin's aid, Wart's dreary life is transformed. He is able to move through hitherto unimagined fantasy worlds, all of which is supposed to prepare him for his future role as an adult "in the real world."

The film, in other words, is a simulation of the Disney theme park experience, something like a trip to Disneyland itself. For rather obvious commercial reasons, many of the amusements at Disneyland are derived from characters and situations from Disney animated features, one entertainment flowing inseparably into the other in a circulation like a Möbius Strip. Indeed, whether the occasion for the opening of Disneyland in July 1955 was to promote the films and the television show, or whether the films from 1948 on were made to both promote and to be incorporated in the theme park confounds a simple chicken-or-egg dialectic. Many of the film projects certainly seem to have been chosen for their potential adaptability as attractions at the theme parks: The animated features released after 1948 but before the opening of Disneyland were *Cinderella* (1950), *Alice in Wonderland* (1951), *Peter Pan* (1953), and *Lady and the Tramp* (1955). In addition, in 1950 Disney expanded into live-action feature films, beginning that year with *Treasure Island*. *20,000 Leagues Under the Sea* was released in 1954, *Davy Crockett, King of the Wild Frontier* in May, 1955, and *Third Man on the Mountain* in 1959. This latter film lead to the invention of the Matterhorn attraction, while *20,000 Leagues* lead to the Submarine Voyage, creating a closed loop between the films and the park. (On June 14, 1959 the then Vice-President, Richard Nixon, dedicated the Matterhorn, the Monorail, and the Submarine Voyage at Disneyland.) In short, the theme parks are simulations of the films, with the film projects chosen with an eye towards their potential as simulations at the theme parks. Executives at Universal Studios, for instance, must have at some point noticed the loopiness of Disney films and theme parks, followed suit and created their own theme parks. Universal's *Jurassic Park* (1993) is an example of a film that incorporates the device of an amusement park that can in turn be looped back and simulated in a (real?) theme park. (Author Michael Crichton modeled *Jurassic Park* on the 1973 film he wrote and directed, *Westworld*, which featured the break down of simulacra in an amusement park, a film probably inspired by Disneyland.) The theme parks and films create a spiraling effect, creating what Baudrillard figuratively calls simulations of simulations, or simulations of nothing.[11]

One of the strengths of the Arthurian legend is its great flexibility, and the particular uses of the legend we have discussed in this chapter surely do reveal just how flexible those limits are. Yet the films discussed in this chapter tend to reveal the validity of E. D. Hirsch's observation, in *Cultural Literacy*, that knowledge tends to be transmitted according to stereotype and cliché. The use of the Arthurian legend in these films is at its farthest reaches, in figurative terms a kind of catachresis, in which the barest minimum of the features of its typical characters are invoked. "King Arthur" is a character in *Siege of the Saxons*, but beyond the name, the character in this film and the character in the received legend have scant features in common. There is a figure named "Merlin" in *The Sword in the Stone*, but he shares minimal features with the character as depicted in Malory; they seem to be connected only by name and by their supernatural powers as "wizard." Nonetheless, the films have contributed to the continued vitality of the legend.

NOTES

1. On this point we do not think that Slotkin would disagree; the features he identifies represent cold war political commonplaces—and by cold war we mean a world polarized into two competing camps engaged in mutual subversive activity, which would include the period preceding World War II as well. Noam Chomsky has argued this in his *Rethinking Camelot: JFK, the Vietnam War, and U.S. Political Culture* (Boston: South End Press, 1993). For example, William Wellman's *Beau Geste* (1939) contains a rather extended allusion to the Arthurian legend. Gregory L. Ulmer's *Heuretics* also draws on Slotkin's observations; Ulmer remarks on the propagandistic function of *Beau Geste*, by observing that the film disguises it purposes "by formulating public, historical events in terms of private or personal conflicts" (86). Ulmer concludes that the film was preparing the country to go to war.

2. See Alan Lupack, "An Enemy in Our Midst: *The Black Knight* and the American Dream," in Kevin J. Harty, ed., *Cinema Arthuriana* (29–39), who argues that the film enacts a rags-to-riches fantasy.

3. At this point we should acknowledge *Prince Valiant*, yet another film released the same year as *The Black Knight* which employs an assortment of Arthurian characters. The film is putatively based on Harold R. Foster's comic strip which began in 1937. *Prince Valiant*'s use of "Viking" invaders suggests a possible influence on *The Black Knight*, though we suspect this invoking of a similar outside enemy is a matter of convergence rather than direct influence. Both films employ the "enemy within" theme; we have repeatedly stressed this theme as a commonplace in many early 1950s films; the point hardly needs reiterating

4. Christianity and Judaism, rather like America and Russia, can combine forces to fight the enemy, however, as in a film contemporaneous to *The Black Knight*, *Ivanhoe*, where the Jewish patriarch, Isaac, not only lends financial support to Ivanhoe's efforts to raise the ransom and rescue King Richard (the Lionhearted), but also is willing to risk the freedom of his daughter, Rebecca, in order to free his Christian king. Ivanhoe's behavior is thus identical to Slotkin's El Cid, in his insistence that his personal honor require to act as the "champion" of the nation, against the private and selfish considerations of rival contenders.

5. We are indebted to Frank McConnell's book, *Storytelling and Mythmaking: Images From Film and Literature* (New York: Oxford University Press, 1979).

6. We suspect that Columbia preferred to recast and slightly revise *The Black Knight* rather than rerelease it, given that Alan Ladd, Ephraim Katz has noted, had, in November 1962, "nearly been killed by an 'accidental' self-inflicted gunshot wound" (*The Film Encyclopedia* 676). Ladd's puzzling decline (*13 West Street*, released in June 1962, was a fine suspense film) was probably in some related to the decision to remake the film. At the time of his death at age 50, in January, 1964, Ladd's career had been in a decline, and his death "came as a result of an overdose of sedatives mixed with alcohol, possibly intentional" (676).

7. There is, of course, no narrative precedent for a daughter named Katherine especially in the absence of a queen, though the 1949 *A Connecticut Yankee in King Arthur's Court* provides Arthur with a niece. It is noteworthy, however, that in the Old French Prose Romance, *Perlesvaus*, Arthur and Guinevere have a legitimate son, Loholt, whose untimely death causes Guinevere herself to die of grief.

8. See Martin Jay's *Marxism and Totality* (332ff.), however, regarding Goldmann's recognition of the differences between Being and totality. We should point out that Goldmann's purpose is to show how Heidegger's *Being and Time* (1927) is virtual rewrite of Lukács's *History and Class Consciousness* (1923) with all the Marxism removed. We have also profited from Richard Wolin's *Labyrinths: Explorations in the Critical History of Ideas* (Amherst: University of Massachusetts Press, 1995), in which Wolin argues that Western Marxism—especially the Frankfurt School version—was basically a secularized variant of Jewish messianism, with the thought of Walter Benjamin a prime example.

9. The analogy is drawn from Margaret Cohen, *Profane Illumination: Walter Benjamin and the Paris of Surrealist Revolution* (Berkeley: University of California Press, 1993), p. 240. Cohen is discussing Benjamin's exchange of figures to explain the process of ideology, namely his move from the figure of the *camera obscura* (which Marx used) to the figure of the phantasmagoria, a popular nineteenth-century entertainment. At issue is Benjamin's moving away from the figure of the *camera obscura*, a device that "mechanically reverses the world out there in the darkened chamber of thought," to the phantasmagoria, a "magic lantern" that "inverts painted slides that are themselves artistic products" (240). We trust that our use of the analogy has not done violence either to Baudrillard's or to Benjamin's thought; employing over-simplifying analogies risks creating problems at a deeper level.

10. "The Nine Old Men," named after the nine chief justices of the Supreme Court, was Disney's affectionate name for the animators who had worked with him the longest. With the exception of Les Clark, who joined Disney at the Hyperion Street studio in 1927, the rest of the Nine Old Men joined Disney in the 1930s: Wolfgang Reitherman, 1933; Eric Larson, 1933; Ward Kimball, 1934; Milt Kahl, 1934; Frank Thomas, 1934; Ollie Johnston, 1935; John Lounsbery, 1935; and Marc Davis, 1935. John Culhane reports that by the time of *The Rescuers* (1977), "the nine had dwindled to five": Les Clark and Ward Kimball had retired, Marc Davis was designing rides for Disneyland and Disney World, and Eric Larson was training artists. Lounsbery died in 1976, the same year Kahl retired. Reitherman was the last of the nine to retire ("The Last of the Nine Old Men" 10). Culhane also reported that the Nine Old Men was an "animation team that was nonexistent . . . anywhere in the world. Disney and his team developed a technique, and then a style; and together they created many of the great works of the animated film" (10). Our reason for citing Culhane is to indicate that the phrase "Disney film" is largely inaccurate; it was Disney working with these men who invented the technique and style associated with that studio today.

11. W.J.T. Mitchell uses a scene in Crichton's *Jurassic Park* as a model for what he calls "the debate between realism and irrealism" (*Picture Theory* 358). He sees the figure of John Hammond, the entrepreneur who conceived of the park, as a "showman, the P. T. Barnum of *Jurassic Park*" (359). Whereas Mitchell uses the figure of P. T. Barnum, in this study we have used the Wizard of Oz to capture a figure like Walt Disney, who is a much more complicated figure than that of a mere entrepreneur. Mitchell notes that Spielberg's movie of *Jurassic Park* "eliminates nearly all traces of political or economic debate and confines the narrative strictly to the service of spectacle and speculation" (360n. 22), a surprising comment considering that Spielberg is the Disney of the "After Walt" era; of course his films emphasize spectacle. For the bad science the film presents, see Stephen Jay Gould on *Jurassic Park* in *Past Imperfect*, Ted Mico et al., eds., 31–35.

5

The Arthurian Legend
as Hollywood Epic

All my films use the Arthurian legend as a template; it happens to
a large extent unconsciously. But there you have the classic wound
that won't heal, which is very much part of that.
—John Boorman (*Film Comment* · July/August 1995)

In this tale I am a fake god by occupation, and a magician by inclination. Merlin is my hero. I am the puppet master. I manipulate
many of the characters and events you will see, but I am invented,
too, for your entertainment and amusement.
—Arthur Frayn (Zardoz) in John Boorman's *Zardoz* (1974)

Excalibur (1981) deserves a chapter unto itself because it is both complex and
controversial. The film has been the subject of considerable critical inquiry,
some of it negative, although there can be little doubt that it has earned a place
in the *Arthurian* canon, at least, and it has done so rather quickly at that. Certainly it is one of the most frequently discussed films that employ the legend,
and judging from the critical attention it has received, even academics have
embraced it despite their initial skepticism.

Nearly every objection to the film is related to its putative distortion of the
"historical facts" of Arthur's life and times, whatever those historical facts might
be, or to the wrath of the academic purists who, taking the film's credit "Adapted
from Malory's *Le Morte d'Arthur*" in its strictest sense, find disappointment
because Boorman doesn't merely transpose his "source," unadulterated, onto the
silver screen.[1] Boorman himself, it seems, has been able to grasp a concept that
has, inexplicably, eluded his critics. He observes, "I think of the story, the
history, as a myth. The film has to do with *mythical* truth, not historical truth;
it has to do with man taking over the world on his own terms for the first time"
(*Film Comment* 31). In chapter 1 we addressed the issue of verisimilitude.

Arthur belongs to the world of romance—he has been relegated to the world of imaginative literature—which means, as James Douglas Merriman has asserted in *The Flower of Kings*, that the legend was, from its inception and will remain, ahistorical (25).

We find it also worth reiterating that it is futile to assess a filmic version of the legend by narrative standards, even when a director acknowledges a literary source or influence. The formal requirements of film demand that it be encountered and assessed by those conventions that govern it and not by literary expectations. Boorman's ability to transpose the tyrannical literary tradition he inherited to the filmic medium and to also transform the material, to infuse it with his own signature, born out of his own vision, is in part what makes *Excalibur* such a compelling film.

Even critics who have written favorably about this film seem perplexed by it or hesitant to grant it the stature it has nonetheless achieved. Perhaps this can be explained by the complexity of *Excalibur* and by its initial resistance to any convenient Hollywood generic label. As we mentioned in chapter 3, the film does owe a debt to some of the Hollywood melodramas, especially to *Knights of the Round Table*, in that in it there are lessons to be learned about what material is expendable and what is essential and, even more important, the manner in which characters and their roles can and must be conflated when working within the time restrictions inherent in the medium of the film. From the 1954 production Boorman has also perhaps borrowed some scenes not found in Malory's *Morte*, which *Knights of the Round Table* also credits as its literary source, such as the sword play between Arthur and Lancelot when they first meet. We have also discussed how a film such as *First Knight* has, in turn, borrowed from *Excalibur* in its highly stylized, lush imagery, even though the effect is quite different.

Boorman reveals that he read John Cowper Powys's novel *A Glastonbury Romance* (1937), with which he was quite taken: "I read it when I was about 18; I read all his novels. He was very unfashionable—F. R. Leavis said it was rubbish—so it was never taught anywhere. *Glastonbury Romance* is about the conjunction of the Arthurian legend and the Christian legend. That set the pattern for me, really" (*Film Comment* 55–56). This is a revealing remark because it testifies to Boorman's lasting fascination with the legend. It is also valuable, though, because it demonstrates another of our principles discussed in chapter 1—that popular and not academic endeavors have been largely responsible for the legend's transmission. F. R. Leavis—august literary critic—found Powys's novel to be "rubbish," but from this "rubbish" sprang one of the sources for *Excalibur*, which has contributed to the revitalization of the legend.[2]

Excalibur shares elements with Arthurian melodramas and with films that employ the quest, and yet neither of these comparisons will yield an accurate description of what the film is, but will only do a disservice to all the films involved. This is because Boorman's Arthurian production more closely approximates the epic form. It does feature the love triangle, to be sure, and it also depicts a grail quest that is pre-Christian (*not* the quest for the "Holy Grail"), but the film's complexity makes it subsume and transcend these categories. Yet it bears instead a striking family resemblance to the Hollywood epic, especially those films that have chosen for their subject religious themes. Indeed, like the epic tradition in literature, such films frequently take as their theme the establishment of a religion or a nation.[3]

EXCALIBUR AS EPIC

To elucidate this point, we wish to review some essential features of a model Hollywood epic in order to compare and contrast *Excalibur*'s features with them. We have chosen as a model for comparison a film from late Classical Hollywood by a director whose name is metonymically associated with the extravagant Hollywood epic, Cecil B. DeMille.[4]

DeMille's biblical epic *The Ten Commandments* (1956) seems the most apt because its subject matter, like that of *Excalibur*, is tied to a tyranny of tradition. If Boorman had to take into account the long and complex narrative tradition of the Arthurian legend, DeMille had to contend with one perhaps more formidable, the book of Exodus and the story of Moses. A similar feat was accomplished, however, by the great English epic poet John Milton who, undaunted by Genesis, rewrote the story of the Fall in *Paradise Lost* and displayed a remarkable originality. Like Milton, DeMille and Boorman locate "cracks" or points of entry to open up texts that seem to be impregnable. Moreover, the source material of both films comes heavily weighted with a seemingly iron-clad tradition apparently impossible to overthrow, one that appears to demand a special faithfulness in the rendering of cherished figures. The two films are twenty-five years apart (1956 and 1981, respectively), the first, as stated above, coming from the period of late Classical Hollywood, the other from the "New Hollywood" of independent producers.[5] Both directors have enjoyed renown and reputation; both DeMille and Boorman merited an entry in Sarris's canonical text *The American Cinema*, Boorman's entry at the time based on the strength of only two films, *Point Blank* (1967) and *Hell in the Pacific* (1968). *The Ten Commandments* and *Excalibur* share a number of schemata worth pointing out.

Although both films, it would seem, draw from a source material that must remain inviolate, close scrutiny shows that this is not the case. In a highly unusual spoken "preface" in which DeMille himself addresses his audience directly to introduce *The Ten Commandments*, he claims to have depended on texts other than the Bible to construct the story of Moses: The "ancient texts" of Philo, Josephus, Eusebius, and Rabbinical Midrash. He penetrates the seemingly iron-clad story by arguing for what he calls the "missing years" of Moses' life—a span of about thirty years from Moses' infancy to maturity that are elided in Exodus. Thus, much of Moses' life could be surmised, inferred, in short, invented. In *Excalibur* the credits indicate that Malory's *Morte* is the source text, but this is deceptive, co-writer Rospo Pallenberg and Boorman having drawn freely from a number of sources as well as from their own treasonous creativity.[6]

We must emphasize that although *The Ten Commandments* and *Excalibur* may be in some way linked to a distant quasi-historical figure, both films represent the imaginations and signatures of their writers more than the texts claimed to be their putative sources. As stated earlier, DeMille claims to have faithfully adhered to the texts of Philo, Josephus, Eusebius, and rabbinic midrash, but as Alan F. Segal points out in his essay on *The Ten Commandments* in *Past Imperfect: History According to the Movies*:

What DeMille fails to mention is that because all these sources were written more than a millennium after the Exodus, scholars consider them irrelevant to the task of assessing the historical accuracy of biblical events. However much scholars may enjoy reading them and however relevant they may be to the time of Jesus (during which many of them were written), they have little to offer when it comes to ascertaining the truth of biblical history. (De Mille actually relied just as much on modern romances—including Dorothy Clarke Wilson's *Prince of Egypt*, J. H. Ingraham's *Pillar of Fire*, and A. E. Southon's *On Eagle's Wings*.) (36)

The situation is somewhat analogous to Boorman's case. While he asserts in the film's credits that the film is based on Malory's *Morte*, this is in fact only partly true. Boorman's sources, as well as influences, are many. DeMille, however, would have us believe that he gleaned every possible historical source, and that he is recreating "the truth" of Moses's life with factual accuracy. Boorman's representation of reality does not pretend to be rooted in historically accurate truths about Arthur—scant as those are—but rather in timeless psychological truths. Both DeMille and Boorman do, however, credit a source or sources that they then alter freely to suit their own artistic aims. If we review the prominent features in these two films, we can see that, despite some differences, they have much in common.

One of these differences should be addressed immediately. Because *The Ten Commandments* is a product of late Classical Hollywood, it features a stable of Hollywood stars—Charlton Heston as Moses, Yul Brynner as Rameses, Anne Baxter as Nefretiri, Edward G. Robinson as Dathan, and Cedric Hardwicke as Seti. In contrast, *Excalibur* features a virtually unknown cast, at least at the time of its release: Arthur is played by Nigel Terry, Guinevere by Cherie Lunghi, Lancelot by Nicholas Clay; the only actor with substantial film acting experience is Nicol Williamson (Merlin), the only actress Helen Mirren (Morgana). This is, apparently, precisely what Boorman wanted. He deliberately chose actors with low profiles, those who would not bring with them off-screen *personae* that might impinge upon his particular treatment of the legend.

On a formal level, both works resemble dramatic epics in that they must overcome elisions and provide for time lapses in order to cover the entire life span of the hero—and even beyond, in terms of their cosmology. The films are dynastic and vast in scope; thus, the directors must devise ways to move the plot ahead swiftly, sometimes several decades, in order to satisfy the time constraints imposed by the filmic medium on such lengthy and ambitious subject matter. In *The Ten Commandments*, which is three hours and thirty-nine minutes long, DeMille himself provides the voice-over narration, serving as the oracular narrator who reads passages from Exodus to fill in the narrative gaps. Boorman tries more subtle methods, eschewing the voice-over narration for more formal innovations, although he does not entirely escape the use of such a voice-over, as we will see below. Unlike DeMille, Boorman risks confusing his audience by his formal technique. He conflates characters, functions, and images to provide links. For instance, Boorman claims that his co-writer, Rospo Pallenberg, devised at least one of the "several bold jumps forward in time," one of which was having "Uther Pendragon, Arthur's real father and the 'primogenitor' of the whole saga . . . drive the sword into the stone, rather than Merlin, as in Malory" (Harlan Kennedy, "The World of King Arthur According to John Boorman" 33). At that point they cut, jumping ahead eighteen years to the moment when Arthur will pull it out. Another device to indicate time transitions is with aging or at least changed faces, once with Arthur and another time with Morgana and Mordred. The above quotation also shows the dynastic nature of the film—Uther is the "primogenitor." Moses leaves a legacy to the Jews by naming his successor as well. Both works, then, focus on an entire generation.

Both films emphasize the importance of the law, and the epic heroes— Moses and Arthur—are entrusted by some supernatural force with the tablets or the sword that serves as a symbol of their election and of the law. Moses dwells alone on Mount Sinai for forty days and forty nights awaiting the law, and at last he receives it in the tablets upon which are inscribed the Ten Commandments. But the reception of these laws also proves to his discouraged followers that Moses is the genuine item—the true deliverer. In Boorman's film, Uther himself, once he learns that he is "not the one" to bring the law, plunges Excalibur into a stone in order to prevent it from falling into unworthy hands. The sword is the symbol of leadership and the law, and only the true heir, the law-bringer, can remove it.

Both the tablets and the sword empower the heroes and serve as liberating forces to a people, but they also demand adherence to a code represented by that law. When his reign draws to a close, the hero must relinquish the symbol of his power. Moses, himself unable to enter the Promised Land, gives over his staff— with which he has worked so many miracles—to Joshua, who is instructed to lead the Jews across the River Jordan. Moses also instructs him to place the five books of the law, the *Pentateuch*, in the same ark that bears the two tablets upon which the law is inscribed. Likewise, at the moment of his death, Arthur relinquishes Excalibur, commanding Perceval to cast it back into the lake, where it will remain "until another king" comes to claim it.

The protagonist, the law-bringer, is a natural born leader, dynamic and charismatic. He not only commands the love and loyalty of other men but is also attractive to women, and he is able to rely upon supernatural assistance as well. Although both films do contain a love interest, this element does not dominate the plot. The love triangle in *The Ten Commandments* is comprised of Rameses, Moses, and Rameses' sister, Nefretiri. The next pharaoh will be named by the current pharaoh, Seti, who plans to choose either his own son, Rameses, or his adopted nephew, Moses. Egyptian custom apparently dictated that the daughter of Pharaoh was to mate with the heir apparent, even when it involved incest, as it would and does when Nefretiri is forced to become the sister-wife of Rameses. Her love is for Moses, who returns her affection until he discovers his true identity as the son of a "Hebrew slave." But the triangle is subsumed by the power struggle, since they are one and the same: The man who wins the right to be named the next pharaoh also wins the girl.

The incest motif (which we will discuss at length later in this chapter) has interesting connections with the Arthurian legend, however, even though the plot is worked out differently, as is the love triangle. Family upheavals and jealousies, it would seem, make for dramatic possibilities, and love triangles seem most interesting when they are tied to a power base as well. Igraine, for instance, is coveted for her beauty, but she also becomes a trophy to be possessed by the dominant male in a deadly power struggle between Uther and the Duke of Tintagel.

Both films depict an elect or designated ruler who comes from apparently humble origins, although this turns out to be true in neither case. The protagonist's identity is concealed from him and those whom he will eventually lead, and in each case his true parentage is hidden from him, only to be revealed when he is poised to assume his role as leader of the people. The infant Moses is found among the bulrushes by Pharaoh's sister, Bithia, a grieving and childless widow.[7] The infant is wrapped in a "Levite cloth" that indicates he is the son of "Hebrew slaves," yet she adopts it despite Pharaoh's edict that all the Hebrew male infants should be put to death, and she subsequently names the child Moses. Merlin demands possession of the infant born of Uther and Igraine and names him Arthur; the mage then places him in a foster home but does not reveal his identity even to his foster father, Sir Ector.

Not until Moses, through his compassion, has gained great popularity among the enslaved Jews he is sent to rule and is about to be named the next pharaoh for having built the city of Goshen for Seti does he discover his true origins and face an immediate dilemma: He must choose to be the next pharaoh and marry the beautiful Nefretiri, whom he loves, or turn his back on this opportunity and on his adoptive mother's love and kindness in favor of remaining with his biological family, who are slaves. He opts for the latter, of course, and his true destiny—to lead the Hebrews out of bondage and into the Promised Land—eventually becomes manifest. Moses himself—ostensibly an Egyptian oppressor—turns out to be "the deliverer" the Jews have awaited. Likewise, the young Arthur unwittingly pulls the sword from the stone when, acting as his foster brother's squire at a joust, he allows Kay's sword to be stolen and hastily grabs for the one no man has been able to free from the rock where

Uther thrust it. The kindly but alarmed Sir Ector, also ignorant of Arthur's true identity, tells the youth to "put it back," after which Arthur removes it again with ease in front of the powerful contenders for the throne. He reluctantly learns of his true parentage when Merlin arrives to reveal it; strife among the nobles breaks out, and the young man flees into the forest, loathe to be king and doubting his ability to rule. Yet he is the deliverer upon whom Britain has awaited.

In both films one religion displaces another. The religion of the Egyptian pharaohs is a false one that doesn't acknowledge the "god of the Hebrews." Moses frees his people by demonstrating that his god is more powerful than pharaoh's, by curse of drought, turning the water of the Nile red, and other miracles. Finally, Pharaoh himself is responsible for the curse that inadvertently brings death to his own son by declaring that the firstborn child of all slaves shall be killed. Instead, the "Hebrew God" kills the firstborn of all Egypt, including pharaoh's own son. In *Excalibur*, Merlin realizes that the time of Arthur is a time "for men," not gods, and that he must find other worlds to inhabit. During Arthur's marriage to Guinevere, apparently performed under the auspices of a Christian priest, Merlin and Morgana lament the passage of the pagan gods. Morgana approaches the mage and claims to be "a creature" like him, one who invokes the older gods and religious rites that survive despite the rise of the new Christian faith.

Both films also feature what we shall call "oracular voices" that emanate from inanimate objects. In *Excalibur*, the grail questions Perceval twice, prompting him to reveal the insight that "the king and the land are one." "I am that I am" speaks twice to Moses also, once from the Burning Bush and again when he inscribes the Ten Commandments on the stone tablets. There are important distinctions to make here, however. The oracular voice of the grail speaks to Perceval while he is in a delirious state, after he has been hanged to a tree by the armored automata Mordred controls. His first encounter with the grail is thus a private, solitary vision that occurs in an apparent state of trauma-induced hallucination. The second time the oracular voice speaks to Perceval is after he emerges from the waters of a stream, having shed all his armor and most of his clothing in an act of "purification" that prepares him for the truth of the grail, that "the king and the land are one," and thus also that the voice of the grail is actually Arthur's. In contrast, Moses' encounter with the voice of God is not intimated to be caused by hallucinations or delirious visions, although Moses, like Perceval, has to undergo a period of "purification" by wandering without food or water about the desert until his spirit is "ready for the maker's hand."

These schemata, of course, are attempts to sketch general similarities, not argue for a one-to-one correspondence between the two films. Certainly, the broad similarities neglect major differences between the two epics, in particular the absence of certain features in Boorman's film that are essential to DeMille's. For example, a crucial feature of DeMille's film is his idealization of motherhood and the mother as the moral center of the family and, by extension, civilization. It goes without saying that a critical plot point is when Bithia, throughout the film a sympathetic figure, saves the infant Moses' life, responding to powerful maternal drives. Later in the film, the "old slave woman" Moses saves from being crushed to death is, ironically, his biological mother, although at that time Moses is unaware of who she is, thus suggesting a natural bond between mother and child.

When Nefretiri admits she killed Memnet to prevent her from exposing Moses' origins, Moses immediately seeks out his adoptive mother, Bithia, to confirm the story. A key scene in the film depicts the moment in the slave hovel when the two mothers, one the adoptive mother and the other Moses' biological mother, both declare their love for Moses. Later, during the night in which the god of the Hebrews kills the firstborn of Egypt but spares the Jews (the origin of Passover), Bithia opts to stay with Moses and his family rather than to stay in pharaoh's palace, and even follows him into exile. Moses' wife, Zipporah (Yvonne De Carlo), is also a motherly figure, the symbol of a silently enduring, long-suffering, eternal love.

Another important distinction that must be drawn between the films has to do with the visual styles of the two directors. DeMille's visual style is static, largely composed of a series of *tableaux vivants*, while Boorman's visual style is kinetic, largely a modernist derivation of *cinéma-vérité* techniques.[8] In his 1977 study, *Dreams and Dead Ends*, Jack Shadoian makes a perceptive comment about Boorman's *Point Blank* (1967), one that applies to his other films as well:

The film confuses us because the world we expect to be present in the film isn't there, is negated by both form and content. As our expectations are denied, we must scramble to deal with what in fact we are given, which we feel makes deep sense but is not something we can arrive at by our ordinary distinctions. The film's emphasis on de-humanized characters and its deliberately disordered exposition align it with elliptical, anti-narrative, anti-psychological trends in other media. Boorman's cinematic excesses, inversions, and disjunctions construct a context in which his quixotically determined hero approaches absurdity. The film plays havoc with what is real and what is not, and its environments are visually distorted. (309–310)

Boorman is a modernist, DeMille an anti-modernist, and thus their two films represent two contrasting ways of depicting historical—or quasi-historical—events on film.[9] For the heuristic, as opposed to the hermeneutic, principle of *Excalibur* is not that of narrative, where events follow each other in a causal-chronological order, like that of a dream. Instead, it is one of repeated images, much like a poem (e.g., the repeated image of the sword Excalibur) and, frequently, of events that occur simultaneously. It also employs startling visual images and landscapes intended to *suggest* meaning and invite interpretation rather than supply it. Of the importance of landscapes in his films, Boorman comments, "The landscape is essentially the externalization of the inner state of the characters . . . [so that] finding it and photographing it in the right way is enormously important because you're trying to express the spiritual/psychic elements of the character" (*Film Comment* 54). He confesses, "There's always a key image and a particular way of doing it that inspires me before I make a picture. In *Excalibur* it was the sword rising from the lake" (*Film Comment* 49). In addition to a central image, it is also instructive to note, Boorman seeks a tune or song that expresses what he is trying to convey in a film: "Once you get it and all the actors can hear it, they respond and you're all singing the same song. With a film like *Excalibur*, it's heightened, isn't it? It's a mythic register" (56).[10]

EXCALIBUR AS ADAPTATION OF MALORY

Excalibur cannot really be described as an "adaptation" of Malory at all, but rather, as a criticism of it—a text that acts as a "corrective" to it. Like T. H. White before him, Boorman's work enjoys a complicated relationship with its professed pretext. Part of the academic resentment expressed toward the film surely does derive from the misleading credit at the conclusion of the work, indicating that it is an adaptation. Boorman invokes Malory because he wishes to indicate that his film is epic in scope and dimension; that is, it is a portrayal of the entire received legend (for which Malory is so largely responsible) and not just a portion of it. But Boorman does not wish to be enslaved by Malory's work, nor will he allow his own creative impulses to be curtailed by it. Therefore, his assertion that "Malory was really the first hack writer" (Kennedy, "The World of King Arthur" 33) is inexplicable unless it reveals his struggle with a strong Arthurian precursor. Boorman borrows the adumbration of the legend from Malory as well as its tragic grandeur, but a close examination of the two texts makes it very clear that *Excalibur* is a Jungian reading of the legend, one superimposed over the Malorian structure, which is then transposed onto the screen through the sequence of images.

Let us first review Boorman's "source" by recalling Merriman's identification of "the essential Arthurian story or, in Platonic terms, the ideal story, as it manifests itself in Malory" (*The Flower of Kings* 22), to which we alluded in our first chapter. We begin with the details of Arthur's parentage, followed by the brief mention of his foster family, Sir Ector and Sir Kay. Malory then recounts Arthur's rise to power under the tutelage of Merlin: He pulls the sword from the stone, overcomes the rebellious kings, and unites Britain, after which he marries Guinevere (despite Merlin's warning that she and Lancelot are destined to love one another). Although Merriman does not consider Arthur's incestuous liaison with Morgause and the engendering of Mordred to be part of this essential story, nonetheless it is present in Malory, and it does bring about dire consequences. For a while the kingdom prospers, but at the same time the adulterous affair begins and we see, in the Tristram section, the general breakdown of chivalric values among the knights. The holy grail appears at Camelot and all the knights pledge a vow to seek it, but only three—Galahad,

Perceval, and Bors—enjoy success on the quest (Lancelot receives a partial vision, but his sin prevents him from a complete experience of the beatific vision). After the quest the adultery causes more dissension when it is made public. Arthur is forced to seek revenge for Lancelot's accidental slaying of Gareth and Gaheris as he rescued the queen from the stake and, while the king does so, Mordred usurps the throne in his absence. This division of the kingdom leads to civil war: Mordred and Arthur mortally wound each other, although the latter may have sailed off to Avalon to be healed. In Malory's work, Lancelot and Guinevere then live out the remainder of their days in contrition and die holy deaths.

Boorman's *Excalibur* does not follow the order of events outlined above. His alterations of this material are useful in discerning his own mythic reading of the Arthurian legend, revealing the degree to which he reworks the inherited material to obtain a Jungian inflection. Generally, the opening scenes of the film are faithful to Malory's text: Uther is embroiled in a bitter battle with the Duke of Tintagel, covets his wife (Igraine), and relies upon Merlin's magic to slay his enemy and satisfy his lust. From this union is born Arthur, whom Merlin demands as payment for services rendered. He then places the infant in the protective custody of Sir Ector until such time as Arthur should be called upon to act as deliverer to the British people. Once the young Arthur pulls the sword from the stone, there are those who oppose him and he must first prove himself by the sword and by his courage.

After Arthur meets and marries Guinevere (against Merlin's warning, as in Malory), Boorman's film takes a very different turn than that of his ostensible pretext. Enter the adult Morgana, Arthur's half-sister and the "creature" who relentlessly pesters Merlin in an effort to learn his lore. She succeeds in seducing Merlin and serves as the nemesis to the Round Table. Boorman conflates three characters from Malory's text and creates an entirely new figure in Morgana. First, in Malory's work Arthur unwittingly sleeps with his aunt, Morgause of Orkney, who then gives birth to Mordred, Arthur's cousin-son. In addition, Malory includes Nenyve, a lady whom Merlin "felle in dotage on" (76) but who "was ever passynge wery of hym and wolde have bene delyverde of hym, for she was aferde of hym for cause he was a devyls son" (77). She eventually entraps the mage because "allwayes he lay aboute to have hir maydonhode" (77), and his prediction of his own shameful destiny is then fulfilled. Morgan le Fay, Arthur's half-sister in Malory, continually intrigues against him, but unsuccessfully—her only feat is to steal the scabbard that sheaths Excalibur, one that could have made Arthur immortal.

Boorman's Morgana works against Arthur and his court from the time she arrives at Camelot for the wedding. She tries subtle means of discord and even prompts Gawain (Liam Neeson) to accuse Lancelot and the queen of adultery. Moreover, she persuades Merlin to reveal to her, at last, "the sacred charm of making," which entraps him, but this event occurs simultaneously with the scene in the woods where Lancelot and Guinevere have satisfied their physical desire and are discovered by Arthur, who thrusts the sword between them. As Arthur buries Excalibur in the ground between the guilty lovers, Merlin is shown to be entrapped in the "dragon's breath" of his own making but also impaled by Arthur's sword. On the same night, Morgana uses her magic to make herself over into the likeness of Guinevere and sleeps with her half-brother Arthur so that she can conceive Mordred. Thus she subsumes the roles of Morgause, Nenyve, and Morgan le Fay.

In doing this, Boorman has economized, as he must, in order to fit the complete legend into two hours and twenty minutes on the screen. But these changes are also enormously important in other ways. Boorman virtually omits the long Tristram section of Malory's text by showing one effective scene in which Arthur proudly alludes to the prosperity of his kingdom, while this scene also reveals—through Gawain's accusation—that the Round Table has already been undermined by the sin (in thought, at least) between Lancelot and the queen. When Arthur sees for himself, soon after, the fruition of the love between his best knight and his wife, he is wounded psychically, relinquishes the symbol of his power, and engenders Mordred on Morgana. (When the lovers awake and see the sword, Lancelot starts up in alarm and exclaims: "A king without a sword; the land without a king!") This is very different than in Malory's text where, it is suggested, Arthur "had a demyng of" (674) the affair between the two but tolerated it because he did not wish to lose his best knight or his wife. Moreover, the adultery creates havoc only when it is made public and Arthur is forced, through the wiles of Mordred and Aggravaine, to acknowledge it.

In Boorman's film Arthur rides into the forest knowing he will find the lovers there because just prior to his departure he had asked Merlin whether they were together and Merlin had confirmed that they were. When Arthur comes upon the lovers, it is a private and not a public moment, so that the hurt Arthur receives is personal, leaving him vulnerable to Morgana's "charm," which results in Mordred. Moreover, we see the ineffectiveness of the Christian faith when, in a scene directly following the unhallowed birth of Mordred, a priest prays for protection against "Morgana's unholy child" and is answered immediately by a lightning bolt that strikes Arthur to the ground, wounding him and creating the need for the quest to heal him.

It strains one's credibility to see Malory's grail section as the source of inspiration for the quest in *Excalibur*. In his edition of Malory, Eugène Vinaver avers that "Malory's *Tale of the Sankgreall* is the least obviously original of his works. Apart from omissions and minor alterations, it is to all intents and purposes a translation of the French *Queste del Saint Graal*, the fourth branch of the thirteenth-century Arthurian Prose Cycle" (758). Although this claim that Malory was at his least original here has been widely disputed, it is clear that his quest is the quest for the holy grail, the pseudo-relic that sprang most probably out of the imaginative efforts of Cistercian monks. Thus, Malory compares earthly and celestial codes of behavior and shows that the kingdom has fallen into "evyll lyving" and this is why the grail has been withdrawn. Galahad accomplishes a number of foreordained tasks, among them the healing of the wounded king (who is *not* Arthur). Perceval and Bors, though sorely tested, do also earn a place at the reenactment of the Last Supper in the Castle Carbonek. Lancelot can peer in, but for this he is wounded for twenty-four days, and cannot partake of the actual supper. All the rest perish or meet disgrace on this Christian quest for this pseudo-relic. Malory also recounts the history of the grail and its keepers, absent, of course, in *Excalibur*.

Boorman's quest conversely is initiated by Arthur's wound, which renders him an ineffective man and ruler and lays his kingdom to waste. Moreover, it is Arthur himself who instructs the knights to search for the grail (in Malory, Arthur sits by helplessly as the knights swear the vow and then laments this rash pledge). In *Excalibur* the ailing king tells his knights that "Only the grail can restore leaf and flower." When the most sincere of his followers, Perceval (Paul Geoffrey), asks where to search, the king weakly responds, "Portents, signs . . . follow."

Nearly all the knights perish on this quest. Lancelot goes insane and becomes a kind of mad prophet or reformer who hurls angry accusations against the Round Table amidst the wailing and lament for the dead, so familiar in the wasteland that Arthur's kingdom has become. (In Malory, Lancelot is humbled on the quest and turns to God, but he backslides after this, resuming his affair with the queen. At the end of Malory's text he finally renounces his love and dies the death of a saint, but this, as we shall see, is altered in Boorman's film.) At last, only Uryens (Keith Buckley) and Perceval are left. It is Uryens, at the moment of his own death at the hands of the treacherous Mordred, who urges Perceval to keep searching for the grail, since he is the "last" of the quester knights. The others have all met failure, either succumbing to the harsh elements of heat or cold or, finding their way across the wasteland to the castle that houses Morgana and Mordred, meeting with a humiliating and hideous death, being hanged from trees to have their eyes pecked out by ravens.

Perceval himself had found his way there once before meeting Uryens, but he had failed. Meeting the child Mordred (Charley Boorman), who wears a gilded mask (the design of which was resurrected from *Zardoz*), Perceval is asked, "You seek what Arthur wants? That thing they call the grail?" To which Perceval responds, "I do." Inside the castle, Morgana taunts the knight and offers him several chalices via the use of various automata knights, but he refuses to drink. Apparently this is a test that Perceval—like others before him—has failed because Mordred says, "He's no good, mother. Take him to the tree." Perceval is strung up like his predecessors and has a vision of the grail; in this vision an oracular voice asks him, "What is the secret of the grail? Whom does it serve?" But Perceval cannot answer. He is saved, by chance, when the rope on which he hangs is cut by the rowel of a dead knight's boot swaying from a branch just above him. One can understand why after this he is loathe to continue the quest. Only when he happens upon a mob of crazed mourners, led by Lancelot, and is chased into a stream of water does Perceval undergo a kind of baptismal purification that enables him to succeed in his second encounter. This time when asked, "Whom does the grail serve?" he can now correctly identify that it is Arthur himself, and when questioned, "Have you found the secret I have lost?" Perceval says, "Yes. You and the land are one." This smacks of Jessie Weston's pagan vegetation rituals, not of Christian doctrine, indicating that Boorman has strayed far from his Malorian source, even hearkening back to a rite that precedes Chrétien although, like him, he does use Perceval as his grail hero.

It is possible to identify similarities between the use of the grail material in Boorman's film and in some of the productions we will discuss in chapter 6 on the postmodern quest as well, in that *Excalibur* does not portray the grail or its significance in Christian terms. Instead, it is much more indebted to Jessie Weston's concept of the grail as a survival of earlier pagan rites, which we will discuss in more detail in the next chapter. It differs from the films examined in that chapter, however, in that it does not present the quest as postmodern, only pagan. Boorman himself has confessed that he first got interested in the legend by reading T. S. Eliot's "The Wasteland," which acknowledges Weston as its source, and then he went on to read Weston's *From Ritual to Romance*. This lends credibility to our supposition in chapter 1 that Weston, partly through Eliot's poem, is a main contributor to the popular transmission of the legend. One can trace *Excalibur*, then, to Boorman's exposure to Weston. Once Perceval divines this secret, he finds himself with the cup in his hand at Arthur's side and begs him to drink, which heals both the king and his land. It is worth noting that there is no Galahad in *Excalibur*, no maimed king except Arthur himself, and no reference to the grail as the "holy" grail.

Boorman likewise freely alters the conclusion of this purported "adaptation" of Malory. In the *Morte*, Arthur and Mordred do battle, after which the king either dies or sails off to Avalon, followed by the conclusion of Malory's text with the final meeting between Lancelot and Guinevere, who has repented of her sin and now resides in a convent. When she refuses to resume their affair, Lancelot himself renounces the world and dies a holy man, after he himself buries the deceased queen next to Arthur.

Excalibur portrays a final meeting, not between Lancelot and the queen, but between Arthur and Guinevere before he battles Mordred, a scene in which Arthur, inexplicably and in a complete reversal of Malory, asks for Guinevere's forgiveness. Tennyson had likewise usurped Lancelot's meeting and appropriated it to Arthur, and Boorman even steals a line from Tennyson's work. In Boorman's film, it turns out that Guinevere has kept Arthur's sword for him through the years, since the day Arthur plunged it between her and Lancelot. Now that he is healed, she returns it to him. Whereas Tennyson's queen is contrite, it is Boorman's king who begs the queen's forgiveness for having blamed others for his own shortcomings. Guinevere replies: "I loved you as king and sometimes as husband," offering as a reason for her adultery, "One cannot gaze too long at the sun," an almost verbatim quotation of, "But who can gaze upon the sun in heaven?" uttered by Tennyson's Guinevere in the "Lancelot and

Elaine" idyll (l. 123). Boorman's Arthur confides in her that he hopes they can be reconciled one day, "when I owe no more to the future. It is a dream I have." He takes his leave of her and is also reconciled with Lancelot, who comes to his knightly senses during Arthur's battle with Morded and wins the day, but dies when his "old wound" is reopened in Arthur's service. Thus, Boorman rearranges Malory's ending, concluding instead with Arthur's last fight with Mordred, his mortal wounding and commanding of Perceval to throw Excalibur back into the lake, and his sailing off to Avalon—a conclusion heavily indebted to Tennyson. No doubt Boorman imagined this ending a more dramatically charged and mythically significant conclusion than that found in Malory, whose work is concerned with Christian repentance, regeneration, and the peaceful death of two reformed adulterers.

Boorman features Arthur as the most significant figure because he is interested in the mythic and epic dimension of the Arthurian story, not in the melodrama or the quest alone. "I've often been accused of yearning for a lost golden age that never existed, but central to my philosophy is the notion that there was a harmonious period and something went wrong, something was lost through some terrible act, a wound, and ever since we've been trying to struggle our way back to it. My way of trying to do that is through filmmaking" (*Film Comment* 58). Like dreams, films should touch something deep within us, a truth that resides, since the advent of Christianity, buried in our collective memory, but which can be reached through visual images that thus function like the Jungian dream. This is why the Arthurian story has had such a profound impact upon Boorman's imagination: It speaks of an ideal world lost, but if it was lost, then perhaps, through an ardent quest it can be found again and the "old wound" healed. Let critics scoff, Boorman cares little:

I have a theory about a good story. We know it already, we've heard it a thousand times, but it holds us, we listen, we want to know what happens next. Why? I think we're hearing echoes of some deep pattern of early happenings in the human race that is now being repeated. Listen carefully to the echoes of myth. It has much more to tell us than the petty lies and insignificant truths of recorded history." (Cited by Strick in *Sight and Sound* 171)

EXCALIBUR AS A JOHN BOORMAN FILM

As we note in the epigraph that begins this chapter, Boorman observes that the Arthurian legend has served as a "template" for all his films, an admission he was making to at least two interviewers during the filming of *Excalibur* in 1980. Harlan Kennedy, writing in *American Film* (March 1981), comments:

Boorman's whole movie career might be seen as leading to this point—the igniting of the mythical spark in a story which has long been his most cherished movie project. Boorman's earlier films are crammed with presaging hints of the Arthur legend: from the name itself popping up in a key role in *Zardoz* (Arthur Frayn, sage and wizard) to the quest motifs, the notion of "heroes" struggling toward a source of meaning and resolution in a world of flux. (37)

Boorman has also stated that when given the opportunity to direct his first feature film, he proposed an adaptation of John Cowper Powys' *A Glastonbury Romance*.[11] It is clear from interviews that he never abandoned this hope, but it is also obvious that he found the Arthurian material "flexible" (Boorman's term) enough to fold into other stories. One of these films was the aforementioned *Zardoz*, which we speculate represents a sort of "compromise" attempt to film the legend, cloaking it in a veneer of science fiction. When this film and *Excalibur* are juxtaposed, some startling similarities emerge, each film shedding light on the other.

Boorman remarked to Philip Strick (*Sight and Sound*) that, "I've been trying to raise the money for this film [*Excalibur*] for ten years. Five years ago [1975], all I got was embarrassed smiles when people were confronted with the Merlin story" (170). The year 1975 predates, of course, *Star Wars* (1977), a film that Boorman thinks is nothing more than a "straight transposition of the Arthurian story—Guiness is the Merlin character, Mark Hamill is the boy Arthur suddenly chosen to be King, it's very clear" (*Sight and Sound* 170). No doubt Boorman used this argument to obtain funding for *Excalibur* sometime in the late 1970s.

The *Star Wars* trilogy does indeed borrow its structure from the Arthurian legend, and it also shares several qualities with the epic genre. Like Moses and Arthur, the epic heroes discussed earlier, Luke Skywalker is raised by a foster family. He does not know his father's identity until at a crucial moment it is revealed to him that his father is Darth Vader. Like Moses and Arthur, Luke is also of the "elect," one of the chosen, in that the "force is with him," and empowers him. He is a deliverer, a liberator from the Empire and its evil emperor. Moreover, this trilogy features "Jedi Knights," a group of individuals who, after rigorous initiation, learn to control the force bestowed upon them, using it to serve either good or evil ends (Darth Vader, we are told, has been "seduced by the dark side of the force").

It is arguable that there are two figures partially modeled on Merlin and his role: Yoda, Luke's teacher, who is a kind of wise hermit "creature," and Ben (Obi-wan) Kenobi, who is Luke's mentor and a quasi-father figure to him. There is also a possible love triangle with incestuous overtones between Luke, Princess Leia, and Han Solo. Luke and Leia are siblings, but they do not learn this until late in the trilogy, and their attraction to each other is obvious, creating a rivalry between Luke and Han for her affection. Finally, although the ending is an inversion of the Arthurian legend, it has similarities. Here, the son, Luke, is good (as opposed to the evil Mordred) whereas his father, Darth Vader, has served evil (as opposed to Arthur, who has served good). They do become embroiled in a final deadly battle, but Luke manages to convert his father back to the cause of good: Luke "heals" or redeems the moribund Vader at the conclusion of the trilogy. Thus, Boorman has good cause to assert that *Star Wars* is a transposition of the legend—all this, without a single overt allusion to the *Matter of Britain*. The mythic structure is what arguably qualifies it as Arthurian.

Using the chronology Boorman provides above suggests that "the Merlin story" would date back to 1970, sometime after the completion of *Leo the Last* (1970). (Of course, other interviews suggest that Boorman had an interest in filming "the Merlin story" back in 1964–1965, when he had his first opportunity to direct a feature motion picture.) His next film turned out to be *Zardoz* (1974), however, a story which Boorman has indicated dates from 1972. In the "Preface" to his own novelization of *Zardoz*, dated September 1973, Boorman writes:

I wrote *Zardoz* in 1972 at my home, a lost valley in the dreaming hills of Wicklow. It came out closer to a novel than a screenplay. Gradually I worked it into a film form that proved too radical for most of the studios. Finally I got some backing and shot the movie [in Ireland] in our local studios, Ardmore, and locations around my house between May and July, 1973. (v)

Whatever film Boorman wished to develop next is unclear, although it seems to have been a project named *Merlin*. In any case, that project was interrupted in order for him to direct *Exorcist II: The Heretic*, a film Boorman worked on from roughly October 1975 to December 1976 and released in the summer of 1977. In her book *The Making of Exorcist II: The Heretic*, Barbara Pallenberg indicates that while this latter film began post-production work at National Film Studios in Bray, Ireland, in November 1976, Rospo Pallenberg was also present "mainly because he [had] started writing Boorman's next film, *Merlin* (202).[12] The title of this project changed at some point, however, for in the 1980 *Sight and Sound* issue that discusses the film we now know as *Excalibur*, the film is referred to as *Knights* because the first choice for title, *Merlin Lives*, presented copyright problems. Sometime, however, before its release in May 1981 it became *Excalibur*, a title chosen either by Boorman or by Orion executives or arrived at through a mutual decision by both.

The key film in the above chronology, as we have suggested, is *Zardoz*, which shares a number of important features with *Excalibur* despite *Zardoz*'s science fiction setting (set in the year 2293). *Zardoz* also represents Boorman's retelling of L. Frank Baum's story *The Wonderful Wizard of Oz*, as the conflation of syllables within the title allows one to find "Zard-oz."

The god Zardoz, an immense floating stone head with the face carved into a distorted grimace, dwells in heaven, a place known only as Vortex. Zardoz is the god of the Exterminators, a warrior caste whose mission is to rape, plunder, and murder the Brutals, who represent a caste of farmers and villagers in the Outlands. When they are out on a raid, the Exterminators wear masks which, except for their color, red, rather than gold, are identical to that worn by Mordred in *Excalibur*. The film's protagonist, Zed (Sean Connery), experiences a moment of *dianoia* when he realizes that the god he and the other Exterminators have been worshipping is a fake god. During an attack on a Brutal village, Zed is lured into a decaying library by a figure he later learns is Arthur Frayn—the magician who is also the manipulator of the fake god, Zardoz. There he is shown a book titled *The Wonderful Wizard of Oz*, which Zed decodes as the source of the fake god's name, Zardoz; he determines that his mission as an Exterminator has been a sham, a manipulation in the name of some unhallowed cause.

Desiring the truth behind Zardoz, Zed hatches a plan to gain access to Zardoz. During the Brutals's seasonal offering of grain, the baskets of which are dumped in Zardoz's mouth, Zed hides himself under the pile of grain. When he is sure that Zardoz is aloft, he emerges from the pile of grain, shoots the surprised Arthur Frayn (who is resurrected later, however), and rides the head into the Vortex. The humans who live in the Vortex are Eternals, members of an intellectual caste who have devised eternal life. (They share many of the features of H. G. Wells's Eloi in *The Time Machine*.) Because Arthur Frayn is an Eternal, his body undergoes "reconstruction" and he returns later in the story, reprising his "magician" role.

The Eternals discover that, in addition to his physical superiority, Zed has a powerful intellect, perhaps as great as theirs, and thus they wish to kill him. Zed enters the Vortex as an Exterminator but emerges as a liberator. By penetrating the Vortex, he brings death with him, something many of the Eternals, ironically, desire.

Besides the conflation of the Arthur figure with the figure of Merlin, *Zardoz* also features the quest structure, premised on Zed's need to know the truth about his god. His quest allows him to become a liberator of sorts, the sword-wielding "deliverer" many of the Eternals, ironically, awaited. Moreover, the Eternals's condition is seen as effete, as sterile, because they can neither live nor die. Recall that in *Excalibur*, Arthur without Excalibur "can neither live nor die," and longs for one of his knights to bring him the grail. All these features are shared with *Excalibur*. In addition, two moments in *Zardoz* share dialogue similar to that found in *Excalibur*.

The first moment has to do with Zed's desire to know the secret of immortality the Eternals have invented, a secret hidden in a place known only as the Tabernacle.[13] For help in his cause, Zed approaches May, an Eternal who seems to have a premonition of Zed's real identity. We reproduce the dialogue as found in the actual film (in Boorman's novelization it is slightly different):

> *Zed*:   May, I want your help.
> *May*:   You're here to destroy us, the Tabernacle.
> *Zed*:   I want the truth.
> *May*:   You must give the truth to receive it.
> *Zed*:   I'm ready.
> *May*:   It'll burn you.
> *Zed*:   Then burn me.

The dialogue here is similar to that between Merlin and Morgana in *Excalibur*, when Morgana follows Merlin into his cave to learn from him "the sacred charm of making." Recall that Merlin and Morgana witness present and past events unfolding before them: The naked Lancelot and Guinevere embracing among the rocks and trees, King Arthur, with Excalibur drawn, approaching them and, between, Igraine embraced by the armored Uther:

> *Morgana*:   More. Show me more. Show me the dragon. Tell me
>   the sacred charm of making.
> *Merlin*:   Even though such knowledge would burn and blind
>   you.
> *Morgana*:   Then burn me.

In both scenes, the one seeking forbidden knowledge puts himself (or herself, as the case may be) at the mercy of the one possessing the knowledge. The knowledge is of an occult kind: In *Zardoz* the knowledge is the secret of eternal life; in *Excalibur*, the knowledge is a mystical power that can dominate reality. In effect, the power wanted is the same.

Another point of similarity between the two films is the image of the dragon. A critical moment in *Zardoz* occurs when Consuella, an Eternal who views Zed as a beast and wants him killed, realizes that in her desire for his death she has become the predator and refuses to continue her hunt. Again we quote from Boorman's novelization of the film:

> "In hunting you, I have become you and I have destroyed what I
> set out to defend."
> " 'He who fights too long against dragons, becomes himself a
> dragon'—Nietzsche." (110)

Jung's term for this Nietzschean insight is "dissimulation," or projective identification, a psychic process of *association* (rather than *dissociation*), or mimetic fusion, whereby Self identifies with Other, magically "absorbing" it to keep it from disappearing and abandoning the helpless Self to its own resources. We argue that the recurring reference to the "dragon" in *Excalibur* demands to be read in a Jungian fashion, following Boorman's lead.[14]

We suggest that in a Jungian reading the "dragon" becomes a synonym for the mythical snake or world serpent, the Worm Ouroboros, which is rendered in the image of a snake swallowing its own tail. This is the primal dragon, a frequent symbol in world mythologies. The Jungian historian of myth Erich Neumann refers to this snake as "the serpent which at once bears, begets, and devours" (*The Great Mother* 30), while the great historiographer of esoteric and occult religions Hans Jonas calls this serpent "a huge dragon whose tail is in its mouth" (*The Gnostic Religion* 112–13).

Recall the dialogue exchange between Merlin and Morgana as she follows Merlin into his cave to learn from the sacred charm of making:

Morgana: What is this place?
Merlin: Here you enter the coils of the dragon. Here my power
            was born. Here all things are possible and all things
            meet their opposites.
Morgana: The future?
Merlin: And the past.
Morgana: Desire?
Merlin: And regret.
Morgana: Knowledge?
Merlin: And oblivion.

The "coils of the dragon" where "all things meet their opposites" invokes the circular image of the snake swallowing its own tail. Indeed, a snake is shown slithering among the branches of the forest when, early in the film after drawing Excalibur from the stone, Arthur goes in search of Merlin and is told to "relax in the arms of the dragon," and later, snakes are shown crawling among the rocks of Merlin's cave when he invokes the dragon for Morgana.

Boorman ascribes to the dragon a generative principle, a maternal force, as within its coils Merlin's power was "born," the source of Merlin's occult creative powers. The image of the coiled serpent swallowing its tail, the serpent that "at once bears, begets, and devours," Erich Neumann was to argue, in *The Origins and History of Consciousness*, is reflected in the mythology of the "Mother Goddess":

This early stage of conscious-unconscious relations is reflected in the mythology of the Mother Goddess and her connection with the son-lover. The Attis, Adonis, Tammuz, and Osiris figures in the Near Eastern cultures are not merely born of a mother; on the contrary, this aspect is altogether eclipsed by the fact that they are their mother's lovers: they are loved, slain, buried and bewailed by her, and are then reborn through her. (46–47)

We acknowledge that it might be argued that the image of the coiled dragon swallowing its own tail, in which "all things meet their opposites," is an image that unconsciously invokes the poststructuralist paradigm of reflexivity, the *mise en abyme*, which can be also be captured in the image of mirrors facing each other, what Jorge Luis Borges was to call a "specious infinity." It is an image that is also, remarkably, and perhaps more importantly, connected to the question of incest and hence to the myth of the Oedipal double, a myth that is also invoked in *Excalibur*.

John T. Irwin, in his book *The Mystery to a Solution*, amid a discussion of Jung's *Mysterium Coniunctionis*, Adam Kadmon, the Tetragammaton and the *Kabbala denudata*, and Borges's story "Death and the Compass," observes that "incest is a structural correlative of doubling. Which is simply to say that incest is the form of (re)union necessarily implied by the notion of an originary (self-generative) being, a being that must double itself in order to reproduce" (51). He continues:

Thus the joining of the letters [in the gematria of YHVH] is not simply a double marriage but a marriage born of doubling, an incestuous union. . . . This balancing of a direct and reflex movement in the generation of emanations, of feminine mirror images, suggests the simultaneous progression/regression characteristic of a double-mirror structure, the kind of structure Borges had in mind when he described "the three inextricable persons" of the Trinity as "a strangled, specious infinity like that of opposite mirrors." That the double marriage of masculine and feminine letters in God's name (a marriage of doubles) is incestuous is only to be expected. (51)

Boorman's imagining of the Arthur story is riddled with mirrored doubles: the same hidden within the appearance of difference (Morgana as Guinevere), the different within the appearance of same (Uther as the duke). Arthur is seduced by Morgana (as Guinevere) just as Igraine is seduced by Uther (as her husband); Morgana is Igraine's daughter (same), Arthur is Uther's son (same); they are mirrored doubles. However, a mirror reverses left and right, producing a *chiasmus*: The Arthur-Mordred doublet. The Greek myths of Narcissus, Nemesis, and Echo become unavoidable associations. We again turn to John T. Irwin for help on this issue:

[The] tendency of the narcissistic self to find its own reflection wherever it looks is frequently evoked in incest scenarios where the self's inability to break out of the circle of self-love is dramatized as a character's inability to break out of the family circle (that ring of faces resembling his own) in choosing a love-object. The extremes of incest and suicide represent in effect the poles of love and hate in the self's relationship to itself and, as in the nature of polar opposites, they tend to reverse into one another. The self's incestuous entrapment within the family becomes a form of self-destruction, and the self-destructive duel with a double becomes an incestuous *Liebestod*. (213)[15]

"Come, father, let's embrace at last," Mordred says to Arthur, and they do, each realizing—seeking—his own (suicidal) death as well as that of the other, in the culmination of the incestuous Liebestod which *Excalibur* enacts. As Irwin observes, "In the Oedipus myth, incest's disintegrative effect on the notion of kinship (considered as a differential ground of the self) is symbolized by the proliferating self-destruction, like a chain reaction in a house of mirrors"(215).[16] (The application of this insight to Shakespeare's *Hamlet* is so strong it must be mentioned.) The "disintegrative effect" also dissolves the relationship between mother and child, Mordred having first brutally strangled his mother, Morgana, whom he can no longer recognize as his mother. As René Girard observes, in *Violence and the Sacred*, "Between patricide and incest, the violent abolition of all family differences is achieved" (74).[17]

A "chain reaction in a house of mirrors" is literalized in the climax to Boorman's *Zardoz*. Zed gains entrance to the center of the Tabernacle, which is nothing less than a house of mirrors. Once within the Tabernacle, Zed draws his pistol and begins to destroy the mirrors, a moment that has to be considered Boorman's deliberate visual homage to the hall of mirrors climax in Orson

Welles's *The Lady From Shanghai* (1948). While most certainly an homage, we also suspect the conclusion of *Zardoz* has a more occult import, a Jungian reading suggesting that at the level of personal psychology it is Zed's moment of individuation, that is, the elevation and integration into consciousness of his shadow archetype, symbolized in the mask of the Exterminator that is reflected in the mirrors he destroys.

A final affinity between these two films is the importance of dreams in each. In *Zardoz*, for instance, Zed is asked by Consuella why he likes to sleep, to which he responds, "Because I have dreams." She is astonished and notes to herself that in this primitive specimen the conscious and unconscious minds are split, requiring the need for dreams. Boorman told Michel Ciment: "The essence of *Zardoz* came to me in a dream; and since I believe, as Jung claimed, that these myths exist inside us, I was waiting for them to be released, to emerge into the light" (*John Boorman* 140). In *Excalibur*, Arthur is able to "resurrect" Merlin on the eve of his final battle because he is able to reach him in "the land of dreams." And Arthur had earlier told Guinevere in their last meeting the he was the stuff of "future memory." The Jungian inflection can scarcely be missed here: To Boorman, dreams are a vital part of our existence, not simply our mental life. Moreover, Boorman's message is amenable to the gnostic vision to which Jung was drawn as well: We are all strangers here. Our dreams are a register of our desires, ambitions, fears, and of our lost—or perhaps forgotten—collective heritage.

NOTES

1. "Adapted" is the operative word here. While other versions, including the 1954 *Knights of the Round Table*, have claimed indebtedness to Malory, they have suggested that they were "based" upon the *Morte*. But Boorman uses "adapted," we think, to suggest that he is trying to transpose the entire received legend as found in Malory (even though he uses other versions than Malory's, and his own imagination as well) to indicate that he is working towards this ambitious end.

2. This book of Powys's was reissued in 1995, indicating either continued or renewed interest in it, despite Leavis's invective against it. Moreover, in an article published in the *Times Literary Supplement* (December 5, 1995), critic Jerome McGann argues that Powys's work met with hostility because, with *A Glastonbury Romance* he attempted to employ the conventions of the medieval romance genre, which were antithetical to those of realism. This does not help us much to explain Boorman's fondness for Powys, however. Powys (1872–1963) lived in the United States for many years, and the 1932 publication of *A Glastonbury Romance* occurred first in the United States. In 1931 Powys, along with Ben Hecht, Alexander Woollcott, and Theodore Dreiser founded the Fortean Society after Charles Fort's death. (For information on Charles Fort see chapter 2 note 11.)

3. Similar epics would include Anthony Mann's *El Cid* (1961) and also his *Cimarron* (1960), both of which address the theme of founding and/or serving a nation. *Legends of the Fall* (1994) is also an epic which explores the issue of what it was to be part of the frontier scene, and it also activates the Tristram legend, referring to it and creating an incestuous love triangle. On a superficial level, *Legends of the*

Fall resembles *A River Runs Through It* (1993), in that both films feature Brad Pitt as the pivotal character and both are set in Montana. But the true precursor for *Legends of the Fall* is Mann's *Cimarron*: Both are frontier epics (one set in frontier Oklahoma, the other in a Montana that is scarcely more settled) that ask difficult questions about patriotism and portray heroes who ultimately stand up against government corruption. Both deal with generations of families, and both have a love triangle with a twist. Moreover, the hero of *Cimarron*, Yancey Cravet, abandons his wife and remains absent for twenty-five years; the hero of *Legends of the Fall* also abandons his wife for a very long, though indeterminate period of time. Interestingly, the female protagonist (the analogue to Iseult of Ireland in the love triangle) of *Legends of the Fall* is played by Julia Ormond, cast the next year as Guinevere in *First Knight*.

4. We are aware, as is Andrew Sarris, that "the mere mention of Cecil B. DeMille will evoke complacent laughter in some quarters, and bristling patriotic speeches in others" (*The American Cinema* 91). DeMille remains interesting ecause of his historical importance and because of his anti-modernist aesthetics (see note 8).

5. Orion Pictures was formed in early 1978 after Arthur Krim, the head of United Artists for 27 years, left with four other United Artists executives and named the new company after the constellation Orion, which supposedly was composed of five stars (not true). During Krim's tenure as head of United Artists (1951–1978), that studio garnered both 108 Academy Awards and immense profits, leading to Krim's legendary status within the film industry. For a discussion of the Krim departure from United Artists, and the formation of Orion Pictures, see Steven Bach's *Final Cut: Dreams and Disaster in the Making of Heaven's Gate*. (New York: Morrow, 1985). *Excalibur* had to have been among the first projects Orion approved; Orion's first major success was the 1979 film directed by Blake Edwards, *10*, starring Bo Derek.

6. Actually, the question of sources is almost impossible to untangle. While there is no question that Boorman drew from Malory's *Morte*, he was also, as we have indicated, influenced by Powys' *A Glastonbury Romance*, Weston's *From Ritual to Romance*, Tennyson's *Idylls*, C. G. Jung's theories of dreams and archetypes, Jung's speculations on the figure of Merlin—a figure with whom Boorman identifies, as did Jung—and also Boorman's own interest in the occult. In short, the film is emblazoned with the multitudinous sources of these sources as well as his own signature. Besides *Excalibur*, Boorman's interest in the occult emerges most clearly in the films *Zardoz*, *Exorcist II: The Heretic*, and *The Emerald Forest*—the period immediately preceding *Excalibur* and just after. Boorman told Michel Ciment, "I was more interested in works deriving from the legend, such as White's *The Once and Future King*, which really marked my childhood. Then, at school, it was *Idylls of the King*. . . . But I'd never studied the original texts. It was later that I came to them, and I was extraordinarily impressed by them . . . especially . . . *Parsifal*" (*John Boorman* 192).

7. In Exodus 2:5–10 it is Pharaoh's bereaved daughter, and not his sister, who finds the infant and adopts it—so much for DeMille's adherence to his "sources."

8. We have profited from Sumiko Higashi's essay, "Antimodernism as Historical Representation in a Consumer Culture: Cecil B. DeMille's *The Ten Commandments*, 1923, 1956, 1993." In Vivian Sobchack, ed., *The Persistence of History* (91–112). Higashi persuasively argues that DeMille's *mise-en-scene* "dated back to an antimodernist tradition that mediated the experience of twentieth-century modernity for generations of filmgoers" (91) and that his visual style is derived from early twentieth-century practices of historical pageants that "reenacted inspirational scenes" (93), all of which constituted a civic form of dramatic noesis utterly outside the halls of academe.

9. See Richard C. Bartone, "Variations on Arthurian Legend in *Lancelot du Lac* and *Excalibur*," in Sally K. Slocum, ed., *Popular Arthurian Traditions*, in which

Bartone argues that "*Excalibur* constitutes the medieval world as dream" (150). We might elaborate on this point slightly, adding to Bartone's observation that the medieval past is the dreamtime—in a Jungian reading, the birth of consciousness.

10. *Leitmotivs*, or repeated images, as well as musical harmony, are suggestive of Wagner, whose music Boorman employs liberally in the film (*Parsifal, Tristan and Isolde*, but perhaps most importantly, "Siegfried's Funeral March" from the *Götterdammerung*). But the connection is thematic as well as aesthetic. He claims that the German "Ring" legend beloved of Wagner is "almost a kissing cousin to the Arthurian story. Both are parables of the birth of consciousness from dormant nature and of the quest for destiny. And both begin with the image of a piercing, luminous object emerging from water (the sword from the lake, the Rhinegold from the Rhine) and go on to tell of a chosen hero (Arthur, Siegfried) waking a primitive land from its sleep of barbarism" (*American Film* 34).

11. Boorman told Gavin Smith, "When I was asked to do a feature film, the first thing I tried to do was a modern version of John Cooper [sic] Powys' *Glastonbury Romance*. . . . I couldn't get it made, as you might imagine" (*American Film* 55–56).

12. Pallenberg's information may be slightly incorrect; in *American Film* Boorman told Harlan Kennedy that, "'I wrote the original script myself,' and continued, 'but at some point I got stuck on it. It was a bit too long and convoluted. So I got Rospo in'"("The World of King Arthur" 33).

13. When the Tabernacle is finally revealed, it is shown only to be accessed via a warehouse in which the Eternals have stored the busts of past gods. When the Eternals discover the identity of Zed as the deliverer, they run riot, smashing the busts of the gods, just as Zed has "smashed" his own god, Zardoz. This is a feature also shared by *Excalibur*, as the pagan gods acknowledged by Merlin are replaced by the Christian god.

14. We again cite the *Sight and Sound* issue (Summer 1980) which features Philip Strick's article on Boorman. Boorman told Strick: "I'm very attracted to what Jung sees in Merlin; he interprets him as part of the alchemical tradition. . . . So in the film, Merlin is disappearing, fading out as rational man takes over the world. The magic is still there, but it's no longer part of the foreground, it has passed into the unconscious" (170).

15. In his *Paradise Lost*, one of John Milton's most striking inventions is his explanation of origin of Sin and Death (personified concepts), for which he employs the incest model, intensified by that of inversion and repetition. Satan begets Sin out of the left side of his head; he becomes enamored of himself in her, rapes her, and she then gives birth to Death. Death, in turn, rapes his mother, Sin, who then repeatedly gives birth to a pack of beasts that then crawl inside of her and eat at her bowels. Since orthodox Christianity does not allow for Sin and Death to originate with God, this is Milton's way of explaining its inception in the solipsistic structure of incest. The Greek myths of Narcissus, Echo, and Nemesis are unavoidable associations.

16. René Girard, in *Violence and the Sacred*, comes to the same conclusion as Irwin, observing, "Oedipus's monstrosity is contagious; it infects first of all those beings engendered by him. The essential task is to separate once more the two strains of blood whose poisonous blend is now perpetuated by the natural process of generation. Incestuous propagation leads to formless duplications, sinister repetitions, a dark mixture of unnamable things" (75).

17. Just as Morgana had used the sacred charm of making to trap Merlin, Merlin turned it back on Morgana by dissolving the magic that disguised her age. This principle of violent reciprocity is called by Girard "mimetic violence," in which two agents, desiring the same object of power, become enmeshed in ever-increasing reciprocal acts of violence—until a catastrophe occurs. Again, Irwin's "chain reaction in a house of mirrors" is the metaphor which so aptly captures this process.

6

The Arthurian Legend
as Postmodern Quest

> Is dreaming of the Middle Ages really a typical contemporary or
> postmodern temptation? If it is true—and it is—that the Middle
> Ages turned us into Western animals, it is equally true that people
> started dreaming of the Middle Ages from the very beginning of
> the modern era.
> —Umberto Eco, "Dreaming of the Middle Ages" (65)

In his *Postscript to "The Name of the Rose,"* Umberto Eco comments rather
skeptically that the word postmodernism "is applied today to anything the user
of the term happens to like" (65). We tend to agree with Eco, and believe
therefore that our use of the word postmodern demands explanation given the
many catalogues of features promulgated by recent scholarship. While we have
learned much from the studies written by Brian McHale on postmodernism, our
use of the word is derived from John Barth who, while admitting he finds the
word "awkward," says that it is also "faintly epigonic, suggestive less of a
vigorous or even interesting new direction in the old art of storytelling than of
something anti-climactic, feebly following a very hard act to follow" (qtd. in
McHale, *Postmodernist Fiction* 3). Despite the varied approaches to postmodernism, we find the epigonic feature of the concept to be most compelling.
Harold Bloom calls this epigonic feeling belatedness, and that is an important
feature of the films discussed in this chapter. These grail quest(ion)ers tend to
suffer from belatedness, hampered both by the self-consciousness of their
enterprise and by the fear that they are latter-day Quixotes, chasing a chimera.
The films themselves demonstrate a belatedness, drawing on generic features and
stereotypes from the long gone golden age of Classical Hollywood. Speaking of
the inspiration for his *Knightriders* (1981), director George Romero avows that
the film "is in the idiom, in the genre of the old Robert Taylor/Cornel Wilde

films" ("George Romero on *Knightriders*" 25). Moreover, the sentiment of all the filmmakers can be adequately expressed in what Romero says about the patchwork nature of *Knightriders*: "I'm not just drawing from the Arthurian legend, but from all over the culture map" (25).

Brian McHale sees Samuel Beckett as one of the important twentieth-century writers who made the transition from modernist to postmodernist poetics, and we found that Beckett's work provides us with two key characteristics that have governed our understanding of these quest(ion)ing films. One is that the quest(ion)ers seek that which is both ineffable and Unnamable, and so they remain in some sense loners, dwelling with a strange, solitary gnosis. The other characteristic is that the questers are true epigones, but epigones driven by Beckett's own particular formulation of the feeling of belatedness: "I can't go on, I will go on." Despite the idiosyncracies each film displays, we believe that in their portrayal of isolated and anxiety-ridden questers in search of a redemptive grail (even if the the reality of the quest is internal) they can be considered illustrations of the postmodern quest.

Knightriders (1981)

George Romero's *Knightriders* (1981) takes considerable liberties with the Arthurian legend. It is, after all, the only film that has dared to graft the *Matter of Britain* onto the "biker film," a genre that, in his article "Camelot Twice Removed: *Knightriders* and the Film Versions of *A Connecticut Yankee in King Arthur's Court*" Kevin J. Harty identifies as a subgenre of the "American film western" (114). This fusion may well account for the inordinately long running time of the film (146 minutes), although readers who know the conventions of medieval romance should find themselves in familiar territory: The loose structure and episodic nature of the film clearly does resemble the Arthurian narratives of writers from Chrétien to Malory. Romero's innovations have been scorned as well as praised, but the timing of the film's initial release is probably what accounts for its box office failure: It appeared the same week as Boorman's *Excalibur* and was allowed only a limited release—in New York, Los Angeles, and Florida (Harty, *Cinema Arthuriana* 114). Although its debut was short-lived, its release on video has allowed Arthurian enthusiasts to become acquainted with it and contributed to its cult status as well.

We believe that rather than view the biker film as a subgenre of the western, as does Kevin J. Harty in the article cited above, it is more useful to see it as a subgenre of the "juvenile delinquency" films that emerged in the 1950s.[1] In particular, we believe the biker film had its origins in highly stylized ruminations on delinquent culture such as those found in *The Wild One* (1953), which starred Marlon Brando and Lee Marvin as rival motorcycle gang leaders.[2] About the character Johnny (Brando), James Gilbert has argued that he is riven with ambiguity and potential violence—a prominent characteristic of later juvenile delinquency heroes. On the other hand, he is clearly not an adolescent, but not yet an adult either, belonging to a suspended age that seems alienated from any recognizable stage of development. He appears to be tough and brutal, but he is not, nor, ultimately, is he as attractive as he might have been. (*A Cycle of Outrage* 182).

We argue that Billy of *Knightriders* (Ed Harris) shares many of the features of Brando's Johnny as Gilbert reviews them here, yet we do not mean that Romero's film is heavily indebted to 1950s delinquency films (although he certainly knows *The Wild One*). Indeed not, for the biker film went through a significant transformation in the 1960s, and it is precisely this transformation that makes *Knightriders* intelligible.

Gilbert observes that "by the end of the 1950s, Hollywood had ceased to treat the subject with any seriousness. Instead, youth culture films relied on stereotypes developed from more serious films, but voided of any content. Formulaic explanations took the place of complex or ambiguous portrayals" (192). Films such as *High School Confidential* (1958), which featured delinquent stereotypes such as fast cars, sex, drugs, and rock 'n roll, became the benign Bikini Beach films of the early 1960s.[3] By the end of the decade, the biker film was fused to the "road movie" to become the now legendary *Easy Rider* (1969), in retrospect nothing more than a puerile Roger Corman-like "B" movie (stars Dennis Hopper, Peter Fonda, and Jack Nicholson had all previously acted in Roger Corman films).

Joan Mellen, in *Big Bad Wolves: Masculinity in the American Film*, draws analogies between the Brando of *The Wild One* and the twin protagonists of *Easy Rider*, observing that the Dennis Hopper and Peter Fonda characters are "dropouts, doing their own thing, making a religion of sexual freedom, letting their hair grow long as they deck themselves out in absurd regalia" (281)—features of *Knightriders* as well. Yet only through the character played by Jack Nicholson, an American Civil Liberties Union lawyer who specializes in defending hippies, "are we given any attempt to grant some substance to this rebellion, some vision of an alternative society" (282). Mellen concludes her discussion of *Easy Rider* by saying that we "are left with an ambivalent film that has as its core a macho sensibility and a belief, too infantile to carry any conviction, that a real man enacts his masculine defiance by racing down highways on a revved-up motorcycle accompanied by a buddy who understands him" (283).

In many respects, *Knightriders* is a mature revision of such 1960s biker films as *Easy Rider* in that it envisions a band of dropouts and would-be hoodlums who have formed what would appear to be a fully functioning alternative society. Billy is not Brando or Hopper or Fonda, nor is he the lecherous Nicholson, though he stands outside of his society and refuses to abide by its corrupted and corrupting institutional practices (the film features corrupt law enforcement officials as well as corrupting enticements such as corporate sponsorships). If *Knightriders* shares any similarities with the western, it is because Billy is the spiritual heir of male loners such as Gary Cooper in *High Noon* or Alan Ladd in *Shane*, for instance; but more to the point, a loner such as Brando in *The Wild One*. The critical difference is that Billy's severe personal code is intelligible, while Brando's remains unarticulated, private.

Although this merging of the Arthurian legend with the biker movie is perhaps the film's most striking quality, Romero also takes other artistic risks as well, introducing still more innovations, primarily with his unusual portrayals of characters among Arthur's *entourage* whose identities have been well established and, with few exceptions, have remained relatively fixed. Sometimes the effect is comic, but other alterations serve to work toward the economy necessary when the narrative tradition is translated into another—in this case—dramatic form. For instance, as we shall see in the ensuing discussion, Morgan (Tom Savini) in this picture is male. Oddly enough, there *is* a certain logic to this "sex change," since despite their different genders, he is very much like his namesake of the received legend: Both have enormous sexual appetites and both oppose Arthur politically. Yet neither Morgan is directly instrumental in bringing about Arthur's demise. In presenting a character named Morgan who is male and who acts as a usurper, this film also follows an early tradition of the Tristram legend in which there is a male character who usurps the land ruled by Tristram's father. Sigmund Eisner's *The Tristan Legend: A Study in Sources*, outlines the early Welsh sources of this portrayal of a male Morgan, and traces his appearances in Tristram romances as famous as Thomas of Britain's (80-82). Whether *Knightriders* borrows consciously from this tradition is, of course, uncertain, but it does offer an interesting alternative to the usual depiction of a Morgan who is the stereotypical *femme fatale*.

The film also features Merlin (Brother Blue), a black man with butterflies tattooed on his face. He is a retired physician who now serves as the king's traveling medicine man and spiritual adviser, his New Age "head doctor." The film's king is not named Arthur, but Billy, and there is no Guinevere either, although there is Billy's companion and queen, Lady Linnet (Amy Ingersoll), and a love triangle that remains in the background.

Finally, like T. H. White's *The Once and Future King*, *Knightriders* uses anachronisms freely (the entire story smacks of the Society for Creative Anachronism of which such phenomena as Renaissance fairs are made), especially in its inclusion of characters from the Robin Hood legend. White, we will recall, incorporates the latter into his episode that portrays Morgan le Fay, and *Knightriders* borrows the figures of Friar Tuck (John Hostetter), who displays the same weaknesses we have come to associate with stereotypes of this clerical order as they are presented by Chaucer and Shakespeare, for instance: Gluttony, an over fondness for drink, and a sexual intemperance as well. Tuck serves, then, as an analogue to the lecherous Nicholson character in *Easy Rider*. The anachronisms go hand in hand with the film's propensity to call to attention the artificiality of the group and its activities: The music played at the jousts is taped (there is a van with a sound man to operate the equipment) and the lances are "rigged" to break easily to prevent serious injury during the tournament, another way in which *Knightriders* contains postmodern expression.

Ostensibly Romero's film is set in 1970s America, although the precise time is vague (Romero shares with director David Lynch the propensity for setting his films in indeterminate or equivocal time periods.). It tells the story of a group of bikers and an array of other misfits who, under the direction of "King Arthur," alias Billy (Ed Harris) form an itinerant Renaissance fair. The trouble is that whereas Billy believes ferociously in a strict code of honor that does indeed hearken back to the lost world of Arthurian romance his followers, try as they might, cannot find the conviction to join him in his private world. And as we shall see in our ensuing discussion, it is precisely this that makes the film postmodern: Despite the superficial trappings of the 1960s—the film depicts a group of people trying to live communal lives of brotherhood and cooperation— each man *is* an island, after all.

Oddly enough, while Arthurians such as Norris Lacy have praised *Knightriders* for its innovations, Romero himself insists upon allying his Arthurian film (metonymically, at least) with more traditional (i.e., "serious") films of the 1950s and 1960s.[4] For instance, in an interview shortly after the film's release, Romero confesses: "I love genre films. One of the films for which I have a real soft spot in my heart is all the old Robert Taylor, Cornel Wilde films" (25). And in the same essay, lest the reader miss the point, Romero reiterates: "*Knightriders* is in the idiom, in the genre of the old Robert Taylor/Cornell Wilde films" (25). Thus, with *Knightriders* as well as with the horror genre for which Romero has become most famous (e.g., his 1967 *Night of the Living Dead*), Romero insists repeatedly that his efforts hearken back to an earlier age of filmmaking, one that was more creative and less superficial. Moreover, himself an independent filmmaker (Laurel Productions), Romero clearly respects Cornell Wilde for the same reason. What makes Romero's *Knightriders* different from Robert Taylor's *Knights of the Round Table* or Cornel Wilde's *Sword of Lancelot* is that whereas those films are melodramas—a lucrative genre in the 1950s and 1960s, as we saw in chapter 3—his is a film of the 1980s and thus provides its audience with a postmodern angle to an old story.

Romero's remarks about the idea of wedding the Arthurian legend with the biker film and using the Renaissance fair as a premise are equally revealing:

With *Knightriders*, it's not just borrowing from the Arthurian legend, but from all over the culture map. And many of the film's images have to do with America. . . . But the motorcycle culture seemed to fit the Arthurian story. The bikers are a romanticized image, at least in this country. They have their own culture and attitude of this is us, and the rest of the world is you. That made sense on a pure story level, and as allegory. (25)

Knightriders begins at the end: Billy has already received a wound (both physically and spiritually) and his troupe is falling apart despite his tenacious efforts to keep them bound to his ideals. Truly, he is a wounded king, perhaps a loose conflation of King Arthur and the grail king. To bolster this supposition, one can point to intimations of his sexual impotence in the film. Although *Knightriders* opens in the woods with a naked Linnet and a nude Billy, the audience does not catch them *en flagrante*. Instead, Billy stands in a pool of water scourging himself, and as the film progresses it is clear that Linnet stays with him out of a sense of duty, not romantic desire. Early in the film, the audience detects an attraction between Linnet and a noble knight, Allen (Gary Lahti), with whom she eventually ends up—when Billy is "deposed" by the ambitious Morgan, he releases Linnet and in effect gives her away to Allen. If in fact Billy is impotent, this would have interesting connections with *Excalibur*, of the same year; as we saw in the previous chapter, in that work Arthur and the grail king are fused for the sake of economy. Moreover, it makes for an interesting reading when one thinks of Jessie Weston's assertions that the grail king can be traced to pre-Christian fertility and vegetation cults, and her discussion of anthropological studies that have uncovered cultures where the deposition and assassination of impotent kings was still practiced at the same time she was writing in the 1920s.

At any rate, Billy is an idealist whose vision could not be said to fail him in the end, although it must remain his own solitary dream; it cannot be realized fully in the modern material world, but this is true in spirit to the received legend—the tragedy of Arthur is his inability to sustain the image of the mighty Round Table and its chivalric code of behavior. Challenged by "the curse of commercialism," represented by the Disneyfied world of advertising and by the blind ambition of the would-be king, Morgan, Billy's dream of a principled group that sticks together begins to become unhinged. Even those closest to him try in vain to preserve his rapidly disintegrating ideal. And although Morgan is Billy's ostensible "adversary," it is really the corrupt world of promoters and their self-serving ends that present the true threat to his vision. In fact, while Morgan initially jumps on the bandwagon and agrees to become part of a commercial dog-and-pony show, he becomes disillusioned, realizes why Billy objects so vehemently to such offers, and rejects his contract out of hand as soon as he becomes the new king.

Morgan is not an evil nemesis, just an immature and short-sighted rival, but he does mature as the film progresses (one might say he learns from his mistakes) so that he is at last a worthy successor to Billy, if not actually his epigone, another means by which we can identify the film as postmodern. To counter Morgan's repeated challenges to Billy's authority, the film features the king's faithful champion, Allen. As mentioned previously, the film early on hints at a long-standing but sublimated desire between Allen and Linnet. After the first episode in which Allen champions the wounded Billy's cause and frustrates Morgan's efforts to gain control, he takes up with a young woman from the local town, who serves as an Elaine figure, just as Allen functions as a kind of Lancelot. This girl, named Julie Dean (Patricia Tallman), conceives an instant crush on Allen, and Linnet casts a jealous glance at her. Allen, essentially honorable in all his dealings, if a bit temporarily confused by the upheaval at Billy's "court," finally deposits the girl at her home and, we learn eventually, waits for Linnet to be free.[5] As we have mentioned, Billy does free Linnet once he is deposed by Morgan. What is notable is that Allen champions Billy's cause to the end, even though it becomes obvious that he is in love with the queen, Linnet. Thus, although there is a love triangle lurking in the background of this film, it is featured not as a prominent part of the story but rather as an aside to Billy's efforts to will his vision into existence. The attraction between Allen and Linnet is not brought to the fore until Billy has lost his crown, an event that serves as a harbinger of his imminent death.

There are plenty of grotesqueries in *Knightriders*. Horror writer Stephen King makes a cameo appearance as a cynical onlooker at the first "jousting tournament." Then there is the "fat slob jerk" father of the Elaine character who lapses into a drunken stupor when he attends the tournament and who, we learn in a later scene, regularly beats his wife. There are also episodes that feature the gross food orgies and the frantic coupling of Friar Tuck with an overweight photographer employed by the promotion company that convinces Morgan to sign a contract. But despite its penchant for the bizarre, incongruous, and grotesquely humorous, *Knightriders* is tragic; and as we shall see, one might even argue that it is tragic in the formal or classical sense, as is the Arthurian legend itself. In its blend of the comic and tragic genres, *Knightriders* is not unlike T. H. White's *The Once and Future King*, in which the comic mode of the first book, "The Sword in the Stone," gives way to the tragic spirit of "The Candle in the Wind" (book four). The successful melding together of two distinctly different generic conventions is laudable because of the difficulty of the task.

After the first tournament a young boy (also named Billy) searches for the king, whom he addresses as Sir William, and asks him to autograph a picture that had appeared in a motorcycle magazine entitled *Cycle Riders*. Billy is offended that he has been featured in such a degrading publication—"This is like Evel Knieval or something. It's not what we're about"—and refuses to sign it, arguing that such a negative perception is demeaning to his principles and to the *raison d'être* of the group. He hurts the boy's feelings, so Morgan autographs the picture, thus revealing his own failure to grasp Billy's ideals. When Billy is later pressured to sign a contract that would transform his group into a veritable three-ring circus, he also refuses. Again Morgan steps in, agreeing to try the promised lifestyle of the rich and famous. He takes some of the *entourage* with him. But others hold fast to Billy's ideals; although they themselves cannot always understand his highly personalized code, their love for him commands their loyalty.

When at last Morgan defeats Billy's champions—the king himself suffers from a wound that refuses to heal, and each time he attempts to defend himself it reopens—he graciously concedes his authority, embraces Morgan, crowns him, and leads Linnet to Allen's side. Billy then takes swift leave of Merlin and company and departs alone—*except* for one lone companion, a recent addition to the group, who trails the deposed king at a respectful distance and serves as a sort of silent squire. This figure is shadowy, deliberately so perhaps; his function appears to be purely allegorical, but Billy had earlier anticipated his arrival at court and had expressed his apprehension toward this event. Billy had repeatedly received a warning dream that predicted his own demise by a challenger with a black bird on his shield. The black bird is one of the repeated images in the film. It appears as the film opens, is worn on the shield of the mystery knight, and is present at Billy's funeral. When Billy shares his dream with Merlin, the latter does recount the story of Arthur's engendering of Mordred and its consequences, but he then suggests to Billy that we make our own destinies by believing in omens and dreams.

At this suggestion, Billy demurs, however, averring, "You taught me too good, magician. You taught me to believe. That blackbird's gonna git me." But Merlin responds, "Yeah, maybe you'll make it happen yourself. Destiny's gonna get ya'. Like the *real* King Arthur." Merlin then recounts his version of Arthur's "lechery" and engendering of Mordred, the legendary Merlin's advice to drown the babies in order to prevent Mordred from slaying Arthur one day, the child's survival as a foundling whom Merlin subsequently raised not knowing he was Mordred, who does indeed kill Arthur, but "only his body," not his spirit. As it turns out, Billy's dream does not come true—at least not the way he imagines.

Once Morgan has departed with a group of Billy's followers, a true malaise afflicts the rest of the king's *entourage*. Billy refuses to travel until the black sheep—led by the prodigal son—return to him. Meanwhile a tournament is held, presumably to raise money, and we see by the insolent behavior of the bystanders how little they understand Billy's conception of what he and his followers represent. A group of locals challenges the knights and Billy himself defends the honor of his troupe when he fights the youth with the black bird on his shield, known after simply as Indian (Albert Amerson). Billy defeats the youth and makes him yield, but this strife opens his old wound. After this, Indian is always near Billy, although he has no spoken part in the film. But it is as though in overcoming Indian Billy overcomes his fear of death or apprehension of the future; he is prepared for his impending death.

Billy first revisits a town where a redneck deputy sheriff had framed and then brutally beaten one of his followers, named Bagman (Don Berry), apparently a reformed pothead. This was because Billy had characteristically stood by his principles and refused to pay bribe money to the deputy, even though Morgan and others urged him to be pragmatic and pay off the deputy: "We're not paying this rat-pile heap of dog-shit a goddamn cent," insists Billy. Refusing to let Bagman spend the night in jail alone, Billy looks on helplessly from an adjoining cell while the deputy brutalizes him. Before they leave, Billy threatens the deputy, warning him that one day he will return to redress this injustice. And this is exactly what he does. He comes upon the fat deputy unawares in a cafe and delivers a *contrapasso* in the form of a beating every bit as severe and humiliating as the one the deputy had visited upon Billy's friend, in a scene nearly as grotesque as the food fight in *Animal House* (1978). We might add that as in the juvenile delinquency films, Romero also caters to a teenage audience here, providing numerous variations on the chase scene and the demolition derbies portrayed under the guise of jousts. An appreciative crowd in the restaurant applauds when Billy has finished by locking the deputy in the freezer, and Billy's shadow, Indian, leaves wampum—a piece of crafted silver from his belt—to pay for damages.

Billy's next stop is at a country schoolhouse (one of several "time slips" in the film) where, it turns out, the boy who had asked for the autograph is in attendance. The deposed ruler strides abruptly into the classroom, presents the boy with his sword, and then leaves as quickly as he had arrived. This bears similarities to White's conclusion—and that of its filmic descendant, *Camelot*—in that one who believes in the ideal represented by the king is singled out, encouraged, and left with some form of evidence, whether it be a story or a sword, that the king and his society actually existed, presumably to keep the ideal alive. This is a true act of optimism, and in this case it is also a gesture of atonement or recompense for having disappointed the boy earlier.

Another quality that makes this film postmodern is its element of mystery: The audience knows virtually nothing about the characters' early lives. This is particularly noticeable in the case of Billy, where a past would seem to be most in order as an explanation for his singular character. But viewers must accept his enthusiasm for the idealized past depicted in the world of Arthurian romance (and one that is improved upon by Billy's own imagination) as a donnée. Likewise, the intriguing cast of characters who belong to his company seem to be disconnected from their personal histories; we can guess that they are disenfranchised figures, but we are not provided any clues to Linnet's motives for her devotion to Billy—she says she was down on life and then he came along and made her "believe"; she also mentions that she has followed him for two years without question, but why? We learn that Merlin was a physician, and that Steve (Ken Hixon) is a dropout lawyer; that Pippin (Warner Shook) discovers he is homosexual, but we do not know where these characters come from on the psychological or sociological map. Does this matter? In the world of medieval romance, no, but the conventions of modern film might demand otherwise. In an epigonic postmodern world, however, everything seems to fail in achieving a traditional "connectedness."

Billy meets his end happily, though whether deliberately is left open. This ambiguity is, however, important in understanding the film as tragedy. We see him for the last time cruising down the road on his gallant steed of a motorcycle, relieved, carefree, until he begins to show concern for his left hand. He makes motions that suggest he is losing control of it—as though he is having a stroke. He also shakes his head as though to clear it. If this is so, then Billy's death is truly an "accident," and the most we can deduce is that earlier he has had a mere premonition of his own death, which is quite different from willing it.

Otherwise, we can assume only that his death was a suicide when he meets a semi-truck head on. For just prior to this moment, Billy envisions himself in full medieval regalia, galloping along on a great palomino steed in an open field. An ecstatic look plays upon his face, even at the moment of his death. If the viewer sees his death as a suicide, it can only be explained as a suicide of despair, one that had resulted in his deposition and failure to keep his ragged band of misfits united under the common goal of his own ideals. His actions after he is dethroned and up to this moment do suggest that he is preparing for such an end. Yet his ecstatic vision at the very moment of death—his private gnosis—belies the idea of suicide, as does the hint that he is suffering from a heart attack or stroke.

In order to conform to the formal qualities of tragedy, a work must show a reversal of fortune (what Aristotle calls *peripeteia*). That is, although Billy loses position, exchanging an exalted position for a lower one (or more commonly by being an outcast or a corpse), in the process of his fall he also gains superior insight, often having his initial convictions renewed or refined. In its exploration of the ideals it aspires to but cannot attain, tragedy implies optimism. The Arthurian legend surely is tragic in its portrayal of a king and his court who strive after perfection and yet are doomed to fail, and the same might be said for Billy, who fails to communicate his dream and impose his own private strictures on the group, and who is deposed, but who, in the process, has his dream confirmed or strengthened. He fails, but he does not fail himself, nor does his dream abandon him.[6]

The film concludes with his funeral, which includes a gathering of his followers and a tribute to him. His fair death, which allows the viewer a privileged glimpse of his vision, stands as a tribute to his principled character but also testifies to his inability, at last, to communicate and share that vision with others, even those who love and believe in him most.

There is no emphasis upon the love triangle in *Knightriders*, although it is presented in the background; there is no Mordred, although there is plenty of opposition to Billy's ideals; and there is no grail king and no grail quest, even though surely what Billy seeks and the wound he suffers suggests that that component of the legend is present in the background of the film as well. Romero has deftly woven together several genres and taken tremendous risks in his use of the legend. He has surely brought to the fore the splendid but inexorable failure of Arthur and the ideal he represents. And for this reason he has interpreted the *Matter of Britain* for a generation that finds it difficult, in the words of Tennyson "to believe in anything either good or great," but which, nonetheless, feels an intense longing to do so.

The last three films upon which we will focus in this chapter on the postmodern quest all feature the grail branch of the Arthurian legend. The individual search for meaning is surely not peculiar to the *Matter of Britain*, but the trend of films from the mid-1980s to favor the grail material over the love triangle represents a significant change in Hollywood's use of the legend. In some sense, the spiritual quest in these later films is a continuation of a chord struck by *Knightriders*, even though the latter does not expressly employ the grail strand of the legend. Moreover, in all four of these films—*Knightriders* (1981), *The Natural* (1984), *Indiana Jones and the Last Crusade* (1989), and *The Fisher King* (1991)—there *is* a love interest presented, but it is definitely subordinated to the quest for a spiritual ideal.

The Natural (1984)

At first it may appear to be a very strange idea indeed to employ any aspect of the Arthurian legend in a film about baseball, but this is just what *The Natural* (1984), directed by Barry Levinson, does. One might assume that such a film would be doomed to failure, but the combination proved to be enormously lucrative and influential. Clearly the sublime production *Bull Durham* (1988), starring Kevin Costner and Susan Sarandon bears its mark, as does the overtly gnostic *Field of Dreams* (1989), which also stars Costner. But for the purposes of our discussion, *The Natural* is a key film because it is illustrative of our point that a film can be subtle in its use of the legend. Moreover, it need not activate the entire Arthurian corpus to show a recognizable indebtedness, just as films that would seem to be obvious candidates for the label Arthurian—employing characters and elements of plot—may nonetheless violate the spirit of the legend and thus have little of importance in common with it. This is why the ambiguous collocation "Arthurian film" is one that deserves careful attention. Other than a few obvious allusions to it (e.g., a reference to Sir Lancelot and a character named Pop Fisher, who walks with a limp), *The Natural* would apparently have little use for the medieval legend. Yet to borrow a term from John Boorman, the film's "template" is, quite arguably, Arthurian in that it is modeled on the redemptive quest. *The Natural* belongs in this chapter because its quest consists of a secularized spiritualism, a characteristic that defines it as postmodern. The treatment of baseball as a quasi-sacred endeavor is in itself a peculiarly American concept. As early as 1925, in *The Great Gatsby*, F. Scott Fitzgerald had noted this attitude toward the sport. When Nick Carraway meets Meyer Wolfsheim and learns that he had fixed the World Series in 1919, he remarks: "The idea staggered me . . . [and] if I had thought of it at all I would have thought of it as a thing that merely *happened*, the end of some inevitable chain. It never occurred to me that one man could start to play with the faith of fifty million people—with the single-mindedness of a burglar blowing a safe" (74).

The Natural is based on the 1952 novel by Bernard Malamud, although it takes license with that text, notably in its alteration of the ending, an action not unusual for a Hollywood production of any work. For Malamud isn't as optimistic that Roy can resist the temptation of wealth and women (he had, after all, failed the first time), and he leaves the ending ambiguous: Roy doesn't manage a grand slam and the Knights don't win the pennant. Whether this is deliberate on Roy's part or whether the power that dwelled in him has really vanished remains uncertain in the novel. The title shared by the novel and film is in itself significant, though, in that it suggests the idea of "election."

Roy Hobbs (Robert Redford), the main character, is possessed of a gift— the ability to play supernatural baseball—and from the time he is a child he knows that he is destined to greatness. When he is fourteen years old he fashions a bat from an oak tree that has been felled by lightning and bestows upon it the name Wonderboy. This detail probably derives from the Norse legend of the god Wotan who fashions a mighty spear out of a tree he fells. The power in this bat, however, is an illusion, since the talent actually resides in Roy himself, but it takes the entire film for him to realize this. Roy's dream of becoming a baseball great—"the greatest there ever was"—is interrupted for several years by a moment of foolish bad judgment and naïveté (a lethal combination), and this is why the story becomes focused on the redemptive quest. Roy must "heal" himself, but he is also a redemptive figure for the part owner and manager of the team (aptly named the New York Knights), Pop Fisher (Wilfred Brimley), whose ownership is threatened by his partner, a corrupt figure simply known as The Judge (Robert Prosky). Pop's assistant manager, Red (Richard Farnsworth), convinces him to give Roy, a "middle-age rookie," a chance.

The aging Pop wants only two things: He thirsts for a decent drink of water from the dugout's fountain (could it be likened to a draught from a holy chalice?) and to win a pennant before his career comes to an end. Yet before Roy Hobbs is signed on to the Knights by their scout, the season is well advanced, figuratively and literally, and Pop seems to have little hope of attaining his dream. It turns out that The Judge has been bribing several star players to throw games in order to force Pop into retirement. Thus, when Roy refuses to compromise his dream for money, he not only remains true to his own aspirations but also makes Pop's dream realizable as well. Roy's story, then, embodies the myth of the second chance (an American preoccupation rooted in the founding of our country by disillusioned Europeans) and Pop's story the success that can be attained only by the single-minded pursuit of an ideal. They both achieve fulfillment, but each's dream is separate unto himself, and they reach fulfillment only by an unpredictable convergence—yet another aspect of the postmodern "condition."

As in the other three films discussed in this chapter, there is a love interest—though here one might argue for the plural—but it is subordinated to the quest itself. Glenn Close plays Iris, the girl Roy leaves behind when he goes off to seek baseball fame, and she also becomes the source of inspiration to which he must look when his powers are about to fail him at the film's crucial moment. (Evidently she provides him strength when she reveals to him that he is the "natural" father to her teenage son, who is watching Roy in the stand that day. The term "natural" is a nineteenth-century euphemism for "illegitimate.") Is she, then, a kind of Elaine figure, member of the grail family, mother of Galahad, and faithful lover of Lancelot? Possibly, but at any rate she is the positive feminine influence who has to counteract the damage done to Roy by the film's two *femmes fatales*.

The first of these encounters with dangerous fays occurs when Roy leaves home for professional baseball for the first time. On the train, he meets a mysterious woman named Harriet Bird (Barbara Hershey), with whom he becomes immediately fascinated. Harriet remains an extremely enigmatic character in the film, but in his initial conversation with her it is easy to see why Roy is attracted to her.[7] She is great for his already expanding ego, and he lacks the worldly experience he needs to foresee any danger or to be wary of appearances (like the naïve fool, Perceval, of grail lore). Like most young Americans, Roy believes the world is his oyster, and all he needs to do is reach out and take it. (This metaphor and mentality is evident in Willy Loman in *Death of a Salesman*, another work in which characters view sports as a kind of religion.)

Harriet witnesses a display of Roy's extraordinary talent, and she glorifies it by telling him: "It was just like watching Sir Lancelot jousting Sir Tarquine. Or was it Maldemar?" Roy obviously hasn't read his Malory, so Harriet tries another literary avenue: Has he ever heard of Homer? To which Roy responds, "The only homer I know has four bases." Harriet then gives him a crash course in literary history by explaining, not quite accurately, that "he wrote about heroes and kings." She asserts that had Homer witnessed Roy's performance, he would have been moved to write about baseball, too.

Such enthusiasm is contagious, and Roy, ordinarily not very effusive, confides: "Someday I'm gonna break every record in the book. I know I got it in me." Roy then invites Harriet to watch him play ball, but before this promise can be fulfilled, she invites him to her hotel room, shoots him (inexplicably), and then commits suicide, after which the film jumps ahead, audaciously, sixteen years. A baffled audience can only guess at what has occurred in those years, and no motive is ever provided for Harriet's sudden and shocking actions. Roy should have been more cautious in the company he chose to keep, and he pays a heavy price. The ensuing scandal, we learn, is enough to put his aspiring career on ice. Like Perceval, he had arrived at the grail castle, but his ignorance prevented him from realizing his dream.

Once he earns his second chance, Roy astonishes the sports world by breaking records galore; he causes the dramatic reversal of the New York Knights's standings and puts the team in the running for the pennant. His integrity is tested from several sources: among them the team's corrupt owner, The Judge, and an over zealous sports writer, Max Mercy (Robert Duvall), who has exhumed the scandal of sixteen years before and wants to pay Roy big bucks for his life story.

Once again, then, Roy is very nearly robbed of his dream by what turns out to be another dangerous liaison, this time with Pop's niece, who is also involved with another player on the team, Bump Bailey (Michael Madsen). This *femme fatale* goes by the auspicious name of Memo Paris, played by Kim Bassinger.

Although Roy begins a relationship with her, she is under the control of the Judge's partner in crime, a crooked financeer played by Darren McGavin (a role oddly uncredited). Because Roy cannot be bought with money, Memo is enlisted to distract and even poison him, and his life is imperiled. While he is in the hospital recuperating from his "stomach trouble," the old bullet, presumably carried around for sixteen years, is removed. Roy is warned that should he participate in the decisive game, he may risk his health and even his life, but he is undaunted by this.

The climactic moment of the final game occurs because Roy's gift seems to have vanished. Weakened by his illness, he cannot perform the miracle expected of him—until he receives the aforementioned note from Iris. This acts like a token from a medieval damsel in a tournament, breathing new life and fresh resolve into Roy. Wonderboy lets him down when it cracks in two, but Roy now seems to understand that the true source of his talent is internal and so, undaunted, he asks the batboy, Bobby Savoy, for whom he has become a kind of father figure, to choose a replacement for him. It is not an object—be it sword or "relic"—that this quest has as its instrument or as its objective. The grail in this film is indwelling, an ideal. Roy achieves that ideal, but to his teammates it is, after all, only a successful season. It is Bobby and not Roy who selects the bat Roy had helped him fashion, which he had named Savoy Special, and it is with this bat that Roy Hobbs at last hits the homer that secures his dream and also wins the beloved pennant for Pop Fisher. Roy's old wound reopens under the strain, however, and the viewer sees that he is bleeding even before he hits a grand slam.

This, along with the events that follow, taxes the viewer's credibility, but then *The Natural* isn't even striving to be "natural" at all. All sorts of supernatural phenomena occur: A flash of lightning indicates that Wonderboy is about to break, that Roy's power is building; when he hits the homer, the ball knocks out the stadium lights, causing a sort of artificial electrical storm that sends sparks of illumination—a thousand points of light—showering down all over the ecstatic players. This may be a shared victory, but for Roy alone does it offer salvation: The film concludes with a scene that portrays Iris, Roy, and their son in a pastoral field, and not the corrupt ballfield of New York, playing catch. Only after Roy earns his second chance and attains his dream can *The Natural* conclude with the renewed love between Iris and Roy.

It is not surprising to find a mingling of the sacred and secular in this film—a fusion of baseball and religion—since such a marriage is an established American tradition. Athletes regularly attribute their success to God, basketball players make the sign of the cross before shooting a free-throw, and coaches cite scripture to bolster their teams's spirit before a crucial game. For example, the *Omaha World-Herald* reported in its January 30, 1996 edition that Tom Osborne, head coach of the University of Nebraska Cornhuskers football team, quoted the apostle Paul to inspire his players before their 1996 Fiesta Bowl contest (27). Moreover, there is a decided tendency toward the unorthodox in American versions of most recognized religions—from American Catholics who are frequently viewed by Rome as schismatics and mavericks, to the Mormon belief that Christ himself once graced North America with his presence. It is little wonder, then, that *The Natural* should fuse the secular tradition of baseball with the idea of divine election. Roy's quest is a spiritual one, even though it is played out on a sports field, and his redemption comes in the form of a final gnosis, literally a revelatory spark from heaven that serves as an outward manifestation of his grace.

Indiana Jones and the Last Crusade (1989)

> [There is a view of] the Middle Ages [that is one] of so-called *Tradition*, or of occult philosophy (or *la pensée sapientielle*), an eternal and rather eclectic ramshackle structure, swarming with Knights Templars, Rosicrucians, alchemists, Masonic initiates, neo-Kabbalists, drunk on reactionary poisons sipped from the Grail, ready to hail every neo-fascist Will to Power . . .
> Umberto Eco, "Dreaming of the Middle Ages" (71)

Indiana Jones and the Last Crusade (1989), the third of three films featuring Indiana Jones, is most likely the film George Lucas wanted to make when he began the series.[8] Instead, he made *Raiders of the Lost Ark* (1981) but an astute viewer can see that *The Last Crusade* is, in several ways, a remake of the first "Indiana Jones" film. Both films feature cookie-cutter Nazi villains, and both focus on Indiana's battle to prevent a putatively precious relic—the Lost Ark of the Covenant and the holy grail, respectively—from falling into the hands of these comic book antagonists. Perhaps Lucas chose to use the ark because to a popular audience it was then more familiar than the grail which, however, gained notoriety as the decade of the 1980s progressed. Films like *Excalibur* featured it, for instance, as did bestsellers like *Holy Blood, Holy Grail* (1982) and its sequel, *The Messianic Legacy* (1986), both of which maintain that Christ married Mary Magdelene and had children with her, the descendants of whom dwell today in France. They are the keepers of the sacred chalice, which must be hidden from the unworthy. These works also brought the grail legend into the popular arena.[9] At any rate, George Lucas and Menno Meyjes produced the story, which was directed by Steven Spielberg.[10] There are two ways in which this work qualifies as an example of the postmodern quest. The first is in its treatment of the grail itself, including the film's "sources." The second lies in the hero's attitude toward the quest (he is, at the outset a reluctant quester) and the nature of the spirituality the grail quest can afford.

A text extremely useful in unpacking the myriad of issues contained in *Indiana Jones and The Last Crusade* is Morris Berman's *Coming to Our Senses: Body and Spirit in the Hidden History of the West* (1990), which is about the intimate connections Berman sees between the grail legend, Nazi occultism, and the several historical phases of gnosticism: The original phenomenon in the second and third century C. E.; and its reemergence in twelfth- and thirteenth-century C. E. Catharism, Renaissance high magic, and Nazi occultism.

By no means is Berman the first scholar to assert the connection between the origins of the grail in twelfth-century France and heretical movements such as gnosticism, and most certainly he is not the first to puzzle over its origin. Of the many critics who have addressed the origin of the grail, we find that none has stated the problem so succinctly or forcefully as has Jessie Weston. Although we agree with her statement of the problem, we are not in complete agreement with her conclusions; however, there does seem to be considerable merit to what she posits.[11] In the 1913 volume *The Quest of the Holy Grail* (which therefore precedes her more famous *From Ritual to Romance*, 1920), she declares, "As a simple matter of fact there is no ecclesiastical story which connects Joseph of Arimathea with the Vessel (Dish, or Cup) of the Last Supper; ecclesiastical tradition, as such, knows nothing whatever of the Grail" (54). A page later she observes, "Nor, leaving the incidents of the story aside, can the Grail in any way be claimed as a genuine relic" (55). In concluding her dismissal of a Christian theory of origin for the grail, she writes, "Whatever the Grail may be it is not a Christian relic; whatever the source of the story, it is not an ecclesiastical legend" (65). The problem thus stated here is in a conveniently truncated fashion, and although the problem with the Christian theory of origin for the grail has been apparent for decades and perhaps centuries, this has not prevented leagues of Christian apologists from treating Chrétien as an orthodox Christian poet, just as, for example, in his 1994 work *The Western Canon* Harold Bloom exposes the fallacy of treating Dante as poet who expounds upon orthodox Christian ideas.

Regardless of how one might justify Chrétien's text as orthodox, the problem of orthodoxy is even more daunting with the grail poem by Wolfram von Eschenbach, *Parzival*. Despite attempts to treat Wolfram as an illiterate who was nonetheless an original writer of romance and hence a poor reader (or translator) of Chrétien's work (largely based on Wolfram's own remarks in his poem), his work has been recognized as both clever and erudite. Such attempts to pretend ignorance of one's own meaning and sources, Weston observes, are all "eminently satisfactory, so long as the original texts were unknown or ignored" (63). As a matter of fact, it is unclear in Chrétien's text whether the talisman that became known as the "Sangral" or "holy grail" is a dish or cup or platter; in Wolfram's text the object is none of these things but instead, is remarkably, a stone. Evidently, contemporary twelfth-century poets could not even agree on what the talisman was; as Arthur Edward Waite, Weston's contemporary, observed in *The Holy Grail*, Wolfram's *Parzival* "is heterodox." Remarkably, though, he stops short of claiming the work to be heretical (260). Nonetheless, the fact that Wolfram posits a select group of knights who protect the grail, and indeed, suggests that these knights exist outside the church's province, indicates to us a critical problem more severe than simply one of "heterodoxy."

The connections Berman sees between the grail legend, Nazi occultism, and gnosticism suggest the cluster of features, like the stars in a constellation, that inform *Indiana Jones and the Last Crusade*. Otto Rahn, who was later one of Heinrich Himmler's occult advisers and probably a model for the Nazi talisman hunters in *Raiders of the Lost Ark* and *The Last Crusade* was, along with Denis de Rougemont (*Love in the Western World*), one of the promulgators of the idea that romantic or courtly love was originally a kind of gnostic heresy, an expression of the convergent aims of Cathars and troubadours in the twelfth-century Languedoc region of France.

At the same time, Berman's theory (or rather, type of theorizing) points out the danger of hermetic drift in our historical concepts, since it seems bizarre to claim that romantic love and a mystical race theory should possess a common origin. (Berman subsumes them under a very general thesis about western body-hatred.)[12] We have to be on guard against falling into dichotomizing traps with respect to ill-defined concepts. "Gnosticism," for example, is not an idea that admits of a razor-sharp, mathematical definition; instead, like most historically emergent ideas, it seems better characterized as a Lakoffian prototype-based category, or even as a Wittgensteinian system of family resemblances. Different versions of gnosticism may be only remotely related to each other, a fact that is too easily disguised when we refer to them by the same name. We stress this point to illustrate a banal but often neglected point: Because of the absence of a self-evident heritage—the absence of a body of writings that can be called the "definitive" history of "the holy grail"—each contributor is free to construct his own tradition. This situation alone presents a *prima facie* case for a gnostic origin of the grail legend.

Therefore, as one might expect when one begins to examine the bases for this Hollywood film about a fictional search for the grail, one finds that *Indiana Jones and the Last Crusade* incorporates a number of eclectic and esoteric sources. The "official" source, cited in Pollock's biography of George Lucas is, as we have seen, Trevor Ravenscroft's *Spear of Destiny*, which allegedly documents the Nazi interest in religious relics with putative occult powers.[13] Although the film is set in the early 1940s during the Nazi reign, it opens in Utah in 1912 to provide a flashback that accounts for Indiana Jones's love of art and his battle against self-serving treasure hunters. The Nazis, however, are not the primary villains in the film. Indeed, they are rather stereotypical Nazi villains, of the "cultured swine" variety, drawn quite deliberately from Hollywood films of the 1940s and 1950s. Examples would include the Nazi commander played by Erich von Stroheim in Billy Wilder's *Five Graves to Cairo* (1943), Conrad Veidt, who played Major Strasser in *Casablanca* (1943), and Otto Preminger in *Stalag 17* (1953).

The real villains are reckless and rapacious treasure hunters; the master villain, however, is a wealthy American, Walter Donovan (Julian Glover), who seeks the grail and acts in collusion with the Nazis only for his own profit. As we shall see, Donovan believes the grail to be a chalice with powers akin to the proverbial fountain of youth, a cup that can bestow eternal life, a detail that indicates one of the sources for this film can be traced back to Wolfram's *Parzival*, in which the grail, it will be remembered, is a stone that functions as a temporary talisman against death: Anyone who has been in its presence cannot die for a week. At any rate, Donovan's problem is that he is a literalist, and he thinks he can procure the grail so that he can derive from it a kind of vampiric immortality—a prolongation of actual physical life. When Indiana calls him a "Nazi stooge," Donovan scoffs, "If the Nazis want to write themselves into a grail legend and conquer the world, let them—I want eternal life." And it is he who then shoots Dr. Jones (Sean Connery), forcing Indiana to undertake the perilous encounter of the three challenges in order to procure the healing power of the grail for his father, the moribund Dr. Jones.

One of the refreshing aspects of this film is that the heroes are intellectuals, and with the exception of Indiana himself they are neither physically nor ethically accustomed to fighting battles with hands and weapons. Yet heroes they are, and this film comes down firmly on the side of the learned members of society—academics—who are the true guardians of what the grail represents. This secularizing of the grail guardians may be seen as a postmodern element in the film.

This is demonstrated with great humor in two scenes. The first is when Dr. Jones manages to rid himself and Indiana of Nazi pursuers. He uses his wits and his umbrella to scatter a vast flock of seagulls that unwittingly flies up and into the propellers of the enemy's plane, causing it to crash. (He says he suddenly remembered his Charlemagne: "Let the trees be your armies, and the rocks and the birds.") In another scene, which takes place inside a Nazi tank, Dr. Jones immobilizes a soldier by squirting ink into his eye, while a jovial Marcus Brody (Denholm Elliot) remarks: "The pen. The pen is mightier than the sword." We also see this when, in the same scene, Dr. Jones reprimands a Nazi thug by saying, "You should be reading books instead of burning them," since he and Indiana had earlier witnessed a Nazi book burning.

The "bad" intellectual is, interestingly enough, also the "love interest" in the film. Dr. Elsa Schneider (Alison Doody) is enlisted by Donovan, as are the Nazis, to find the grail. Her interest seems to be purely academic and not political or personal, but she is at best mistaken in her belief that intellectuals can take a disinterested stance and be exempt from the moral and ethical ramifications of their actions. Her collusion with Donovan and her collaboration with the Nazis is an assistance of evil, and it is fitting that she should become so seduced by the grail's power that she should lose her life in the earthquake precipitated by her efforts to abscond with the grail and then by trying to recover it—something the Grail Knight (Robert Eddison) had distinctly warned against. Both Dr. Jones senior and Dr. Jones junior, it turns out, have been seduced and deceived by Elsa, a kind of Delilah figure who would betray the grail and its true seekers to the Philistine, Donovan. This potential love triangle involving father, son, and love-object shares affinities with the Tristan legend (uncle, nephew, love-object) but it is never allowed to take precedence over the quest for the grail itself. In fact, it is used primarily for humorous ends (e.g., the unexpected priggishness displayed by Indiana when he is scandalized by his father's uncharacteristic libertinism).

Donovan's myopia prevents him from understanding that the cup grants only spiritual immortality, and then only to the worthy. It cannot be bought, nor can it be wrested away from its keeper (a 700-year-old knight, referred to simply as the Grail Knight). The museum curator and friend of the Jones family, Marcus Brody, warns Donovan, "You're meddling with powers you cannot possibly comprehend"; and another character, Kazim (Kevork Malikvan), who belongs to the Brotherhood of the Cruciform Rose, an oriental secret society that attempts to protect the grail, also cautions Donovan, "For the unrighteous the cup of life holds everlasting damnation." Kazim willingly martyrs himself to protect the secret of the grail.[14] Therefore, when Donovan must distinguish between the simulacra grails and the genuine item, he is at a loss; so is his intellectual hack for hire, Dr. Elsa Schneider. She selects the most ornate of the cups, and Donovan eagerly drinks from it, only to die the hideous death of which Kazim had forewarned him. "He chose poorly," is the deadpan response of the Grail Knight. Indiana, who has passed the three challenges that tested his spiritual worth, as we shall see, chooses the cup of a carpenter, a crude, unadorned one, to which the Grail Knight responds, "You have chosen wisely," and then adds the aforementioned warning, "The grail cannot pass beyond the great seal. That is the price for immortality."

When the film opens, Indiana Jones is established as a champion of artifacts for their scientific and cultural value. In the opening flashback, young Indy insists that the cross of Coronado "belongs in a museum," and he sees to it—years later and at a great personal risk—that that is precisely where it winds up. As a professor of archaeology at an unspecified Ivy League school, Indiana Jones ironically admonishes his class by stating, "Archaeology is the search for facts, not truths," and he impresses upon his students that the search does not include lost cities, maps, or buried treasure. Facts, not truth. If they seek truth, he insists, they can take philosophy courses. He is initially portrayed as a man of science, a positivist who is interested in facts and artifacts, not superstitions and truths. This skepticism contrasts with his father, who has spent his life amassing information about the location of the holy grail. Indiana seems not to grasp his father's commitment to the search for this "relic" (the elder Dr. Jones is a professor of medieval literature) and tells Donovan that his father's "hobby is grail lore." But the audience knows that it is far more than a hobby, that Dr. Jones is a true grail quester.

For instance, after Indiana rescues his father from the Nazi stronghold, a Gothic castle in Salzburg, he is ready to quit the quest and the search for the grail. Angered at this, his father admonishes Indy by saying of the grail: "It isn't archaeology. It's a race against evil." And he implores Indy to go to Berlin in order to stop the "armies of darkness" from procuring the grail. Even in the film's opening flashback the young Indiana bursts into his father's study and interrupts him, but not before we hear Dr. Jones's supplication as he bends over an obscure medieval religious manuscript, "May he who illuminated this illuminate me," revealing what an ardent devotee he truly is. ("Illumination," as we shall see, is precisely what he claims to have derived from his drink from the holy cup.) Moreover, when Donovan avers that the grail can provide eternal youth, Indiana scoffs, "An old man's dream," to which Donovan is quick to respond, "Every man's dream." Finally, at the outset of their quest for the missing Dr. Jones, which soon becomes a quest for the grail itself, Indiana asks Marcus Brody whether he believes in the holy grail, and Marcus responds: "The search for the cup of Christ is the search for the divine in all of us." This question suggests that Indy himself as a true postmodern cannot, at this point, believe in the grail, but Marcus's answer is also postmodern in that the quest becomes meaningful only to each individual and is, in a sense, a quest for identity, or self-knowledge. The intimation is that the grail has become a secular religion (arguably gnostic in its origin) and a highly personalized one at that.

The grail lore or myth that is spun in this film betrays the indebtedness to an array of sources. A brief survey of the grail story as portrayed in *Indiana Jones and the Last Crusade* will be helpful in sifting through the vast number of grail antecedents—or the "grail murk" we discussed earlier. The history of the grail as it is recounted in this film begins with Indiana's first interview with Donovan. The latter unveils a stone tablet or marker and asks Indiana to examine it. Indiana uses his archaeological training to identify it—"Sandstone, Latin, Christian symbol, mid-twelfth century"—and then continues to read it. It is part of a map that points to the Canyon of the Crescent Moon, a place "North of Ankara" (in Turkey) "where the cup that holds the blood of Jesus Christ resides forever." Note here the oriental connection in the ostensible location and also that the directions are at least on a stone, all suggesting that Wolfram's text is a source. Indiana and Donovan also mention that the pseudo relic, the holy grail, was the chalice used at the Last Supper, entrusted to Joseph of Arimathea. Indiana pauses and, still the skeptic, remarks, "The Arthurian legend. I've heard that one before." That the grail is *The Grail*—of the Last Supper and the receptacle of the crucified Christ's blood—eliminates Chrétien as its primary source and suggests that some derivative of Robert de Boron must be the looked to instead. Likewise, the source cannot be Wolfram's work because his grail is a stone and not a cup, although the oriental components of the film surely do derive from his grail romance. The point is that the film has begun its imaginative fusion of sources to create an original tale that is, nonetheless, an amalgam of previous grail stories. We add to the oriental and occult material the secret society of which Kazim is a member, and we clearly see a nonorthodox Christian influence operating in the film, an influence that would also seem to derive from Wolfram.

Donovan and Indiana continue with their version of the grail history. Three brothers, knights of the First Crusade, made a pact to protect the grail. One, the most valiant, stayed behind as the grail's guardian and protector—a role, it turns out, he must play until one stronger and at least his equal in worth comes to replace him. He is the knight whom Indiana meets once he passes the three tests. Of the two remaining brothers, each carried a marker, half of a map that would lead posterity to the grail; but only one brother survived the return journey to France. He told the story to a Franciscan friar, who in turn transcribed it. Donovan's possession of one of these markers proves that the story is true.

The second marker is the one Donovan wants to recover, and he believes it to be in Venice. Led by the copious notes mailed to him by Dr. Jones, Indiana finds this to be so. He and Elsa Schneider discover the second marker in the Venetian catacombs, hidden in the tomb of the third brother, a knight named Sir Richard. With both markers they now have a map, but they need to decipher the clues and, more importantly, overcome the challenges or obstacles present at the site of the grail's location. The clue to the location of the second marker underscores the occult aspect of the grail and its keepers—freemasons ostensibly built encoded messages in their religious buildings, and this film uses that lore for its story. Much of this information about the occult powers of the grail and secret organizations to protect it can be found in works like Ravenscroft's *Spear of Destiny* as well as in bestsellers like *Holy Blood, Holy Grail.*

When Donovan shoots Dr. Jones at point blank range, Indiana must undertake the perilous journey to retrieve the chalice; he must pass the three challenges that prevent the unworthy from entering the chamber where the holy grail is kept. Dr. Jones had found the solution to these challenges in the "Chronicle of St. Anselm" and added them to his extensive grail notes. Each of these challenges is in itself an oracular amphiboly that must be deciphered in order to avoid sudden death. Indeed, the first sight to greet the Jones party when they arrive at the outer site where the grail resides is a decapitated head that rolls to their feet. Donovan and Elsa, who had arrived first, had hired poor natives of the region to use as cannon fodder against these formidable challenges. None has met with success.

As Indiana faces each challenge, his dying father meets each with him, imaginatively, and we can sometimes hear his mutters as he repeats the amphiboly and offers advice to his son. Donovan says to Indiana as he begins this trek, "It's time to ask yourself what you believe," and indeed, the skeptical hero at the opening of the film is now the desperate son who must rely upon his intellectual prowess in order to save his father. The stakes are high, and Indiana knows it. What guides him through the treacherous maze is obviously the training his father had provided him in the past.

The first challenge, known as the "Breath of God," has as its clue "Only the penitent man shall pass." Indiana interprets the clue correctly, uttering to himself, "The penitent man is humble; he kneels before God," and lowers his head in time to avoid being decapitated. The second test, identified as the "Word of God," reads, "Only in the footsteps of God will he proceed." Indiana is faced with a series of marble slabs inscribed with Latin letters; he understands that he must step only on the letters that spell God's name ("Proceed in the footsteps of the word," in this case "Jehovah.") Why Jehovah is associated with the grail is unclear; this is only more evidence of the random assemblage of sources the film uses. Indiana makes a near fatal error when he does not immediately recall that in the Latin alphabet "j" is equal to "i" (a blunder scarcely credible for an archaeology professor, even one under duress, given that he had successfully translated a Latin text earlier in the film). In the nick of time, however, Indiana recognizes his error and proceeds to the last challenge, known as the "Path of God." As we might expect, it is the most perilous. The clue is that "Only in a leap from the lion's head will he prove his worth," which entails literally stepping off a precipice into a chasm and hence to certain death. Quite understandably, Indiana Jones hesitates, gulps, reminds himself "You must believe," and then takes the leap of faith, triggering and landing on a trap bridge that leads to where the grail dwells. Note that he takes the step solely in his desperation to save his father's life, thus making his "leap" a personal one of familial love rather than religious impulse.

Clearly this arduous testing of the hero's spiritual preparation and worth prevents a nonbeliever from achieving entrance into the sanctum. And although Donovan and Elsa have followed Indiana, they follow to no avail, since both meet their deaths. Kazim was right—to the unrighteous the grail grants nothing but eternal damnation. Indiana, now a true grail knight himself, brings the cup to his father and heals him with it. Once Elsa's greed brings about the cataclysmic earthquake, the ancient Grail Knight sadly waves good-bye to Jones and company, who prepare to make a hasty departure.

The conclusion reinforces our reading of this work as postmodern. Both Indiana and his father have partaken of the holy cup, while Marcus Brody and their guide, Sallah (played by John Rhys-Davies, who is in all three "Indiana" films) have witnessed its healing power. Yet the film ends with a jocular exchange between Indiana and his father, as though their relationship had not been altered or they themselves changed by this experience. A running joke throughout the film is that Dr. Jones insists upon calling Indiana junior, which clearly irritates Indiana himself. Only once, when Dr. Jones pleads with his son to relinquish his desire to retrieve the cup from the precipice does he call Indiana by his preferred name, Indiana, the name of the family dog: "Indiana, let it go." He thereby does indeed save his son's life, as his has just been saved by his son. Here, in the film's coda, Indiana asks, "What did you find, Dad?" To which Dr. Jones replies cryptically and perhaps also a bit smugly, "Illumination." This is the one and only word uttered by a character who has devoted his life to the search that has culminated here, a search in which he has nearly died. "And what did you find, junior?" There is no reply from Indiana, just the joke about how he was named after the family dog. Whatever transformative power the grail may have had, it is too subjective and personal to share, even between father and son.

As they are unable to discuss the intimacies of sex (each had slept with Elsa Schneider), so their spiritual lives remain incommunicable as well.

Indeed, their inability to talk to each other is emphasized several times in the film: At the beginning, when Dr. Jones senior refuses to let the young Indiana speak until he has finished his recitation; when, on the German zeppelin, the father asks Indiana what he wants to talk about and this silences Indiana; when their affairs with Elsa Schneider are revealed; and when in the end Dr. Jones comments to Indiana about the incommunicable "illumination" the grail has provided. The equivalencies established here suggest the realm of the fetish.[15] Each man is in some sense an island, even remaining a stranger to his father or son. Each individual is forced to acknowledge that his understanding of others must inevitably be incomplete; there is no book that, in the space of a few hundred pages, can provide the perfect simulacrum of the many years of a person's life. The impossibility of perfect understanding, however, does not negate the possibility of partial understanding. But there seems to be a much bigger issue at work: It is not the enigma that lies between a fetishist and the "reader" of the fetish, but the greater enigma that lies between the fetishist and the Unnamable. That is certainly the message of the Gnostic vision: We are all strangers here, erecting memorials to our own incompressible, unavowable memories.

The Fisher King (1991)

The Fisher King (1991) is also centered on the quest for a spiritual identity that cannot, at last, be shared with another. Written by Richard LaGravenese, the film was directed by Monty Python's Terry Gilliam, who also directed *Monty Python and the Holy Grail*, discussed in chapter 2. Aspects of this film useful for our discussion of the postmodern quest are its treatment of the grail and the source of the idea for the film as identified by its writer.

As we mentioned in chapter 1 in our discussion of the transmission of the Arthurian legend, the grail strand of the legend gained popularity during the 1980s, yet its popularizers are usually not difficult to identify. Richard LaGravenese, the script's writer, remarks in *The Fisher King: The Book of the Film*:

I then happened to read a psychology book by Robert Johnson called *He* in which the Fisher King, or Grail, myth—when paralleled with the male psyche—becomes the story of every man's psychological and spiritual growth. Johnson uses Jungian analysis to explain how a boy, at some specific turning point in his journey from innocence to adulthood, experiences a metaphysical awakening—either consciously or unconsciously. . . . During a brief personal moment of mystical empowerment, the boy "touches" God or the God within—the part of ourselves that is our direct link to the divine; our souls. But being young boys, our innocence, eagerness and naïveté leave us unable to cope with or even understand the enormity of this experience—and so the experience burns us—leaving a "Fisher King" wound. (124)

It is always helpful when a writer shares his or her source of inspiration, and LaGravenese's remarks are revealing for several reasons. First, the source for the grail story in *The Fisher King* is a popular psychology book that applies a Jungian analysis to the medieval legend. The mode of transmission is a "popular" and not an academic one, even though Johnson is a practicing psychologist.[16] (The style of his book, for instance, is simple, with very few technical terms; Johnson uses archetypes and not case studies, and the entire text—there *are* no footnotes—is eighty-five pages, including its three-page Introduction.) This confirms our belief that it is more often through popular than academic outlets that the Arthurian legend is kept alive. Moreover, in his Introduction to *He* Johnson states:

We will be using the French version, which is the earliest written account, taken from a poem by Chrétien de Troyes. There is also a German version by Wolfram von Eschenbach. The English version, *Le Morte d'Arthur* by Thomas Malory, comes from the fourteenth century; but by that time it had been elaborated a great deal. The French version is simpler, more direct and nearer to the unconscious; therefore it is more helpful for our purposes. (x)

Here Johnson reveals a careless disregard for historical accuracy (does he mean that Malory's *source* is fourteenth century, since Malory himself wrote in the fifteenth century?) assuming that his audience neither knows nor cares about such trivial details as dates of composition. Here also, interestingly, Johnson freely "adds" to Chrétien's version, borrowing from other sources to create a story more amenable to his Jungian analysis, without bothering to acknowledge when he has done so. Most telling is his inclusion of the episode in which a boy king is burned by a hot salmon, a detail that LaGravenese discarded, arguing: "I replaced the salmon with a vision of the Grail because it was a more accessible symbol" (124).

Indeed, the salmon story does not derive from a "Christian source" at all but from an ancient Irish story, the "Salmon of Wisdom," recounted, for instance, by Jessie Weston in *From Ritual to Romance* (130). Johnson incorporates the story because it is illustrative of the psychological approach he is using. LaGravenese, on the other hand, understands instinctively that the grail has become a popular, recognizable object. What a long way we have come from George Lucas's substitution of the Ark of the Covenant for the grail—at this point the grail is familiar enough to replace the antiquated (i. e. , pagan) Irish salmon of wisdom.

Another significant factor is that for LaGravenese a Jungian reading of the legend means that one must emphasize in this case not the universal and archetypal, but the personalized nature of God, as he puts it, "the God within," or "a brief personal moment of mystical empowerment." This bears a striking resemblance to Marcus Brody's earlier statement in *Indiana Jones and the Last Crusade*, "The search for the cup of Christ is the search for the divine in all of us"—surely a postmodern and not a medieval sentiment. Spiritual enlightenment thus becomes a question of expanded consciousness, and the quest for the holy grail cannot but represent self-knowledge, which in Jungian terms can be discerned through one's dreams.

It is also fascinating that the key episode in the film, which features a version of the grail myth recounted in a monologue by Parry (Robin Williams), became, as LaGravenese states, "a real community effort, as everyone had an idea about what it meant, or what it should mean. I even got a call from two Los Angeles location people I'd never met, asking why I had cut certain lines from the version they'd read. They then sent me a tape recorded version of the Grail Myth" (133). This suggests that grail stories are both plentiful and popular, and also highly personal.

In the same vein, LaGravenese recalls how each of the artists involved in the film had varied ideas about the grail story. For instance, Terry Gilliam remembered that the fertility of the land was tied to the well-being of the king. LaGravenese himself was more interested in the Jungian psychology. Robin Williams and Jeff Bridges had other ideas and lines from previous drafts that they wanted to be included; but after much debate, LaGravenese recalls, it was decided to tell "the simplest story and let the audience find their own meaning. With Robin's help, I put together what sounded coherent and would be the simplest to play" (133). There is no orthodoxy here, and the "relic" itself is now entirely secularized. It is a goblet with an inscription that reads: "TO LITTLE LANNIE CARMICHAEL FOR ALL HIS HARD WORK . . . P.S. 247 CHRISTMAS PAGEANT 1932," evidently suggesting that he batted or bowled a "247" (118). The connection of the grail with sports is reminiscent of *The Natural* and perhaps even a wry commentary on it.

The Fisher King uses the grail quest to tell a postmodern story about the emptiness of contemporary existence with its obsession for economic and social power; it is about the search to fill the spiritual void created by such vain pursuits. The film's two protagonists are the cynical, narcissistic "shock-jock" and radio talk-show host Jack Lucas (Jeff Bridges) and a traumatized ex-professor and Arthurian enthusiast, Henry Sagan, whose alter identity is known as Parry. Their paths cross when the obnoxious and irresponsible Jack unwittingly goads a psychopathic killer, with whom he regularly converses on his show, into a bloody murder-suicide spree, which results in the violent shotgun death of Parry's wife. This murder occurs before Parry's very eyes, and it is this trauma that induces Parry's amnesia.

After this event Jack, devastated by his own power to control people's lives adversely, quits his talk-show radio job and indulges his own feelings of self-pity and doubt. He drinks heavily and relies upon the love of a video-store owner, Anne (Mercedes Ruehl). One night, in a drunken stupor, Jack strays into dangerous urban territory, is nearly set on fire by two punks, but is rescued by a crazed group of homeless inhabitants of this subterranean haunt, led by Parry. Parry then takes Jack to his underground hovel. The next morning Jack awakes with a terrible hangover, only to have Parry inform him that he is the "one" who is destined to win the grail. Jack is, of course, startled by these rantings, and it is only later, through an accidental conversation with the building supervisor where Parry lives, that he learns why Parry is insane, thus discovering his own role in the tragedy of Parry's existence. But this is one of the many turning points for Jack: When he begins to feel responsible for Parry, his arduous spiritual odyssey is initiated. In terms of the story Robert Johnson tells, Jack has reached into the fire to touch the salmon, but he lacks the spiritual wisdom to avoid being burned. Now he must try to recover from this wound; but until he can overcome his own selfishness, this is impossible.

Jack and Parry share dual roles in the film, that of the wounded king and that of the fool who undertakes the task of healing him. LaGravenese's comments about these complex characters is enlightening:

Parry is, at first, the fool who will lead Jack on his soul's journey. As the movie progresses—especially in the third act—they switch roles; Parry becomes the wounded king and Jack must play the fool to steal the Grail that will save him. I hoped to convey that each man is both fool and wounded king. In other words, you don't need a Parry to find your higher self—he's already inside you. (125)

It is important to observe, though, that until Jack can own up to his own role in Parry's tragedy, he's incapable of undertaking the journey to find "his higher self." What is more, even after he becomes aware of it, he takes several spiritual "wrong turns," reverting to his old dead self. We must stress that *The Fisher King* is first and foremost a story of male friendship and the mutual dependency suggested by that term. LaGravenese did not turn to Johnson's other works, *She: Understanding Feminine Psychology,* nor to *We: Understanding the Psychology of Romantic Love,* but instead his source of inspiration was about one man who heals another, what might now be recognized as male bonding. Thus, although the film does portray in some detail the love interests of Parry and Jack, the romances are not the focus (nor do they seem to be much indebted to Arthurian models usually activated by Hollywood versions of the legend, since there is no triangle and since they both end happily). This is why only Parry and Jack are involved in the episode discussed above in which Parry informs Jack that he is the "elect," or the one the grail has called to its service; the central episode that occurs at night in Central Park, where Parry recounts to Jack the film's version of the grail story; and Jack's "healing" of Parry by retrieving the "chalice" from a Madison Avenue mansion.

What is more, *The Fisher King* does not conclude with the union of Parry and his new love-object, Lydia (Amanda Plummer), once his consciousness and sanity are restored, nor does it end when Jack and Anne are at last reunited. The final scene underscores that this is a film about a spiritual odyssey undertaken by two males whose lives are, quite by chance, inextricably joined—for the duration of the film and beyond. Jack and Parry are once again portrayed in Central Park at night, but this time while they stargaze, the previously inhibited Jack now joins Parry by stripping as well. If we examine each of these key scenes in detail, we can discern with some clarity the film's central vision and its portrayal of the postmodern quest for meaning. We have already explored the first of these episodes, in which Jack and Parry meet and the latter informs Jack that he is destined to be the Grail Knight. Even here Jack resembles more closely a wounded king than a healing knight, but the roles reverse more dramatically as the film proceeds.

The heart of the film is surely the scene in which Parry relates to Jack the story of the Fisher King. The two are wandering around in Central Park at night; much to Jack's dismay, Parry takes off his clothes: "You can't do this! This is New York. Nobody lies naked in a field in New York!" exclaims Jack, who then goes on to castigate himself and question his own sanity: "I mean the man talks to invisible people—he sees an invisible horse—and he's naked in the middle of Central Park. I should be surprised? I'm not surprised. I'm fucking outta my mind to even be here!"

Jack cannot be persuaded to disrobe, but he does lie down next to Parry, who then commences with his story of the wounded king. He admits there are several versions, but that he is most fond of the one in which the Fisher King, as a boy, receives a vision of the holy grail and is told that he is God's chosen one. The boy, however, is blinded by his own hope for power and glory; convinced that he is invincible, he tries to reach into the flame that surrounds the vision of the grail, but he is burned instead. This leaves him wounded and ashamed of his rash action. When he matures and becomes king, he tries to recover the grail, but each failure to do so only deepens his wound. Subsequently, the land he governs begins also to fail and his people starve. The king himself, "sick with experience," starts to die. His knights try in vain to heal him, but one day a fool enters his court. When the fool sees the king's suffering, he asks how he can help, and the ailing ruler says, "I need a sip of water to cool my throat." The fool takes a nearby cup, fills it with water, and offers the king a drink, which subsequently heals him. And when he looks at the cup, the king sees that it is the holy grail, although it appears to be ordinary and he has never recognized it as such. Astonished, the king asks the fool how he could succeed where he and his best knights failed. The fool replies, "I don't know. I only knew you were thirsty." And Parry concludes: "And for the first time since he was a boy, the king felt more than a man—not because he was touched by God's glory . . . but rather by the compassion of a fool."

This closely resembles the version of the story recounted by Johnson in *He*, although LaGravenese substitutes the grail for the salmon. It is actually an amalgam of versions, with an emphasis upon failure caused by the vain pursuit of power and glory, no doubt in order to speak more specifically to Jack's own psychic wound. Here, we see, Parry is the fool who can effect Jack's return to health, but only by serving as the impetus for Jack himself to become a fool— willingly scaling the wall of a millionaire's mansion decked out in bizarre regalia, breaking and entering it to recover a trophy with little inherent value, and then visiting the bedside of the comatose Parry, when he plops the "grail" on Parry's chest in the hopes of waking him. Only by healing Parry can Jack heal

himself, and only by encouraging Jack to play the quester knight can Parry the
fool-wounded king recover his health. In fact, Parry's role as fool is a the result
of his dissociated mental condition, a result of the trauma of the gunman's attack
and his wife's death. His impaired memory prevents him from remembering the
trauma of seeing his wife's head explode. Jack, on the other hand, must humble
himself and take on the fool's role—willingly risk being made a fool of—in
order to heal both Parry and himself.

Each time Parry is relaxed or begins to experience happiness, his memory
threatens to return, to punish him with the horror of his wife's death. This
occurs in the ironic form of a phantasmagoric figure that Parry and the audience
can see, but the other characters cannot. This figure, the Red Knight, appears
when Jack tries to remind Parry of who he really is: "You don't belong in the
streets. You're an intelligent man. . . . You're a teacher. . . . You were a teacher
at Hunter College. Can't you remember?" Parry screams as the vision of the Red
Knight appears, but as Jack comes to Parry's assistance, he is able to hold this
figure at bay, thus only reinforcing Parry's conviction that Jack is "the one" to
recover the grail from its selfish Madison Avenue owner. Parry now feels
protected against the knight and starts out in vain pursuit of him, while an
astonished Jack runs helplessly after him. The Red Knight also threatens to
appear directly after Parry has recited his Fisher King story because telling it
seems to prompt his memory about his former self even though he remembers
that self as another person: "The Fisher King myth has a lot of derivations. I
remember I was at this weekend seminar at Princeton once, and there was this
one speaker. . . Henry Sa . . ." He stops short because he begins to see the Red
Knight; Parry's real name was Henry Sagan, and his scholarly interest was grail
literature. The last time the Red Knight appears is directly after Parry has
enjoyed his enchanted evening with Lydia, Jack, and Anne in a Chinese
restaurant. He has walked Lydia home, confessed his love for her, and extracted
from her a kiss and a promise that she will see him again. As soon as he finds
happiness, the thunder of hooves is heard and the knight reappears. Parry
whispers to the menacing figure, "Let me have this," but to no avail. As he is
pursued, Parry remembers the inducement for his current amnesia—the traumatic
witnessing of his wife's murder. Although two hoods eventually cause the
physical injury that lands Parry in a hospital emergency room, hallucinating, he
sees himself as a victim of the Red Knight and willingly submits to a fate that
has tormented him for so long. It is not his physical wound that endangers his
life but the comatose state induced by his recollection of the trauma. Evidently
Parry's subconscious is blocking his happiness by sending the Red Knight to
torment him with guilt and anxiety.

The Red Knight is derived from Johnson's book *He*, where Johnson's discussion of what this figure represents is very helpful in understanding his
function in the film. The naïve fool Parsifal, has arrived at Arthur's court an
aspiring knight himself, and requests of the king the Red Knight's armor and
horse. Arthur and his court laugh at this request because of the Red Knight's

strength and audacity. He had taken the holy chalice and had flung a flagon of wine into Queen Guinevere's face as an insult; no one could prevent him from acting as he pleased. Thus, Arthur grants the young Parsifal's boon, saying that he may have the armor and horse if he can get it. Likewise, when Parsifal asks the Red Knight for is armor, the latter is amused and invites him to try to get it. Parsifal mortally wounds him in the eye with his dagger, thus laying claim to the armor. The significance of this episode in the grail story, according to Johnson, is that when Parsifal slays the Red Knight "he relocates a very large sum of energy from the Red Knight, that is instinct, to himself, as ego" (22). Johnson argues that this marks a rite of passage from adolescence to manhood. He also finds it significant that although Parsifal fights many opponents, the Red Knight is the only one he slays. The battle with aggressive instinct is the one that each boy must win in order to become a man. Johnson points out that this battle may be fought outwardly, as in a sports competition, or it may be internalized, such as when an individual struggles with the impulse to be a bully. "The Red Knight is the shadow side of masculinity, the negative, potentially destructive power" that must be subdued for maturity to occur (24). This power, though, cannot be repressed but only rechanneled. It is "his aggressiveness," or a "masculine power" each adolescent male needs in order "to make his way through the mature world" (24).

Parry must subsume the Red Knight, not vanquish him, which is why he alternately runs from him and pursues him. He must internalize the violence he has witnessed, but not forget it. If the Red Knight is his persecutor, he is also Parry's past—a reminder of the aggressive violence he experienced in the murder of his wife and the past Parry must come to grips with in order to be whole again. Parry cannot continue on life's journey but will remain frozen, an effigy of his former self in his subterranean world, until he can remember and cope with the source of his traumatic amnesia. Only when he is healed by the grail— that is, when he wakes and says to Jack, "I had this dream . . . I was married to this beautiful woman . . . I really miss her, Jack. Is that okay? Can I miss her now?"—is he free to resume his identity and begin a life with Lydia.

That only Parry can see the Red Knight, that only he can hear the "little people" who inform him that Jack is "the one" to bring about his recovery, and that the grail is a trophy that resides on a shelf in a New York manison all suggests the postmodern nature of this film. Its attitude toward the grail is not one of irreverence, as it is in *Monty Python and the Holy Grail*; instead, it strives to point to the highly private nature of the spiritual quest and the subjective aspect of what the grail is. If it is a bowling trophy to everyone else, no matter. To Parry, and then subsequently to Jack, it is the self-defined object of desire. More important, it is in the quest itself and not in the "grail" that redemption lies. Each person must achieve wholeness in a different way, although the journey itself is a universal one.

In the final scene of *The Fisher King*, Parry has recovered the knowledge of his former self and Jack has recovered an innocence that must hearken back to his prelapsarian self, before his values became corrupted by power and fame. For the pair find themselves in Central Park, not with their lady loves, but together, and this time Jack is naked too. Moreover, Jack joins Parry in "cloudbusting," an imaginary exercise by which they believe it is possible to move the clouds in the sky through an exertion of the will. Jack says to Parry as they gaze at the clouds in the sky: "Hey, they're moving, am I doing that?" which suggests a renewed and childlike faith in himself, one tempered, however, by the remembrance of having thrust his hand in the hot flame.

To understand as postmodern the portrayal of the spiritual quest and of the pseudo-relic, the holy grail, as portrayed in the films discussed in this chapter, one need only compare the films with other, earlier Hollywood productions that also feature the quest. As we discussed in chapter 3, for instance, *Knights of the Round Table* employs the quest for the grail but in a very conventional treatment of that strand of the legend. Even a film as late as *Excalibur* treats the quest, albeit in a conflated and Westonesque fashion, in a manner that has much more in common with its portrayal in medieval narrative than in those films that follow it by only a few years. Perhaps once the story of the grail quest and the holy cup gained wide circulation, Hollywood filmmakers saw it as a vehicle through which to emphasize the individual's search for meaning and the difficulty of attaining insight in a world that would seem to hold so many obstacles.

NOTES

1. We of course recognize that juvenile delinquency films did not originate in the 1950s, but earlier Hollywood juvenile delinquency films generally depicted delinquents confined to the slums of large cities—most often New York City. In the 1950s, however, delinquency was no longer confined to the lower classes, but extended to the middle classes (e.g. , *Rebel Without a Cause*).

2. We are indebted to James Gilbert's chapter "Juvenile Delinquency Films" in *A Cycle of Outrage: America's Reaction to the Juvenile Delinquent in the 1950s* (Oxford: Oxford University Press, 1986); and to Jim Morton's articles, "Biker Films" (140-142), "Juvenile Delinquency Films" (143-145) in the issue of *Re/Search* 10 (1986) devoted to "Incredibly Strange Films." Incidentally, Ken Russell's rarely seen short, *Knights on Bikes* (1956), may have served as the inspirational source for Romero's film. See Thomas R. Atkins, ed., *Ken Russell* (New York: Monarch Press, 1976).

3. See Mark Thomas McGee, *Fast and Furious: The Story of American International Pictures* (Jefferson, N.C.: McFarland, 1984). See also Jim Morton's "Beach Party Films" (146–147) in *Re/Search* 10 (1986).

4. In his essay "Arthurian Film and the Tyranny of Tradition," Lacy compares Eric Rohmer's *Perceval le Gallois* with *Knightriders*: "If I find Romero's film considerably less engaging and admirable than Rohmer's, it is simply that *Knightriders* is the product of a less gifted artist. Yet, unless we are simply offended by the concept and context of Romero's work, it is apparent that he is more creative in his treatment of the Arthurian story—as inspiration, as a flourishing legend rather than an artifact—than is the French filmmaker. It is not simply that Romero has produced something idiosyncratic, although he has surely done that, but that he has chosen an

approach that allows him to build on the legend without becoming its slave" (*Arthurian Interpretations* 4:1 [Fall 1989]: 81). What is puzzling about these remarks is their apparent contradiction. For it is unclear how Romero can be "a less gifted artist" than Rohmer when, in fact, by the essay's own criteria and admission Romero's is the more creative film in its use of the legend in that it does contain the innovations necessary to move from one medium to another, whereas Rohmer's efforts are limited to a transposition from narrative to film. As T. S. Eliot averred, "Immature poets imitate. Mature poets steal." The same might be said of filmmakers.

5. It is interesting that in their study *From Scythia to Camelot: A Radical Reassessment of the Legends of King Arthur, the Knights of the Round Table, and the Holy Grail*, C. Scott Littleton and Linda A. Malcor theorize that the character of Lancelot originated with the Alans in southwestern Gaul and trace the etymology of Lancelot's name as either deriving from "(A)lanz-lot," meaning "the Alans' parcel of land" or from "(A)lans" and "Lot," meaning the "Alans of Lot"—those who lived in the area near the Lot River in southwestern Gaul (98). (See Garland Reference Library of the Humanities, vol. 1795 (New York: Garland Publishing, 1994).

6. The same might be said for Willy Loman in Arthur Miller's *Death of a Salesman*. If one sees Willy's suicide as his admission of defeat, or more particularly of the defeat of his dream, then his is not properly a tragedy. But Willy goes to any extent to protect his dream—what Miller calls his dignity—and believes that by sacrificing his own life his dream will live on through his son Biff. Willy convinces himself that if he has the fifty-thousand-dollar life insurance policy behind him, he can transfer his dream to Biff. "That boy will be magnificent!" he tells himself. Thus his suicide reveals not a defeated man but the triumph of his dream and thus, as Miller asserts, the play contains the optimism necessary for tragedy, even for the "common man." See Miller's important essays on the subject, especially "Tragedy and the Common Man" and "The Nature of Tragedy," reprinted in *The Theater Essays of Arthur Miller* (New York: Viking, 1978). It is also no coincidence that both Willy and Billy meet their end with a crash, a preferred method of death in American literature, perhaps because it offers rich and varied metaphorical possibilities.

7. Harriet's character may be a partial model for Susan Sarandon's role in *Bull Durham*. Although the latter character has much humor and is greatly expanded, both are precociously well-read, ardent idealists—female quixotics who believe in the power of the word. Harriet is not sane, however, whereas Susan Sarandon's character is possessed of a healthy dose of common sense. Harriet is apparently so in love with glory and fame, obviously influenced by her love of heroic literature, that she is willing to commit murder and then suicide to attain it. The common sense and spirit of the character played by Susan Sarandon are reminiscent of Maggie in *Cat on a Hot Tin Roof*, as is the sexuality she exudes, although her love of baseball and sublimated ego raise the concept of baseball to the sublime, much the way Harriet's warped sense of heroism did in *The Natural*.

8. In his book *Skywalking: The Life and Films of George Lucas*, Dale Pollock avers that when, in 1975, Lucas met filmmaker Phil Kaufman and told him of his idea for the "Indiana Jones" movies—"a 1930s-era college professor/playboy hero, a cross between Clark Gable and Dick Powell, who battled the Nazis by day and squired beautiful women in diaphanous gowns to fancy nightclubs in the evening"—Kaufman "saw a way to combine the idea with the legend of the Lost Ark of the Covenant, detailed in *Spear of Destiny*, a book about Adolf Hitler's fascination with religious artifacts" (222). Although Pollock's book, published in 1982, precedes *Indiana Jones and the Last Crusade* by some seven years, nonetheless, he must surely be mistaken here, confusing his artifacts. *The Spear of Destiny*, Trevor Ravenscroft's 1973 bestseller, is not concerned with the Ark of the Covenant but with the recovery of the spear of Longinus, which purportedly pierced the side of the crucified Christ and thus

possessed occult powers. It is much more closely allied with grail lore (the cup also contained the drops of Christ's blood and like the spear was passed down from generation to generation) than to the Ark of the Covenant. George Lucas was not the only artist influenced by Ravenscroft's book, however. No doubt author James Herbert wrote the horror novel *The Spear* (1978) drawing heavily on Ravenscroft's ideas.

9. Note that we are not concerned here with the putative truth of these two texts. To be sure, the texts base their rather audacious arguments on hearsay and "evidence" that for many scholars seems unsatisfactory because it cannot be verified. Rather, we are concerned with the fact that however "impurely," the books keep public interest in the grail alive. For other works that present controversial views regarding Mary Magdalene and the grail legend, see Marjorie M. Malvern, *Venus in Sackcloth: The Magdalen's Origins and Metamorphosis* (Carbondale: Southern Illinois UP, 1975), a work that precedes by some years *Holy Blood, Holy Grail*, and see also *Mary Magdalen: Myth and Metaphor*, Susan Haskins (New York: Harper Collins, 1993).

10. The result is a film that by critical acclaim exceeded the previous two "Indiana Jones" movies. *The Variety Movie Guide* asserts that it is "more cerebral than the first two Indiana Jones films," and that "the Harrison Ford–Sean Connery father-and-son team gives *Last Crusade* unexpected emotional depth, reminding us that real film magic is not in special effects" (294).

11. Weston's views have never been dismissed entirely by the scholarly world. On the contrary, subsequent studies have served to corroborate many of her tenants. See, for instance, Silvestro Fiore, "Les origines orientales de la legende du Graal," *Cahiers de civilisation medievale* 10 (1967), 207–219, in which the author draws analogies between the Perceval story and that of the Egyptian god Horus.

12. The prevailing view that the Cathars participated in the Western expression of body-hatred has been challenged by Ezra Pound, a serious scholar of Provençal and Troubadour culture. Pound argued that the Cathars embodied the spirit of classical paganism that survived Church domination for centuries. The Troubadour poets, therefore, might well have viewed the body and the senses as vehicles for religious experience. Thus, they and the Cathars would have been anti-ascetics; since the Cathars were persecuted and driven from southern France, however, they had no public voice nor did they write their own history. See Robert Casillo, *The Genealogy of Demons: Anti-Semitism, Fascism, and the Myths of Ezra Pound* (Evanston: Northwestern University Press, 1988), especially chapters 2 and 16. For additional information on Pound's thinking see John Kimsey's "The Code of Love: Troubadours, Cathars, and Ezra Pound," in *Gnosis* 18, Winter 1991: 24–31.

13. Morris Berman dismisses Ravenscroft's book. About Ravenscroft's claims he writes: "Ravenscroft . . . claimed that Hitler took peyote; that under the leadership of Dietrich Eckart the Thule Gesellchaft performed occult rituals on selected victims; and that Eckart opened the centers of Hitler's astral (third) body. No evidence whatsoever is cited for these claims, which are completely outlandish" (279).

14. In the Eastern connection and especially the Wolfram influence, as we can see in the story recounted by Donovan about the three knights of the First Crusade.

15. Our position is that the inability to communicate the meaning of the fetish would seem to be essential for a true fetishist. Our understanding of the fetish differs from that put forth by Freud. The later Freud seemed to conclude that the fetishist was not a solipsist. He argues, in *An Outline of Psycho-Analysis,* in his discussion of the fetishist, that "the detachment of the ego from the reality of the external world has never succeeded completely" (60; see also 61). Our position, however, is that Freud most certainly did *not* show, finally, that the fetishist is not a solipsist; he simply defined the fetish as "a compromise formed with the help of displacement" (*Outline* 60) of cathexis from the instinctual object to some signifying object, an effect that

tells us nothing about whether this *signifier as such* is understood by one, ten, a hundred, or one hundred million people. For instance, the example of the foot-fetishist in *Introductory Lectures on Psychoanalysis* provides no help given the narrative's glaring lacunae, as he simply recounts the (illusory?) scene of origin of the fetish, though this explanation tells us nothing of the meaning of the fetish (348–349). He concedes, in "Fetishism" (1927), that it is not always possible "to ascertain the determination of every fetish" (201) though the impossibility of this is unrelated to the critical issue of the meaning of the fetish. What is the fetish? An enduring material object, X, that acts as a signifier of some other object, process or relationship, Y. Fetish is thus to be distinguished from ritual as object is from event, the spatial axis of a related pair whose temporal axis is ritual: The Sacrament of Holy Communion is the ritual, the transubstantiating wine and wafer the fetish. The signified entity, Y, is, in turn, instinctually highly cathected for sexual, religious or economic reasons, or even because of some atypical neurological condition. In the fetish complex the signifier—the fetish object—in turn becomes cathected, acquiring the affective import of the instinctual object. How does the fetish object become cathected? In other words, the question is how it is possible that a signifying object (even one possessing materiality) can provide some part of the satisfaction of the instinctual object. This paradox certainly confounded Freud and would seem to be the primary reason for his interest in fetishism, especially in those cases where the fetish is unrelated to the instinctual object by metonymy, for instance, when a cowry shell is more mysterious than the female foot. Signs may be consumed but they are not nutritious.

16. Johnson's book was first published in 1974; the publishing history is as follows: *He* (King of Prussia: Religious Publishing, 1974); *He* (New York: Harper & Row, 1977); *He* (revised edition) (New York: Harper & Row, 1989).

Filmography

Month and year of release for the films released before 1970 were taken from the following sources: *The New York Times Directory of the Film*. New York: Arno Press/Random House, 1971; and Krafsur, Richard P., ed., *American Film Institute Catalog of Motion Pictures: Feature Films, 1961-1970*. 2 vols. New York: R. R. Bowker, 1976.

A Connecticut Yankee (Fox Film Corporation, April 1931; 93 mins.) Director: David Butler. Producer: William Fox. Adaptation and Dialogue: William Conselman, based on Mark Twain's novel [and *A Connecticut Yankee at King Arthur's Court*, Fox Film, 1921]. Cinematography: Ernest Palmer. Settings: William Darling. *Cast*: Will Rogers (Hank Martin); William Farnum (King Arthur); Frank Albertson (Clarence); Maureen O'Sullivan (Alisande) Brandon Hurst (Sir Sagramore); Myrna Loy (Morgan Le Fay); Mitchell Harris (Merlin).

A Connecticut Yankee in King Arthur's Court (Paramount, April 1949; 106 mins.) Director: Tay Garnett. Producer: Robert Fellows. Screenplay: Edmund Beloin. Cinematography: Ray Rennahan (Technicolor). Art Direction: Hans Dreier, Roland Anderson. Editor: Archie Marshek. Music Score: Victor Young. Songs: Johnny Burke (Lyrics) and James Van Heusen (Music). *Cast*: Bing Crosby (Hank Martin); Rhonda Fleming (Lady Alisande/Sandy); William Bendix (Sir Sagramoure/Clarence); Cedric Hardwicke (King Arthur); Murvyn Vye (Merlin); Virginia Field (Morgan Le Fay); Henry Wilcoxon (Sir Lancelot); Richard Webb (Sir Galahad).

Camelot (Warner Brothers/Seven Arts, October 1967; 180 mins.) Director: Joshua Logan. Producer: Jack L. Warner. Screenplay: Alan Jay Lerner. Cinematography: Richard H. Kline (Technicolor). Art Direction and Sets: Edward Carrere. Set Decoration: John W. Brown. Music: Frederick Loewe. Songs: Alan Jay Lerner and Frederick Loewe. Production Design and Costume

Design: John Truscott. Editor: Folmar Blangsted. Music Supervision: Alfred Newman. *Cast*: Richard Harris (King Arthur); Vanessa Redgrave (Guinevere); Franco Nero (Lancelot); David Hemmings (Mordred); Lionel Jeffries (King Pellinore); Laurence Naismith (Merlin); Pierre Olaf (Dap); Estelle Winwood (Lady Clarinda); Gary Marshall (Sir Lionel); Anthony Rogers (Sir Dinaden); Peter Bromilow (Sir Sagramoure); Sue Casey (Lady Sybil); Garry Marsh (Tom of Warwick).

Unidentified Flying Oddball (Walt Disney Productions, July 1979; 92 mins.) [British title: *The Spaceman in King Arthur's Court*] Director: Russ Mayberry. Producer: Ron Miller. Associate Producer: Hugh Attwooll. Screenplay: Don Tait, based on Mark Twain's novel, *A Connecticut Yankee in King Arthur's Court*. Cinematography: Paul Beeson (Technicolor). Art Director: Albert Witherick. Costume Designer: Phyllis Dalton. Editor: Peter Boita. Music: Ron Goodwin. *Cast*: Dennis Dugan (Tom Trimble/Hermes); Jim Dale (Sir Mordred); Ron Moody (Merlin); Kenneth More (King Arthur); John Le Mesurier (Sir Gawain); Rodney Bewes (Clarence); Sheila White (Alisande); Kevin Brennan (Winston); Ewen Solon (Watkins); Pat Roach (Oaf).

A Connecticut Yankee in King Arthur's Court (A Schaefer/Karpf Production [made-for-television], December 1989; 92 mins.) Director: Mel Damski. Executive Producer: Merrill H. Karpf. Producer: Graham Ford. Co-Producer: James Pulliam. Teleplay: Paul Zindel. Director of Photography: Harvey Harrison. Production Designer: Brian Eatwell. Editor: Rod Stephens. Music: William Goldstein. *Cast*: Keshia Knight Pulliam (Karen Jones) Jean Marsh (Morgana); René Auberjonois (Merlin); Emma Samms (Queen Guinevere); Whip Hubley (Lancelot); Hugo E. Blick (Mordred); Bryce Hamnet (Clarence); Michael Gross (King Arthur).

A Kid in King Arthur's Court (Walt Disney Pictures, August 1995; 90 mins.) Director: Michael Gottlieb. Executive Producer: Mark Amin. Producers: Robert L. Levy, Peter Abrahms, J. P. Guerin. Screenplay: Michael Part and Robert L. Levy. Cinematography: Elemér Ragályi. Editors: Michael Ripps, Anita Brandt-Burgoyne. Music: J.A.C. Redford. *Cast*: Thomas Ian Nicholas (Calvin Fuller); Joss Ackland (King Arthur); Art Malik (Lord Belasco); Paloma Baeza (Princess Katey); Kate Winslet (Princess Sarah); Ron Moody (Merlin); Daniel Craig (Master Kane).

Monty Python and the Holy Grail (Columbia Pictures, April 1975; 90 min.) Directors: Terry Gilliam and Terry Jones. Executive Producer: John Goldstone. Producer: Mark Forstater. Cinematography: Terry Bedford. Editor: John Hackney. Art Director: Roy Smith. Costume Designer: Hazel Pethig. Music: DeWolfe. Songs: Neil Innes. Written and Performed by: Graham Chapman, John Cleese, Terry Gilliam, Eric Idle, Terry Jones, and Michael Palin.

Knights of the Round Table (Metro-Goldwyn-Mayer, January 1954; 116 mins.) Director: Richard Thorpe. Producer: Pandro S. Berman. Screenplay:

Talbot Jennings, Jan Lustig, Noel Langley, based on Sir Thomas Malory's *Le Morte d'Arthur*. Cinematography: Freddie Young, Stephen Dade (Technicolor, CinemaScope). Editor: Frank Clarke. Art Direction: Alfred Dunge, Hans Peters. Music: Miklos Rozsa. *Cast*: Robert Taylor (Lancelot); Ava Gardner (Queen Guinevere); Mel Ferrer (King Arthur); Anne Crawford (Morgan Le Fay); Stanley Baker (Modred); Felix Aylmer (Merlin); Maureen Swanson (Elaine); Gabriel Woolf (Percival); Anthony Forwood (Gareth); Robert Urquhart (Gawaine).

Sword of Lancelot (Universal International, September 1963; 116 mins.) [Released in Great Britain in June, 1963 as *Lancelot and Guinevere*; 117 min.] Director: Cornel Wilde. Producers: Cornel Wilde and Bernard Luber. Associate Producer: George Pitcher. Screenplay: Richard Schayer and Jefferson Pascal. Cinematography: Harry Waxman (Technicolor). Editor: Frederick Wilson. Art Director: Maurice Carter. Music: Ron Goodwin. *Cast*: Cornel Wilde (Lancelot); Jean Wallace (Queen Guinevere); Brian Aherne (King Arthur); George Baker (Sir Gawaine); Archie Duncan (Sir Lamorak); Adrienne Corri (Lady Vivian); Michael Meacham (Sir Mordred); Iain Gregory (Sir Tors); Mark Dignam (Merlin); Reginald Beckwith (Sir Dagonet); John Barrie (Sir Bedivere); Richard Thorp (Sir Gareth); John Longden (King Leodogran).

First Knight (Columbia Pictures, June 1995; 112 mins.) Director: Jerry Zucker. Executive Producers: Gil Netter, Eric Rattray, Janet Zucker. Producers: Jerry Zucker and Hunt Lowry. Associate Producer: Kathryn J. McDermott. Story: Lorne Cameron and David Hoselton and William Nicholson. Screenplay: William Nicholson. Cinematography: Adam Greenberg. Production Design: John Box. Art Directors: Stephen Scott, Giles Masters. Editor: Walter Murch. Music: Jerry Goldsmith. *Cast*: Sean Connery (King Arthur); Richard Gere (Lancelot); Julia Ormond (Guinevere); Ben Cross (Malagant); Liam Cunningham (Sir Agravaine); Christopher Villiers (Sir Kay); Valentine Pelka (Sir Patrise); Colin McCormack (Sir Mador); Ralph Ineson (Ralf); John Gielgud (Oswald); Stuart Bunce (Peter); Jane Robbins (Elise); Jean Marie Coffey (Petronella); Paul Kynman (Mark); Tom Lucy (Sir Sagramoure); John Blakey (Sir Tor).

The Black Knight (Columbia Pictures, October 1954; 85 mins.) Director: Tay Garnett. Executive Producers: Irving Allen and Albert R. Broccoli. Associate Producer: Phil C. Samuel. Screenplay: Alec Coppel. Additional Dialogue by Dennis O'Keefe and Bryan Forbes. Cinematography: John Wilcox (Technicolor). Art Director: Vetchinsky. Associate Art Director: John Box. Editor: Gordon Pilkington. Music: John Addison. *Cast*: Alan Ladd (John); Patricia Medina (Lady Linet); Andre Morell (Sir Ontzlake); Harry Andrews (Earl of Yeonil); Peter Cushing (Sir Palamides); Anthony Bushell (King Arthur); Laurence Naismith (Major Domo); Patrick Troughton (King Mark); Bill Brandon (Bernard); Basil Appleby (Sir Hal); Jean Lodge (Guinevere); Pauline Jameson (Lady Yeonil); John Laurie (James).

Siege of the Saxons (Columbia Pictures, August 1963; 85 mins.) [Released in Great Britain as *King Arthur and the Siege of the Saxons*.] Director: Nathan Juran. Executive Producer: Charles H. Schneer. Producer: Jud Kinberg.

Screenplay: John Kohn and Jud Kinberg. Cinematography: Wilkie Cooper, Jack Mills (Technicolor); Art Director: Bill Constable. Editor: Maurice Rootes. Music: Laurie Johnson. *Cast*: Janette Scott (Katherine); Ronald Lewis (Robert Marshall); Ronald Howard (Edmund of Cornwall); John Laurie (Merlin); Mark Dignam (King Arthur); Jerome Willis (The Limping Man); Richard Clarke (Saxon Prince); Francis De Wolff (Blacksmith); John Gabriel (Earl of Chatham).

The Sword in the Stone (Walt Disney Studios, December 1963; 79 mins. Animated. Technicolor.) Director: Wolfgang Reitherman. Directing Animators: Frank Thomas, Milt Kahl, Ollie Johnston, John Lounsbery. Character Design: Milt Kahl, Bill Peet. Story: Bill Peet, based on *The Once and Future King* by T. H. White. Art Direction: Ken Anderson. Editor: Donald Halliday. Music: George Bruns. Songs: Richard M. Sherman and Robert B. Sherman. Voices: Sebastian Cabot, Karl Swenson, Rickie Sorensen, Junius Matthews, Ginny Tyler, Martha Wentworth, Norman Alden, Alan Napier, Richard Reitherman, Robert Reitherman.

Excalibur (Warner Brothers/Orion Pictures, May 1981; 141 mins.) Director and Producer: John Boorman. Executive Producers: Edgar F. Gross and Robert A. Eisenstein. Associate Producer: Michael Dryhurst. Screenplay: Rospo Pallenberg and John Boorman. Adapted from Malory's *Le Morte d'Arthur* by Rospo Pallenberg. Production Designer: Anthony Pratt. Cinematography: Alex Thomson. Editor: John Merritt. Costume Designer: Bob Ringwood. Original Music: Trevor Jones. *Cast*: Nigel Terry (King Arthur); Helen Mirren (Morgana); Nicholas Clay (Lancelot); Cherie Lunghi (Guenivere); Paul Geoffrey (Perceval); Nicol Williamson (Merlin); Robert Addie (Mordred); Gabriel Bryne (Uther); Keith Buckley (Uryens); Katrine Boorman (Igrayne); Liam Neeson (Gawain); Corin Redgrave (Cornwall); Niall O'Brien (Kay); Patrick Stewart (Leondegrance); Clive Swift (Ector); Clarin Hinds (Lot).

Knightriders (United Film Distribution, May 1981; 146 mins.) Director: George A. Romero. Executive Producer: Salah M. Hassanein. Associate Producer: David E. Vogel. Producer: Richard P. Rubinstein. Screenplay: George A. Romero. Production Design: Cletus Anderson. Cinematography: Michael Gornich. Music: Donald Rubinstein. *Cast*: Ed Harris (Billy); Gary Lahti (Allen); Tom Savini (Morgan); Amy Ingersoll (Lady Linet); Patricia Tallman (Julie Dean); Brother Blue (Merlin); John Hostetter (Friar Tuck).

The Natural (Columbia/Tristar, May 1984; 133 mins.) Director: Barry Levinson. Executive Producers: Roger Towne and Philip M. Breen. Producer: Mark Johnson. Screenplay: Roger Towne and Phil Dusenberry, based on the novel *The Natural* (1952) by Bernard Malamud. Cinematography: Caleb Deschanel. Production Designer: Mel Bourne. Music: Randy Newman. *Cast*: Robert Redford (Roy Hobbs); Robert Duvall (Max Mercy); Glenn Close (Iris); Kim Basinger (Memo Paris); Wilford Brimley (Pop Fisher); Barbara Hershey (Harriet Bird); Robert Proskey (The Judge); Richard Farnsworth (Red); Michael Madsen (Bump Bailey).

Indiana Jones and the Last Crusade (Paramount/Lucasfilm 1989; 126 mins.) Director: Steven Spielberg. Executive Producers: George Lucas and Frank Marshall. Producer: Robert Watts. Screenplay: Jeffrey Boam. Story: George Lucas and Menno Meyjes. Cinematography: Douglas Slocombe. Editor: Michael Kahn. Costume Designer: Anthony Powell. Music: John Williams. *Cast*: Harrison Ford (Indiana Jones); Sean Connery (Professor Jones); Denholm Elliot (Marcus Brody); Alison Doody (Dr. Elsa Schneider); John Rhys-Davies (Sallah); Julian Glover (Donovan); Kevork Malikvan (Kazim); Robert Eddison (Grail Knight).

The Fisher King (Columbia Pictures/Tristar 1991; 137 mins.) Director: Terry Gilliam. Producers: Debra Hill and Lynda Obst. Associate Producers: Stacey Sher and Anthony Mark. Screenplay: Richard LaGravenese. Cinematography: Roger Pratt. Production Designer: Mel Bourne. Costume Designer: Beatrix Pasztor. Editor: Lesley Walker. Music: George Fenton. *Cast*: Robin Williams (Parry); Jeff Bridges (Jack); Mercedes Reuhl (Anne); Amanda Plummer (Lydia); Michael Jeter (Homeless Cabaret Singer); Chris Howell (Red Knight); David Pierce (Lou Rosen); Lara Harris (Sondra).

Bibliography

Aherne, Brian. *A Proper Job*. Boston: Houghton Mifflin, 1969.

Alexander, Caroline. "Waiting for Arthur: A Winter Vigil at Camelot." *Smithsonian* (February 1996): 32–40.

Attebury, Brian. "Beyond Captain Nemo: Disney's Science Fiction." In *From Mouse to Mermaid: The Politics of Film, Gender, and Culture*. Eds. Elizabeth Bell, Lynda Haas, and Laura Sells. Bloomington: Indiana University Press, 1995. 148–160.

Bailey, Adrian. *Walt Disney's World of Fantasy*. Secaucus, NJ: Chartwell, 1984.

Banks, Russell. "*Bambi*: A Boy's Story." In David Rosenberg, ed. *The Movie That Changed My Life*. New York: Viking, 1991. 3–13.

Bartone, Richard C., "Variations on Arthurian Legend in *Lancelot du Lac* and *Excalibur*." In *Popular Arthurian Traditions*. Ed. Sally K. Slocum. Bowling Green: Bowling Green State University Popular Press, 1992. 144–155.

Baudrillard, Jean. *Simulations*. Trans. Paul Foss, Paul Patton and Philip Beitchman. New York: Semiotext(e), 1983.

Berman, Morris. *Coming To Our Senses: Body and Spirit in the Hidden History of the West*. 1989. New York: Bantam, 1990.

Bloom, Harold. *The Western Canon: The Books and School of the Ages*. New York: Harcourt Brace, 1994.

Blum, Daniel. *A Pictorial History of the Silent Screen*. New York: Grosset and Dunlap, 1953.

Boorman, John with Bill Stair. *Zardoz* [novelization]. New York: Signet, 1974.

Burke-Block, Candace. "*The Film Journal* Interviews George Romero on *Knightriders*." *Film Journal* 84 (4 May 1981): 25.

Byars, Jackie. *All That Hollywood Allows: Re-reading Gender in 1950s Melodrama*. Chapel Hill: University of North Carolina Press, 1991.

Cameron, Ian. *Adventure in the Movies*. New York: Crescent, 1973.

Cawelti, John G. *Adventure, Mystery, and Romance: Formula Stories as Art and Popular Culture*. Chicago: The University of Chicago Press, 1976.

Ceram, C. W. *Archaeology of the Cinema*. New York: Harcourt Brace, n.d.

Chadwick, Elizabeth. *First Knight* [novelization]. New York: Pocket, 1995.

Chapman, Graham, et al. *Monty Python and The Holy Grail (Book)*. New York: Methuen, n.d.

Chrétien de Troyes. *The Complete Romances of Chrétien de Troyes*. Trans. David Staines. Bloomington: Indiana University Press, 1993.

Ciment, Michel. *John Boorman*. 1985. Trans. Gilbert Adair. London: Faber and Faber, 1986.

Clute, John. "Edisonade." In *The Encyclopedia of Science Fiction*. Eds. John Clute and Peter Nicholls. New York: St. Martin's Press, 1993. 368–370.

—. "Robinsonade." In *The Encyclopedia of Science Fiction*. Eds. John Clute and Peter Nicholls. New York: St. Martin's Press, 1993. 1017.

Cohen, Margaret. *Profane Illumination: Walter Benjamin and the Paris of Surrealist Revolution*. Berkeley: University of California Press, 1993.

Collier, James Lincoln. *Louis Armstrong: An American Genius*. New York: Oxford University Press, 1983.

Corliss, Richard. "Pretty Ugly." [Review of *Cross of Iron, Aguirre, the Wrath of God*, and *Jabberwocky*] *New Times* (June 10, 1977): 71–73.

Crafton, Donald. *Before Mickey: The Animated Film 1898–1928*. Cambridge: MIT Press, 1982.

Culhane, John. "The Last of the Nine Old Men." *American Film* (June 1977): 10–16.

De Man, Paul. *The Resistance to Theory*. Minneapolis: University of Minnesota Press, 1986.

Dixon, Wheeler W. *The "B" Directors: A Biographical Directory*. Metuchen, NJ: Scarecrow Press, 1985.

—. *The Cinematic Vision of F. Scott Fitzgerald*. Ann Arbor: UMI Research Press, 1986.

Dooley, Roger. *From Scarface to Scarlett: American Films in the 1930s*. New York: Harcourt Brace, 1984.

Dunning, John. *Tune In Yesterday: The Ultimate Encyclopedia of Old-Time Radio 1925–1976*. Englewood Cliffs, NJ: Prentice Hall, 1976.

Eco, Umberto. "*Casablanca*: Cult Movies and Intertextual Collage." *SubStance* 47, 1985: 3–12.

—. "Dreaming of the Middle Ages." In *Travels in Hyperreality: Essays*. By Eco. Trans. William Weaver. San Diego: Harcourt Brace, 1986. 61–85.

—. *Postscript to "The Name of the Rose."* 1983. Trans. William Weaver. San Diego: Harcourt Brace, 1984.

Eisner, Sigmund. *The Tristan Legend: A Study in Sources*. Evanston: Northwestern University Press, 1969.

Eliot, Marc. *Walt Disney: Hollywood's Dark Prince*. 1993. New York: Harper, 1994.

Ellul, Jacques. *Propaganda: The Formation of Men's Attitudes*. 1965. Trans. Konrad Kellen and Jean Lerner. New York: Vintage, 1973.

Epstein, William H. "Counter-Intelligence: Cold War Criticism and Eighteenth-Century Studies." *ELH* 57 (1990): 63–99.

Fell, John L. *Film and the Narrative Tradition*. Norman: University of Oklahoma Press, 1974.

Fitzgerald, F. Scott. *The Great Gatsby*. 1925. New York: Scribner's, 1953.

Forman, Jack Jacob. *Presenting Paul Zindel*. Boston: Twayne, 1988.

Freud, Sigmund. *An Outline of Psycho-Analysis*. Rev. ed. Trans. James Strachey. New York: Norton, 1969.

—. "Fetishism." In *Collected Papers*. Vol. 5. Ed. and trans. James Strachey. New York: Basic Books, 1959. 198–204.

—. *Introductory Lectures on Psychoanalysis*. Trans. James Strachey. New York: Norton, 1966.

Gallagher, Tag. *John Ford: The Man and His Films*. Berkeley: University of California Press, 1986.

Garnett, David. *The White-Garnett Letters*. London: Cape, 1968.

Gilbert, James. *A Cyle of Outrage: America's Reaction to the Juvenile Delinquent in the 1950s*. New York: Oxford University Press, 1986.

Girard, René. *Violence and the Sacred*. 1972. Trans. Patrick Gregory. Baltimore: The Johns Hopkins University Press, 1984.

Girouard, Mark. *The Return to Camelot: Chivalry and the English Gentleman*. New Haven: Yale University Press, 1981.

Godard, Jean-Luc. *Godard on Godard*. 1972. Ed. and trans. Tom Milne. New York: Da Capo, 1986.

Gold, Robert S. *A Jazz Lexicon*. New York: Knopf, 1964.

Goldman, William. *Adventures in the Screen Trade*. New York: Warner Books, 1983.

Gould, Stephen Jay. "Jurassic Park." In *Past Imperfect: History According to the Movies*. Eds. Ted Mico, John Miller-Monzon, and David Rubel. New York: Henry Holt, 1995. 31–35.

Graham, Sheilah and Gerold Frank. *Beloved Infidel: The Education of a Woman*. 1958. New York: Bantam, 1970.

Green, Stanley. *The World of Musical Comedy*. 4/e. New York: Da Capo, 1985.

Haymes, Edward R. "From Romance to Ritual: Wolfram, Arthur, and Wagner's *Parsifal*." In Debra N. Mancoff, ed. *The Arthurian Revival: Essays on Form, Tradition, and Transformation*. New York: Garland, 1992. 174–204.

Harty, Kevin J. "Camelot Twice Removed: *Knightriders* and the Film Versions of *A Connecticut Yankee in King Arthur's Court*." In Harty, ed. *Cinema Arthuriana: Essays on Arthurian Film*. New York: Garland, 1991. 105–120.

Herman, Edward S. and Noam Chomsky. *Manufacturing Consent: The Political Economy of the Mass Media*. New York: Pantheon, 1988.

Higashi, Sumiko. "Antimodernism as Historical Representation in a Consumer Culture: Cecil B. DeMille's *The Ten Commandments*, 1923, 1956, 1993." In *The Persistence of History: Cinema, Television, and the Modern Event*. Ed. Vivian Sobchak. New York: Routledge, 1996. 91–112.

Hirsch, E. D. *Cultural Literacy: What Every American Needs to Know*. Boston: Houghton Mifflin, 1987.

Hoffman, Donald L. "Mark's Merlin: Magic vs. Technology in *A Connecticut Yankee in King Arthur's Court*. In *Popular Arthurian Traditions*. Ed. Sally K. Slocum. Bowling Green, OH: Bowling Green State University Popular Press, 1992. 46–55.

Irwin, John T. *The Mystery to a Solution: Poe, Borges, and the Analytical Detective Story*. Baltimore: The Johns Hopkins University Press, 1994.

Jackson, Kathy Merlock. *Walt Disney: A Bio-Bibliography*. Westport: Greenwood Press, 1993.

Johnson, Robert A. *He: Understanding Masculine Psychology*. Revised Edition. New York: Harper & Row, 1989.

Jonas, Hans. *The Gnostic Religion: The Message of the Alien God and the Beginnings of Christianity*. 2/e. Boston: Beacon, 1970.

Jung, C. G. *Flying Saucers: A Modern Myth of Things Seen in the Sky*. 1959. Trans. R. F. C. Hull. New York: Mentor, 1969.

Katz, Ephraim. *The Film Encyclopedia*. New York: Thomas Crowell, 1979.

Kennedy, Beverly. *Knighthood in the Morte Darthur*. Arthurian Studies XI. Cambridge: D. S. Brewer, 1985.

Kennedy, Harlan. "The World of King Arthur According to John Boorman." *American Film* (March 1981): 30–37.

Ketterer, David. "Mark Twain." In *The Encyclopedia of Science Fiction*. Eds. John Clute and Peter Nicholls. New York: St. Martin's Press, 1993.

—. *New Worlds for Old: The Apocalyptic Imagination, Science Fiction, and American Literature*. Garden City, NY: Anchor, 1974.

—. "'Professor Baffin's Adventures' by Max Adeler: The Inspiration for *A Connecticut Yankee in King Arthur's Court?*" *Mark Twain Journal* 24:1 (Spring, 1986): 24–34.

—, ed. *The Science Fiction of Mark Twain*. Hamden, CT: Archon Books, 1984.

Klass, Philip. "An Innocent in Time: Mark Twain in King Arthur's Court." *Extrapolation* 16:1 (December 1974): 17–32.

Lacy, Norris J. "Arthurian Film and the Tyranny of Tradition." *Arthurian Interpretations* 4:1 (Fall 1989): 75–85.

—. "Mythopoeia in *Excalibur*." In *Cinema Arthuriana: Essays on Arthurian Film*. New York: Garland, 1991. 121–134.

Lagrange, Pierre. " 'It Seems Impossible, But There It Is'." In *Phenomenon: Forty Years of Flying Saucers*. Eds. John Spencer and Hilary Evans. New York: Avon, 1989. 26–45.

LaGravenese, Richard. *The Fisher King: The Book of the Film*. New York: Applause Theatre Book Publishers, 1991.

Lenihan, John H. *Showdown: Confronting Modern America in the Western Film*. Urbana: University of Illionis Press, 1980.

Littleton, C. Scott and Linda A. Malcor. *From Scythia to Camelot: A Radical Reassessment of the Legends of King Arthur, the Knights of the Round Table, and the Holy Grail*. Garland Reference Library of the Humanities, Vol. 1795. New York: Garland, 1994.

Logan, Joshua. *Movie Stars, Real People, and Me*. New York: Delacorte Press, 1978.

Loomis, Roger Sherman, ed. *Arthurian Literature in the Middle Ages: A Collaborative History*. London: Oxford University Press, 1959.

Lumiansky, R. M., ed. *Malory's Originality: A Critical Study of Le Morte Darthur*. Baltimore: The Johns Hopkins University Press, 1964.

Mailer, Norman. *The White Negro*. 1957. San Francisco: City Lights Books, 1970.

Malory, Sir Thomas. *Works*. Ed. Eugène Vinaver. Oxford: Oxford University Press, 1971.

Mast, Gerald. *A Short History of the Movies*. Indianapolis: Bobbs-Merrill, 1976.

Mathews, Jack. *The Battle of Brazil*. New York: Crown, 1987.

McHale, Brian. *Postmodernist Fiction*. New York: Routledge, 1987.

Mellen, Joan. *Big Bad Wolves: Masculinity in the American Film*. New York: Pantheon, 1977.

Merriman, James Douglas. *The Flower of Kings: A Study of The Arthurian Legend in England Between 1485–1835*. Lawrence: The University Press of Kansas, 1973.

Miller, Arthur. *Death of a Salesman*. 1949. New York: Penguin, 1976.

Mitchell, W.J.T. *Picture Theory: Essays on Verbal and Visual Representation*. Chicago: The University of Chicago Press, 1994.

Neumann, Erich. *The Origins and History of Consciousness*. Vol. 1. Trans. R. F. C. Hull. New York: Harper Torchbooks, 1962.

—. *The Great Mother: An Analysis of the Archetype*. Trans. Ralph Manheim. New York: Pantheon, 1955.

New York Times Directory of the Film, The. New York: Arno Press/Random House, 1971.

Pallenberg, Barbara. *The Making of Exorcist II: The Heretic*. New York: Warner Books, 1977.

Peet, Bill. *An Autobiography*. Boston: Houghton Mifflin, 1989.

Pollack, Dale. *Skywalking: The Life and Films of George Lucas*. New York: Harmony Books, 1983.

Porter, Lewis, Michael Ullman and Ed Hazell. *Jazz: From Its Origins to the Present*. Englewood Cliffs, NJ: Prentice Hall, 1993.

Ravenscroft, Trevor. *The Spear of Destiny*. New York: Putnam's, 1973.

Ray, Robert B. *A Certain Tendency of the Hollywood Cinema, 1930–1980*. Princeton: Princeton University Press, 1985.

Robinson, E. A. "Lancelot." In *Arthurian Poets: E. A. Robinson*. Ed. James P. Carley. Woodbridge: The Boydell Press, 1990. 95–179.

—. "Merlin." In *Arthurian Poets: E. A. Robinson*. Ed. James P. Carley. Woodbridge: The Boydell Press, 1990. 15–94.

Rogin, Michael Paul. *Ronald Regan, the Movie, and Other Episodes in Political Demonology*. Berkeley: University of California Press, 1987.

Ruppelt, Edward J. *The Report on Unidentified Flying Objects*. New York: Ace, 1956.

Sarris, Andrew. *The American Cinema: Directors and Directions, 1929–1968*. 1968. Chicago: University of Chicago Press, 1985.

Schatz, Thomas. *Hollywood Genres: Formulas, Filmmaking, and the Studio System*. New York: Random House, 1981.

Schickel, Richard. *The Disney Version: The Life, Times, Art and Commerce of Walt Disney*. 1968. New York: Avon, 1969.

Segal, Alan F. "The Ten Commandments." In Ted Mico, John Miller-Monzon, and David Rubel, eds. *Past Imperfect: History According to the Movies*. New York: Henry Holt: 1995. 36–39.

Shadoian, Jack. *Dreams and Dead Ends: The American Gangster/Crime Film*. Cambridge: MIT Press, 1977.

Shichtman, Martin B. "Whom Does the Grail Serve? Wagner, Spielberg, and the Issue of Jewish Appropriation." In *The Arthurian Revival: Essays on Form, Tradition, and Transformation*. Ed. Debra N. Mancoff. New York: Garland, 1992. 283–297.

Silver, Alain and Elizabeth Ward, eds. *Film Noir: An Encyclopedic Reference to the American Style*. Woodstock, NY: The Overlook Press, 1979.

Sklar, Dusty. *The Nazis and the Occult*. 1977. New York: Dorset Press, 1989.

Slotkin, Richard. *Gunfighter Nation: The Myth of the Frontier in Twentieth-Century America*. 1992. New York: HarperPerennial, 1993.

Smith, Gavin. "Beyond Images: John Boorman Interviewed." *Film Comment* (July/August 1995): 44–46; 49–58.

Spoto, Donald. *The Dark Side of Genius: The Life of Alfred Hitchcock*. 1983. New York: Ballantine, 1984.

Staines, David. "Tennyson, Alfred Lord." In *The New Arthurian Encyclopedia*. Ed. Norris J. Lacy. New York: Garland, 1996. 446–449.

Starr, Nathan Comfort. *The Arthurian Legend in English and American Literature, 1901–1953*. Gainesville: University of Florida Press, 1954.

Strick, Philip. "John Boorman's Merlin." *Sight & Sound* (Summer 1980): 168–171.

Swinburne, Algernon Charles. "Under the Microscope." In *Swinburne Replies*. Ed. Clyde Kenneth Hyder. Syracuse: Syracuse University Press, 1966. 35–87.

Tennyson, Alfred. *Idylls of the King*. Ed. J. M. Gray. New Haven: Yale University Press, 1983.

Tennyson, Hallam, ed. *Alfred, Lord Tennyson: A Memoir by His Son*. 1897. 2 vols. Rpt. New York: Greenwood Press, 1969.

Thomas, Bob. *Walt Disney: An American Original*. 1976. New York: Pocket, 1980.

Thomas, Frank and Ollie Johnston. 1981. *The Illusion of Life: Disney Animation*. New York: Hyperion, n.d.

Thompson, Raymond H. *The Return From Avalon: A Study of the Arthurian Legend in Modern Fiction*. Contributions to the Study of Science Fiction and Fantasy, No. 14. Westport: Greenwood Press, 1985.

Twain, Mark. *The Works of Mark Twain*. Ed. Bernard L. Stein. Vol. 9. Berkeley: University of California Press, 1979.

Index

About the Authors

REBECCA A. UMLAND is an Associate Professor of English at the University of Nebraska at Kearney. She holds a Ph.D. in English from the University of Iowa and has published widely on Arthurian literature.

SAMUEL J. UMLAND is an Associate Professor of English at the University of Nebraska at Kearney. He has published articles on the teaching of literature, film, and film theory. He is the editor of *Philip K. Dick: Contemporary Critical Interpretations* (Greenwood, 1995).

Recover

ISBN 0-313-29798-3

90000>

EAN

9 780313 297984

HARDCOVER BAR CODE